IMAGES
*of America*

# RAINS COUNTY

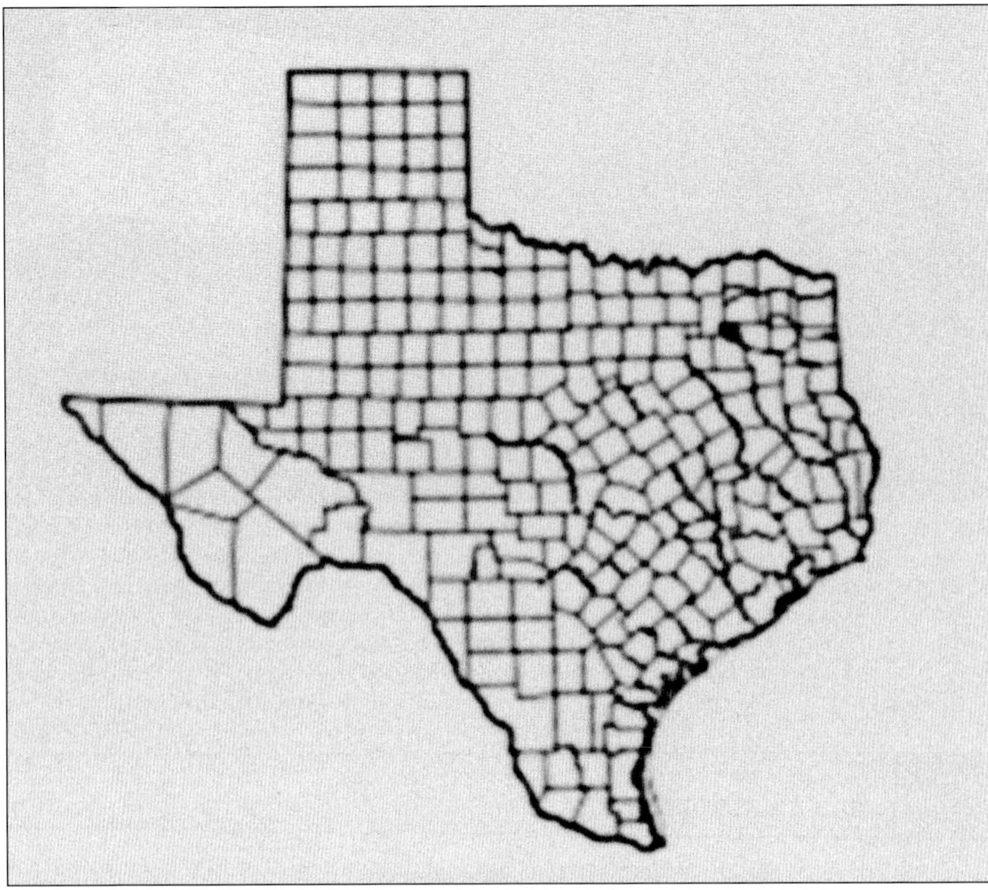

Rains County is in northeast Texas and is the fourth smallest of the state's 254 counties.

**ON THE COVER:** A 4-H pickup leads the Rains County Fair parade around the Emory square. (Courtesy of *Rains County Leader*.)

IMAGES
*of America*

# RAINS COUNTY

Elaine Nall Bay with the
Rains County Historical Commission

ARCADIA
PUBLISHING

ISBN 978-0-7385-7998-6

Published by Arcadia Publishing
Charleston, South Carolina

Printed in the United States of America

Library of Congress Control Number: 2011920845

For all general information, please contact Arcadia Publishing:
Telephone 843-853-2070
Fax 843-853-0044
E-mail sales@arcadiapublishing.com
For customer service and orders:
Toll-Free 1-888-313-2665

Visit us on the Internet at www.arcadiapublishing.com

*This work is dedicated to the pioneers who settled in Rains County and helped form the county. This book is also dedicated to their descendants who preserved their history in word and photographs. "Enjoy the little things in life, for one day you may look back and realize they were the big things."*

# CONTENTS

# ACKNOWLEDGMENTS

The compiler would like to extend her gratitude and appreciation to the Rains County Historical Commission for coauthoring this pictorial history of the county. Unless noted otherwise, all images appear courtesy of the *Rains County Leader.* With the help of Nancy Fenter, the finished project has been made easier for the compiler, who does not currently live in Rains County and does not have day-to-day contact with the residents. The historical information was passed from Nancy to the compiler. Jeri Humphrey scanned and sent photographs, without which there would be a lot of interesting bits of history missing from this book. Thanks to Mary White for taking all of my emails and working to see that what I needed was promptly taken care of. Photographs from individuals are noted on each picture contributed.

# INTRODUCTION

Texas has 254 counties, and is the state with the largest number of counties. Rains County is located in the northeast section of Texas in the Prairies and Lakes region and is the fourth smallest county in the state. Its agricultural industry, which existed at the time of the county's formation, remains today.

A local saying repeated by residents and found in the *Rains County Leader* states, "Come to Rains County where it rains when it wants to." This adage is as suitable today as it was in the past since the county's economic basis is agriculture and cattle.

Caddo Indians settled in the area about 800 AD. In the 1700s, Wichita tribes (Tawakoni and Yscani) moved into what would become Rains County, south and west to the Brazos River. Santa Anna (1794–1876), a young army officer, became dictator of Mexico by 1833 as a result of the revolution he led against the existing Spanish government. Before the Texas Revolution, Santa Anna encouraged people from the United States to settle in the northeastern area of Texas to help protect the land from the Native Americans. Shortly before the Texas Revolution, the Mexican government began to prohibit colonization of Texas, fearful that the Texas inhabitants would seek independence. In early 1836, Santa Anna marched with his powerful army into the Texas province to repress the rebellious Texans. After the Texans were victorious and won their independence from Mexico, many immigrated daily into the Lone Star State.

W.O. Hebisen, owner of the county newspaper, the *Record*, in the late 1890s, declared that the greatest people in the state were those women and men who produced Texas. They were the old settlers who built the schools and churches and established law-abiding communities. They were great because they themselves were peaceable, law-abiding, loving, neighborly, and God-fearing people.

James H. Hooker from Tennessee is assumed to be the first American of European descent to settle in the territory that would later become the county of Rains. At the time he moved to the area, it was known as Flaxweed Prairie because of the tall, thick prairie grasses. Hooker came from Missouri in the 1840s, taking up residence in the southwestern part of Rains County, where he established Hooker's Mill on the Sabine River. William Garrett of Tennessee settled in the northwestern section about the same time. As more and more residents came, communities such as Rice's Point, Sabine Pass, Springville, and Pilgrim Rest were established.

The first white settler in the Point area was William Rice, settling less than a mile east of where the town of Point now stands. When he came to Texas in 1826, Rice first settled in Lamar County. In 1869, J.M. Greer built the first house where the town of Point now stands. Emory Rains (1800–1878) is considered the "Father of Rains County." He and several of his brothers migrated from Tennessee to Texas, where they were given head rights to land by the Mexican government. He represented Shelby County in the Second and Third Congresses of the Republic and in the Convention of 1845, which approved the annexation of Texas to the United States. His most important political accomplishment was the sponsorship of the Homestead Law in 1839, which protected settlers in Texas from the seizure of their homes by creditors.

In 1866, Rains lobbied for the bill to establish Rains County. About 1869, Emory Rains moved to Wood County, which he helped to survey. On June 9, 1870, the legislature approved the formation of Rains County, which was effective in December 1870. Portions of land were taken to form Rains County from four counties: Hunt and Hopkins Counties, formed in 1846, Wood County, formed in 1856, and Van Zandt County, formed in 1848. The bulk of the land for Rains County came from Wood County. The Sabine River travels along the southern border of the county. Creeks that drain northeast into Lake Fork located on the Sabine River are Elm, Cedar, Garrett, Woodbury, Brushy, Sandy, Turkey, Bull and Bear. And there are many springs, with the largest group being the Springville Springs, the source of a stream that flows through the city park in Emory. The Springville community was chosen as the place of business for the first five commissioners. It was later designated as the permanent county seat and renamed Emory. An 1857 plat of Springville shows Ravine Street, which remains in Emory today as the oldest original street.

The first federal census that exists for Rains County dates from 1880, when there were 485 farms and agriculture was the economic base of the county. The staple crop was cotton. Livestock owners raised milk and beef cattle, swine, sheep, and poultry. During the 1940s, the Irish potato and the sweet potato became cash crops. After the decline of cotton in the area in the 1950s, dairy and beef cattle farms became an economic base for Rains County. It has remained an agricultural and rural area since its first settlers arrived in eastern Texas.

According to the US Census Bureau, Rains County today covers an area of 259 square miles, with 232 square miles of land and 27 square miles of water. The three towns in Rains County are Emory, the county seat, Point, and East Tawakoni. Many communities, which were established by a family or a group of settlers, exist in this region.

Still keeping their rural roots alive, the residents of Rains County remember and honor their ancestors who began communities and traditions. One of the attractions is the annual Rains County Founders Day Festival held on the first weekend in May to celebrate the county's heritage. Events include the annual Duck Derby, a quilt show, a 2K Run, a parade, and 42 Domino Tournament, just to name a few. Emory hosts an all-weekend celebration of America's national bird, the bald eagle. The Eagle Festival is held annually on the second weekend of February. Eagle-watching tours on both land and water are conducted. Among the festivities, Native American art and performances are featured.

During mid-September is the annual Rains County Fair held in Emory and lasting for an entire week. It is an old-fashioned country fair filled with events such as a pageant to select Miss Rains County, judging of various farm animals, the downtown parade, and a chili cook-off contest plus many other activities. The first Saturday in December is the annual Christmas on the Square, which features a visit from Santa and Mrs. Claus, tree-lighting in the city park, a Christmas parade, and the list goes on. Each year, a tour of both old and new homes is conducted during December. Over in Wood County is the town of Golden. Each October, Golden hosts a sweet potato festival. This event was aired on the *Oprah Winfrey Show* in October 2004 and January 2005.

Year-round, fishermen and families wanting to camp out and enjoy the outdoors come to one of Rains County's lakes. Lake Tawakoni features campgrounds, and Lake Fork showcases fishermen with fishing tournaments.

The following photographs are a journey into the heritage of Rains County, which still exists today as one of the smallest Texas counties with deep bloodlines.

Y'all come!

# *One*

# Another Day, Another Dollar

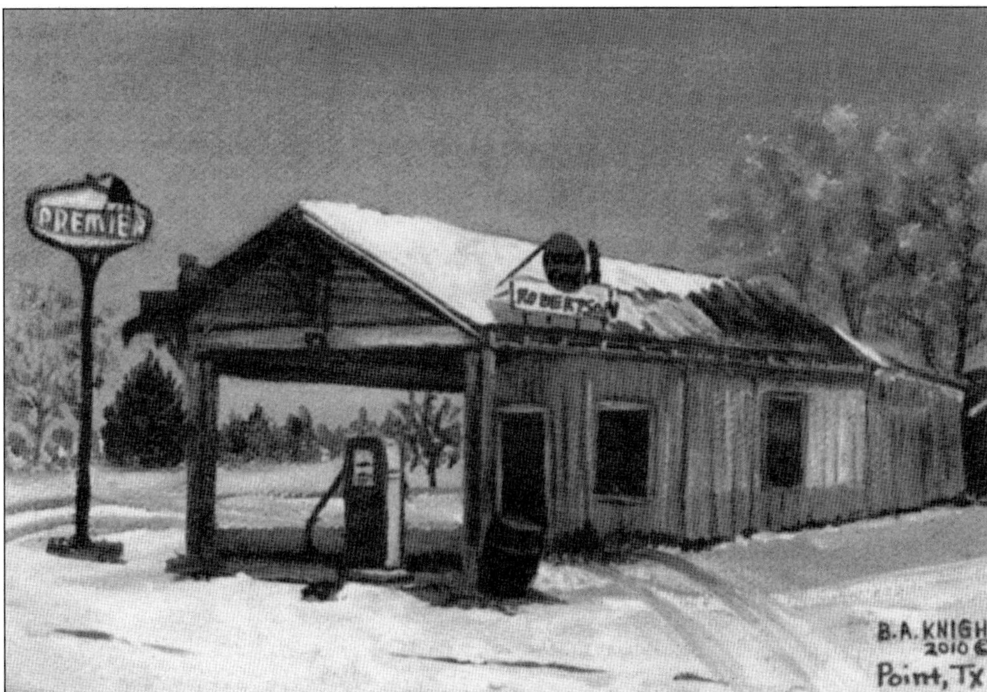


Rains County was, and still is, a rural county. In the early years, the main agricultural business was cotton. The type of farming chosen was for survival and support. Men would stand and watch the clouds hoping for rain. Women would preserve the harvests of crops for the family table. A large number of children guaranteed extra hands in the fields. The many businesses in Rains County operated on credit or cash products and helped support the farming community. The annual income during the early 1900s averaged $800. Positions as clerks and railroad employees netted a higher income, and thus these were coveted jobs. (Original painting courtesy of Brenda A. Knight.)

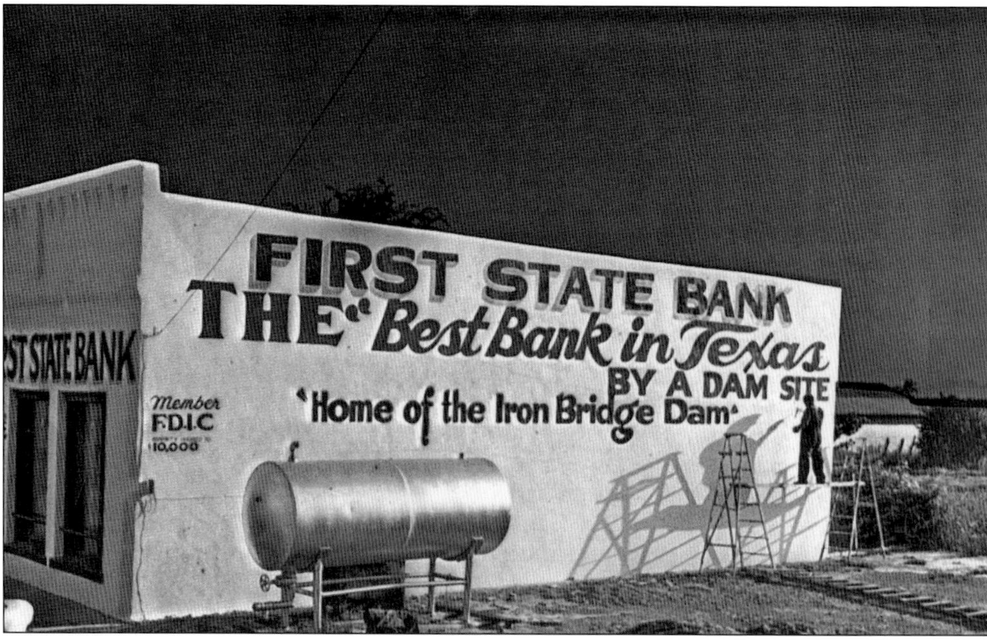


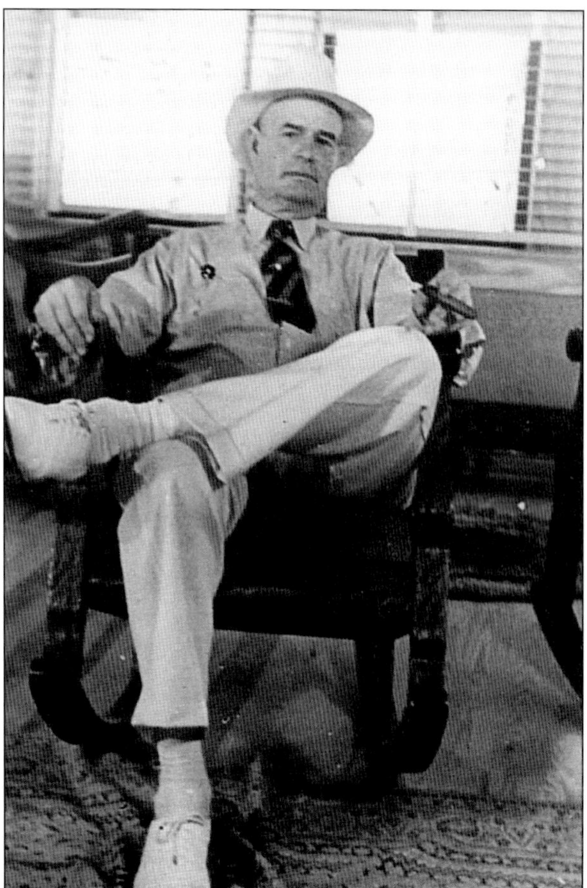

The First State Bank in Point was organized in 1913 and was called the Merchants and Planters Bank. The purpose of the bank was to serve as an exchange for cotton dealers and local merchants. Point had two banks, the First State and the Grantee State Bank, which consolidated in 1917 as the First State Bank (above). The new bank was led by Fannin Caywood Montgomery (left) from 1917 to 1965. A nighttime robbery in 1915 resulted in the death of bank cashier Clarence Glass. (Courtesy of Earnest Cain and Cay Frances B. House.)

Samuel Perry Cain was employed by Uncle Sam for 40 years. He clerked in the Point Post Office under his father, T.M. Cain. In 1916, the younger Cain worked at the Emory Post Office under his sister, postmistress Ada Cain Duffey. In 1920, he became an Emory rural carrier on Route Two, which he served for 19 years. On July 22, 1940, he was placed on the retired mail carriers list. (Courtesy of Jo Ann Turman.)

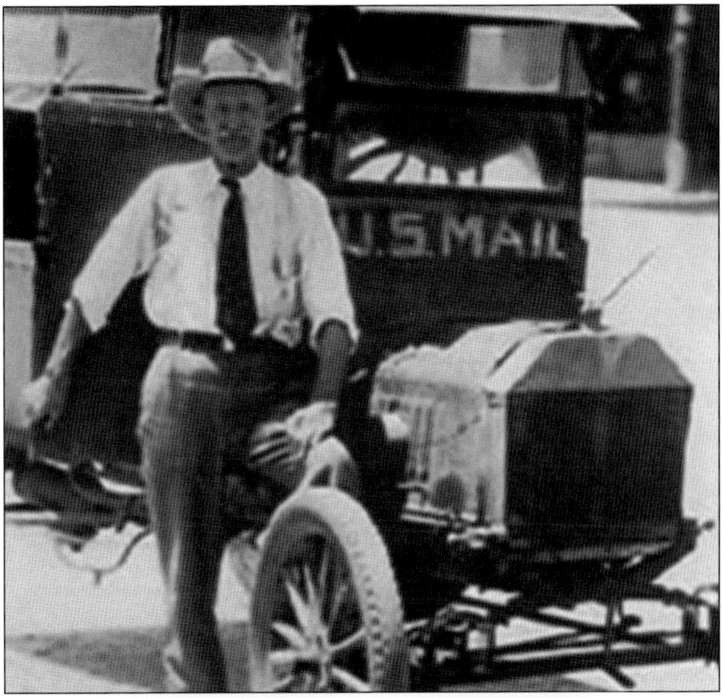


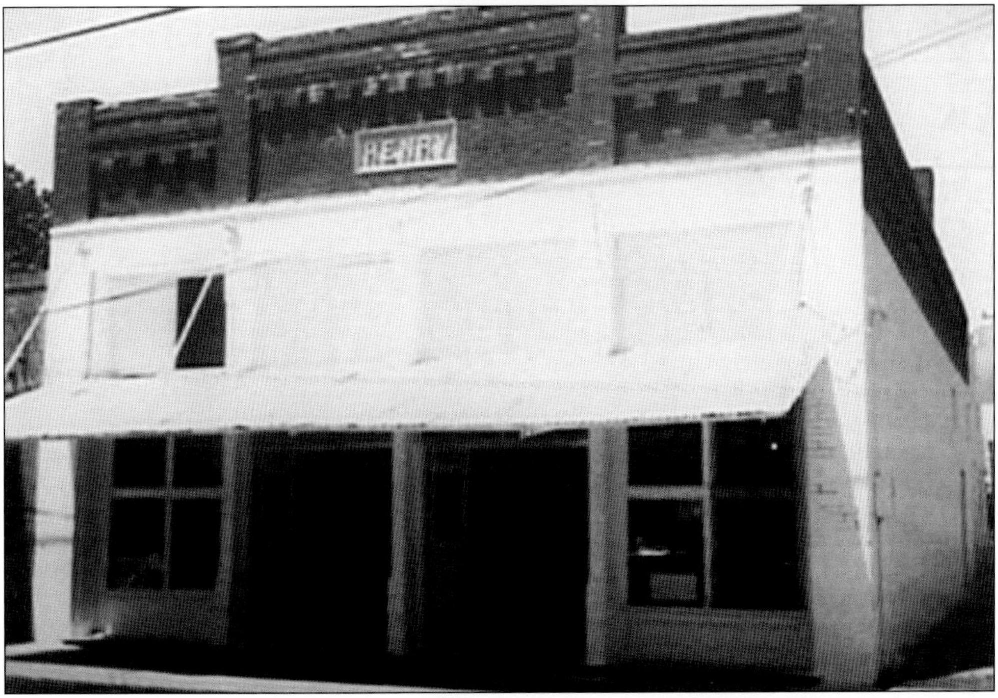


The Henry Building was built and owned by Emma Henry and was located on the southwest corner at the intersection of Quitman Street and Texas Street in Emory. The structure was destroyed in the 1990s. In its earlier days, it was a saloon. Later, the business in the structure was called Henry, Henry & Peeples Merchandise, which was damaged in 1894 tornado. (Courtesy of Ernest Cain.)

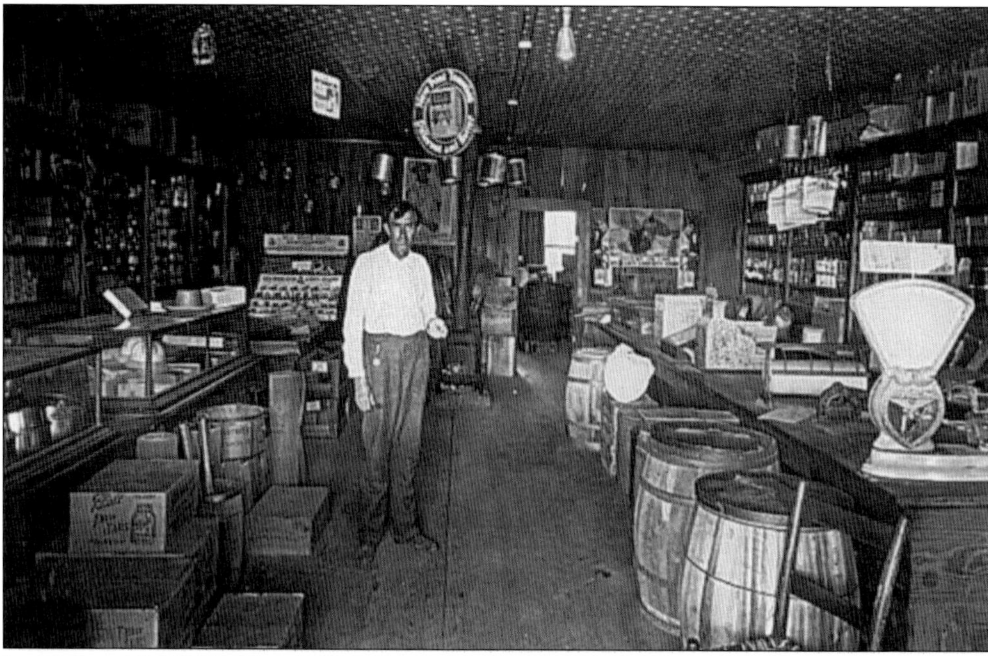

Joe T. Hood (1908–1951) was the son of Bunk S. Hood and Effie Branch. Bunk S. Hood owned and operated the Hood Hardware Store and also served as undertaker in Emory from 1912 until his retirement in 1946. Among the products on the shelves in this photograph are Evangeline corn syrup, Quaker oats, brooms, Granger rough cut tobacco, Lipton tea, and Scott snuff.

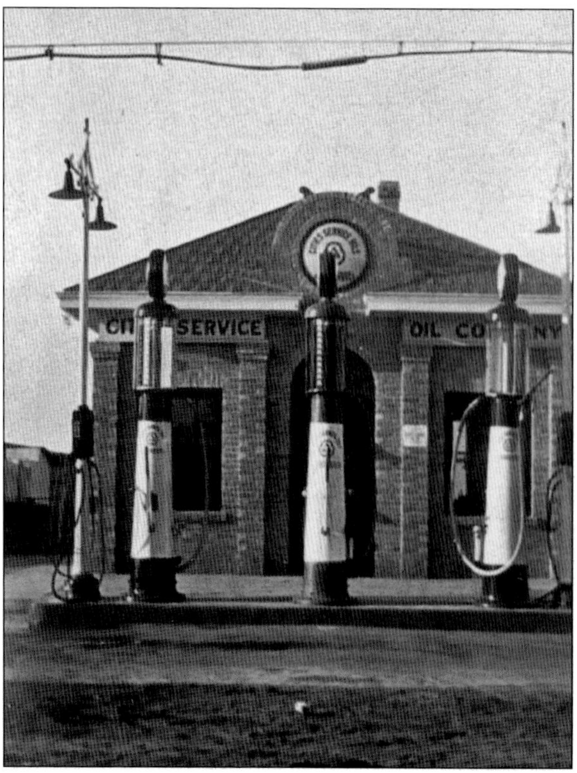


At 18, Bill Barrett, the only child of Ebb and Sennie Sanford Barrett, started working for Chigger Alexander at the City Service Station, later owned by Sam Braziel. Bill Barrett purchased the station from Braziel and reopened it under the name Independent Station. In 1946, Bill purchased two lots on Texas Street and had structures built on the lots. One of the buildings was Barrett's Auto Supply, which he operated for 25 years until he retired in 1971. (Courtesy of Jeri McAree Humphrey.)

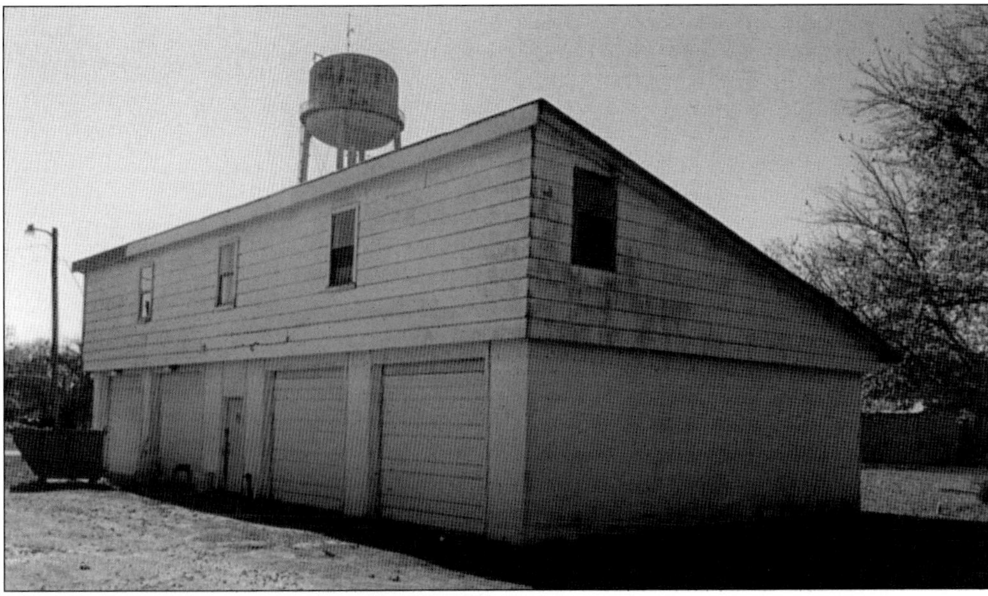

Point volunteer fire department, established in 1948, used a wooden structure with dirt floors on Farm to Market 47. The second fire station, shown above, was across the road in a concrete block building with two bays. Due to roof leaks and the small bays that housed the fire engines, the current fire station was built on Locust Street. (Courtesy of Elaine Nall Bay.)

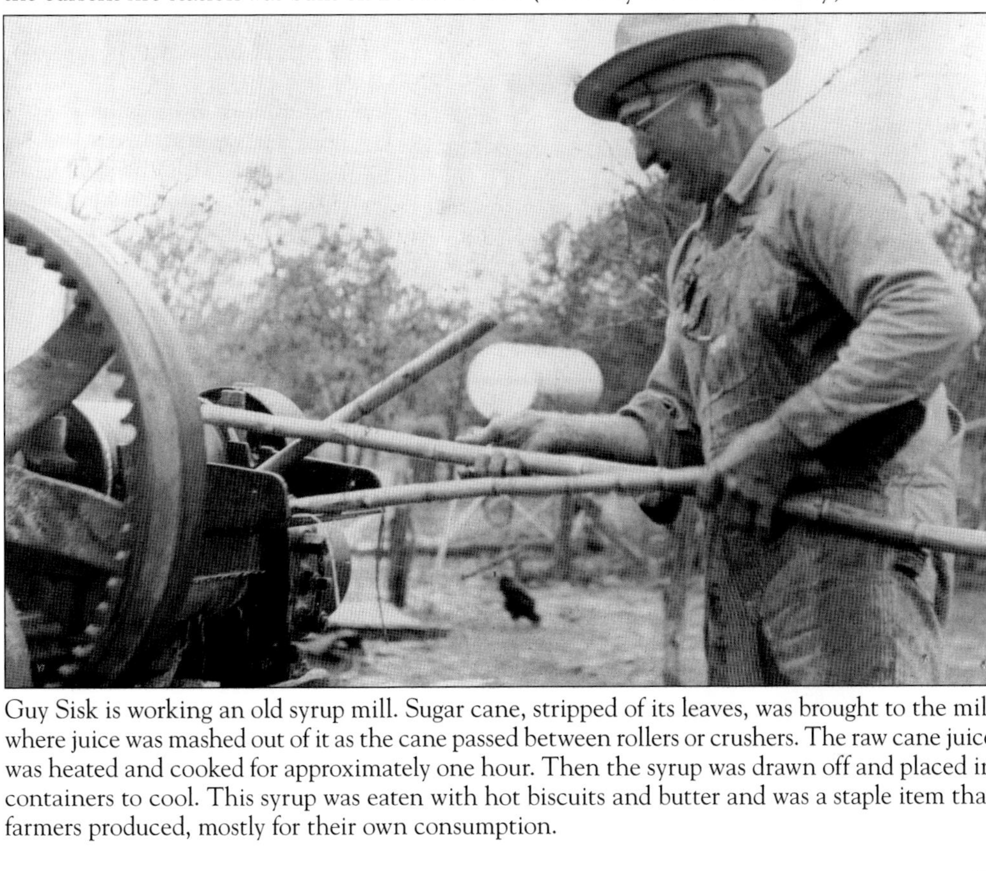

Guy Sisk is working an old syrup mill. Sugar cane, stripped of its leaves, was brought to the mill where juice was mashed out of it as the cane passed between rollers or crushers. The raw cane juice was heated and cooked for approximately one hour. Then the syrup was drawn off and placed in containers to cool. This syrup was eaten with hot biscuits and butter and was a staple item that farmers produced, mostly for their own consumption.

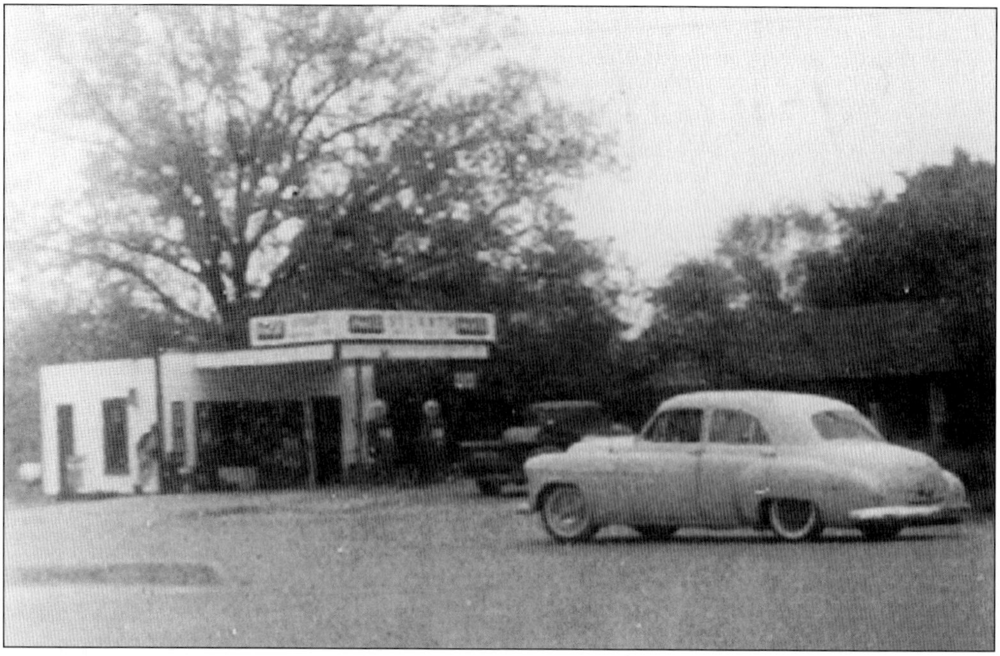

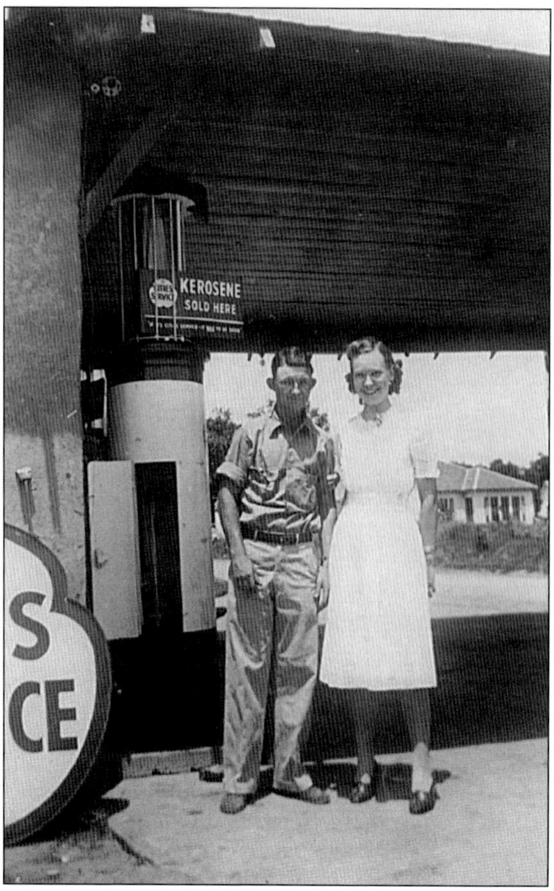


Grover Cleveland Stuart (1892), son of Stephen James "S.J." Stuart and Sarah Jane "Janie" Forbis Stuart, started his business venture as part owner of a dry cleaning shop. Later on, he became full-time owner of Stuart's Service Station, situated on the square in downtown Emory. Bill Barrett built a little stucco service station, City Service Station, on the north side of East Quitman Street, which Joe Peter later operated. Above is the station in the 1940s. It has had the sloping roof removed, new gas pumps installed, and a covered area built for the convenience of patrons. Owners Joe Pete and Flossie Wagley Stuart are standing by the kerosene pump at their service station located on the Emory Square in the 1940s (left). (Courtesy of Jo Ann Stuart Turman.)

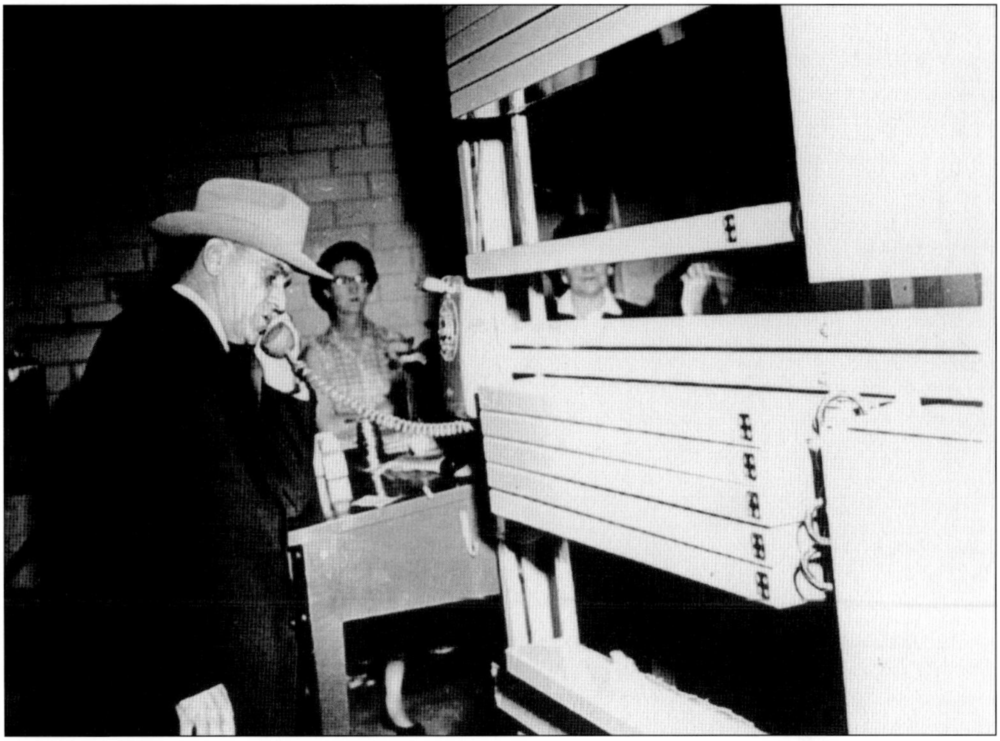

In early February 1922, the *Leader* ran an advertisement from McDaniel Telephone Exchange: "We have moved the Telephone office to the Vincent residence south of the Odd Fellows' Hall, and we want to thank our patrons for the patience with us during this period. Not a single 'kick' was heard and we want to thank you. Also we have our light plant up in shape again and begin service again tonight (Thursday)." Sam Braziel, a former judge, is shown here with teachers Rachel Braziel and Faye Melton at the 1959 telephone company's dedication of the first dial-telephone office in Emory. The white cases to the right of Sam Braziel house the telephone cables.

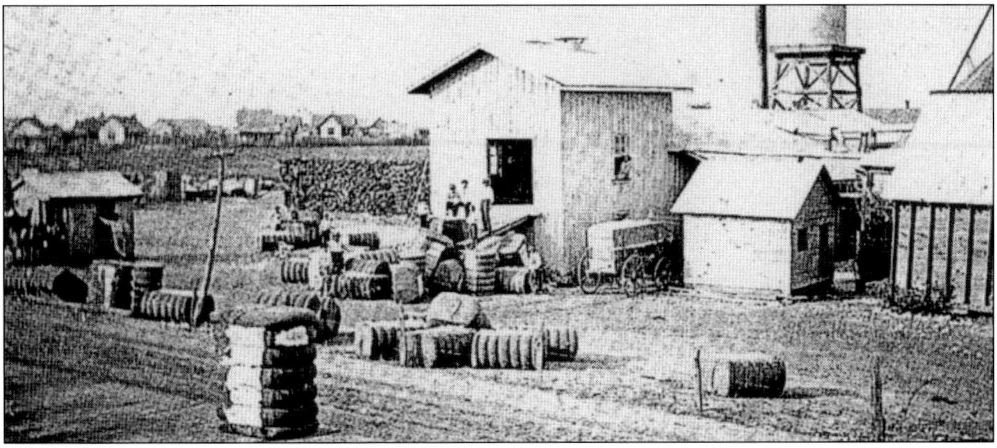

In 1889, W. Fannin Montgomery, father of the Montgomery brothers, installed a gin plant in Rains County. Being the oldest gin in Texas, it was in operation even before Point was established. In 1906, Montgomery sold the business to his three sons, Fannin Caywood (1875–1972), Press Rains (died 1908), and James W. (1878–1930). The business was then conducted under the name Montgomery Brothers. (Courtesy of Cay Frances B. House.)

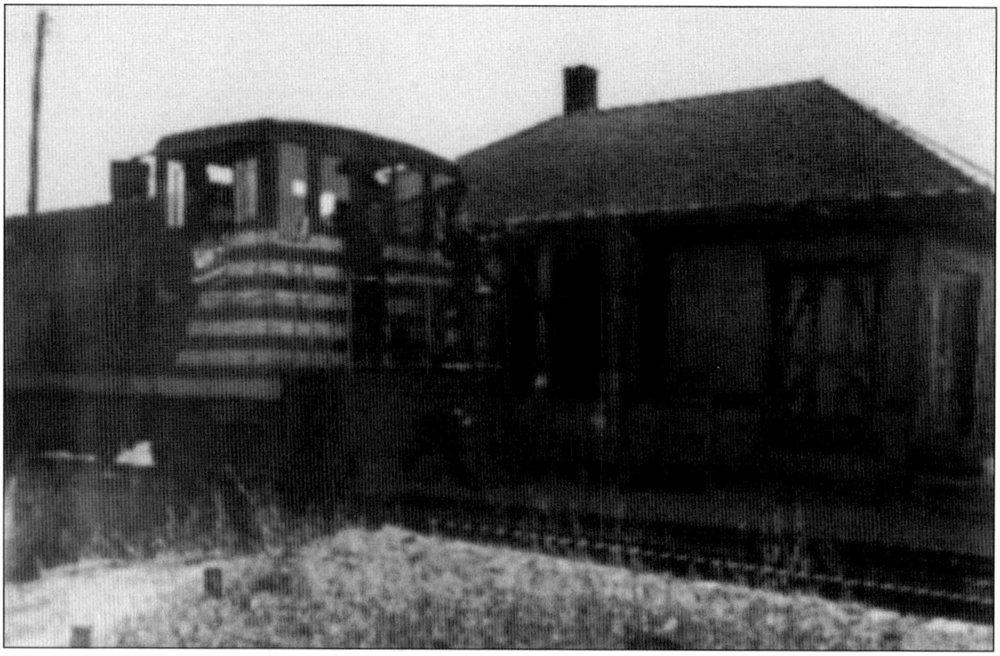

The MK&T railroad line, better known as the Katy, was just to the south of the courthouse square and followed the path that Highway 69 does today. In 1909, the materials to extend the Emory depot were going to be used to build two waiting rooms and a ticket office. The depot still exists today and is currently located on private property in Rains County.

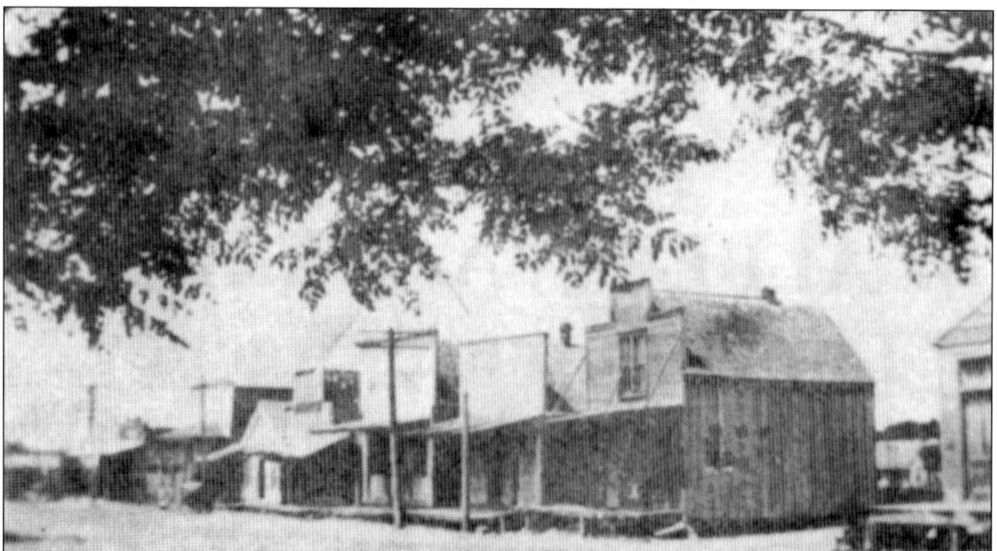

Before the turn of the century, the *Rains County Record reported*, "Infamous Smokey Row saloons were wide-open in 1890, with six saloons selling full blast 24 hours a day. Doc Peeples takes pleasure in setting up to you the best liquor every thrown over a counter in this county." In February 1899, "a Texas Blue norther whistled down . . . in such a severe and unexpected onslaught that . . . glass broke and fell away from the frozen beer in the local saloons" A postcard photograph in the *100th Anniversary of Rains County, 1870–1970*, is the only image of the infamous Smokey Row known to exist. By 1914, it was deserted.

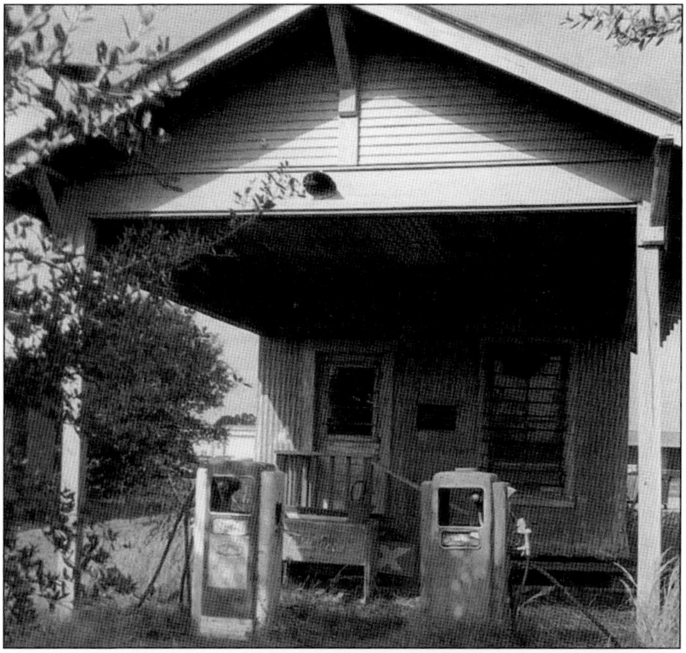

The Robertson Service Station, located in Point, was built of lumber from the old Cozart barn and livery. It was located next to the Point Co-Op Cotton Gin. Clifford and Ida Mae Robertson sold gas for 18¢ per gallon. The little store also carried groceries and automobile parts. After Mr. Robinson's death in 1975, Ida Mae continued to run the station until 1984. The property was later purchased by Marshall and Dorothy Smith, who donated the building to the Rains County Historical Park. (Courtesy of Elaine Nall Bay.)

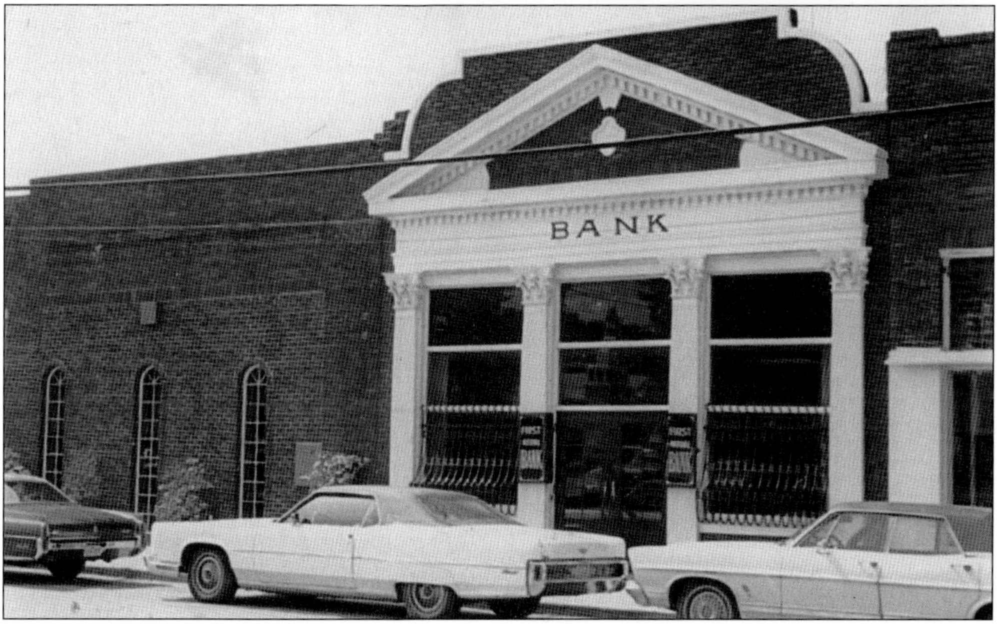


The First National Bank of Emory began business on July 4, 1903, and continues to serve Rains County citizens today. The bank still occupies its original site on the town square. "On the first day that the First National Bank was open for business, the keys to the bank vault were locked on the inside, S.K. McCallon who ran the bank, locked the vault with the keys on the inside when he went to dinner. Upon returning to the bank, he found that he could not get into the vault and had to call on Mr. M.A. (Millard) Vincent, who was handy with tools, to try and open it. After working for an hour or so, Mr. Vincent succeeded in getting the vault door open." This image, from the Rains County Historical Commission's *Rains County History*, shows the bank as it expanded from its original building in 1903 to this one in 1980.

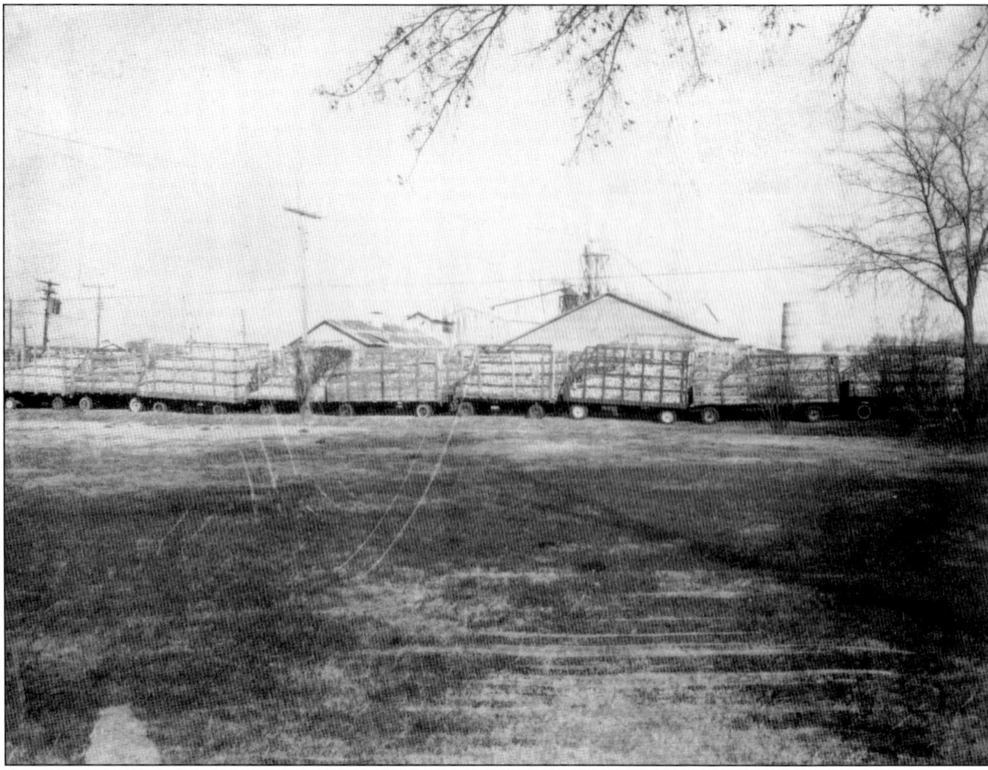

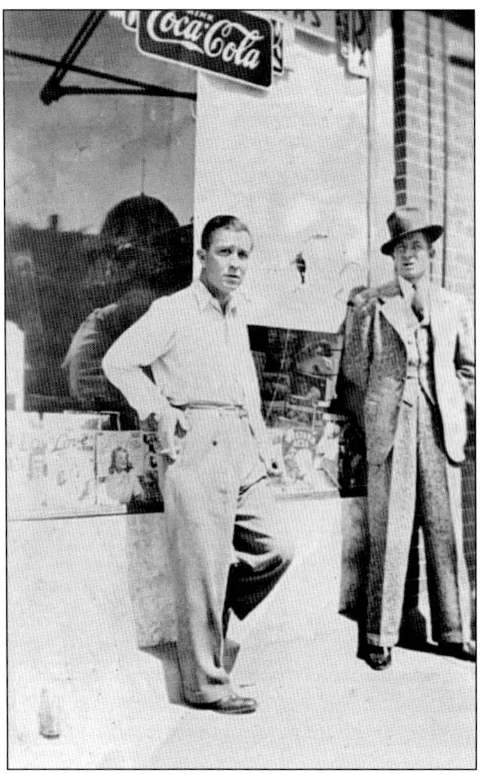


Point Co-Op Gin was organized in the late 1930s by area farmers. The gin housed a Riser Feed Grinder and Molasses Mixer where feed was ground and mixed. The business sold feed in addition to running the cotton-ginning operation. During the 1950s, Point Co-Op Gin was the only gin operating in Rains County.

Jim Nabors (left) and Paz Peeples are standing in front of the Nix Drug Store on the southwest corner of the Emory square in the 1940s. Charles M. Nix (1864–1933) moved his drugstore from Hopkins County to Emory in 1911. His sons Mell, John, and Browning became pharmacists, as did his son-in-law Edwin Brownrigg. They all worked in the Nix Drug Store. When his father retired, Browning Nix purchased the business from the family. (Courtesy of Pat Peeples Adcock.)

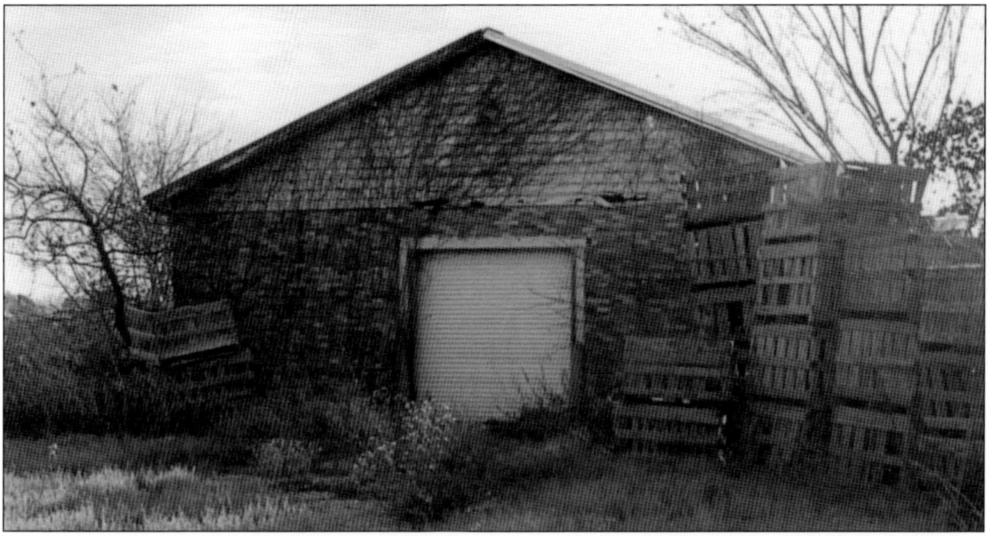

During the 1930s and 1940s, Claud Willis had a regular produce route in Hunt, Collin, and Rockwall Counties. Willis built a large, brick plant for the curing and storage of 30,000 bushels of sweet potatoes. (Courtesy of Ronnie M. Fenter.)

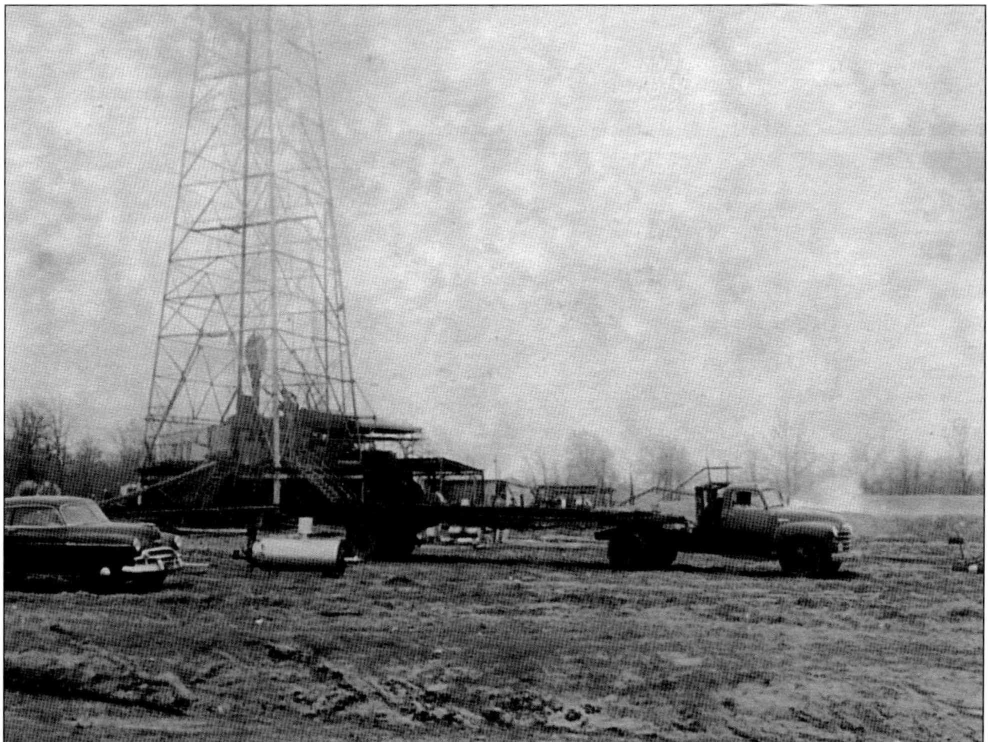

In April 1922, floods and storms swept across Point. Shown here, the deep test four miles west of Point on the J.C. Harris farm was spudded on a Saturday morning without ceremony and is busy pushing the drill downward. The James J. Jeffries derrick on the Corler farm was blown down and completely wrecked. The Texas and Pacific test on the Humphrey farm went through the storm in good shape.

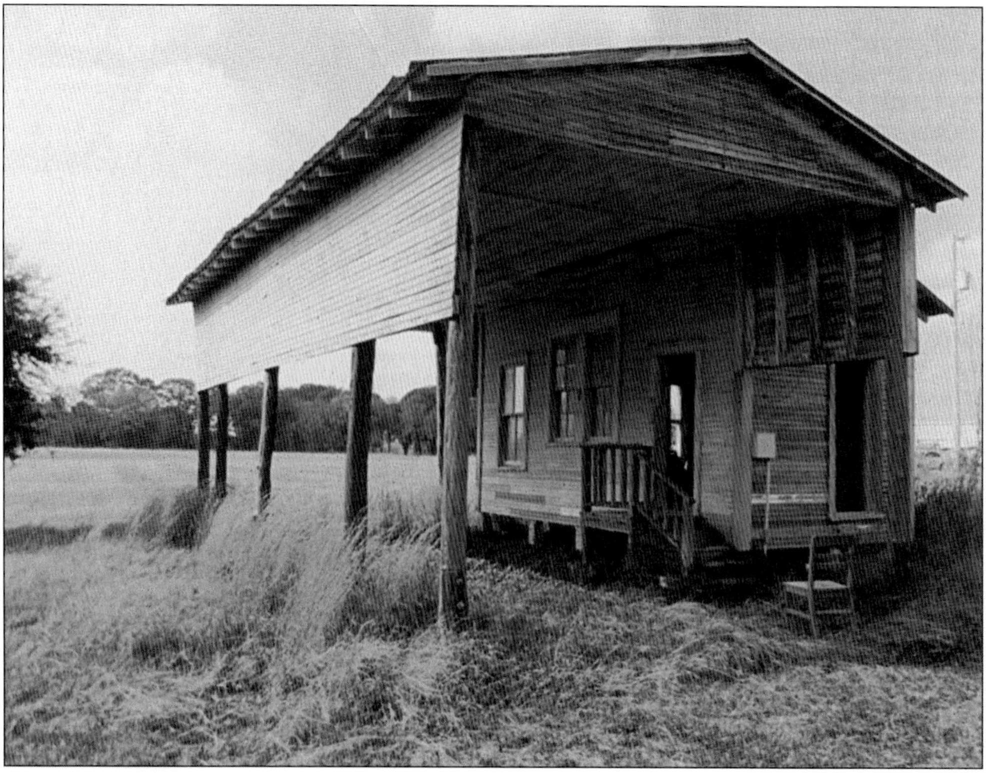

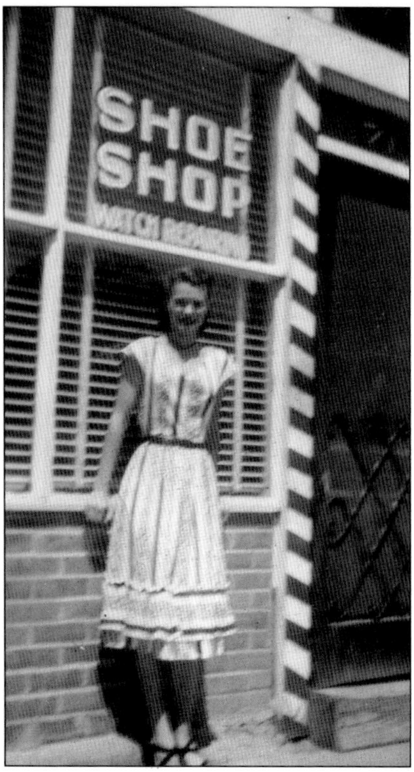


The Point Cotton Gin scales building dates from the 1920s and was used by the Farmers Co-Op Gin, chartered in 1937. The building closed in 1983. This building was donated by Monroe and Louise Hooten and family and is now part of the Rains County Historical Park in Emory—a reminder of when cotton was king. (Courtesy of Elaine Nall Bay.)

Ada Jo Oliver Robertson stands in front of Roy Turner's business, which housed a barbershop, a shoe repair shop, and a watch repair. For some, the most essential of all early day businesses were the local barbershops. As described in *100th Anniversary of Rains County, 1870–1970*, "A man could enter looking as though he had been dragged to town behind his horse and emerge slick-faced, sweet-smelling, and ready for high time in the old town tonight." (Courtesy of Mary A. Cain White)

Henry Doyle Potts's first cattle herd led to his career in agriculture, owning and operating the Potts Feed Store for 47 years. (Courtesy of Maxanne Orsborn Potts.)

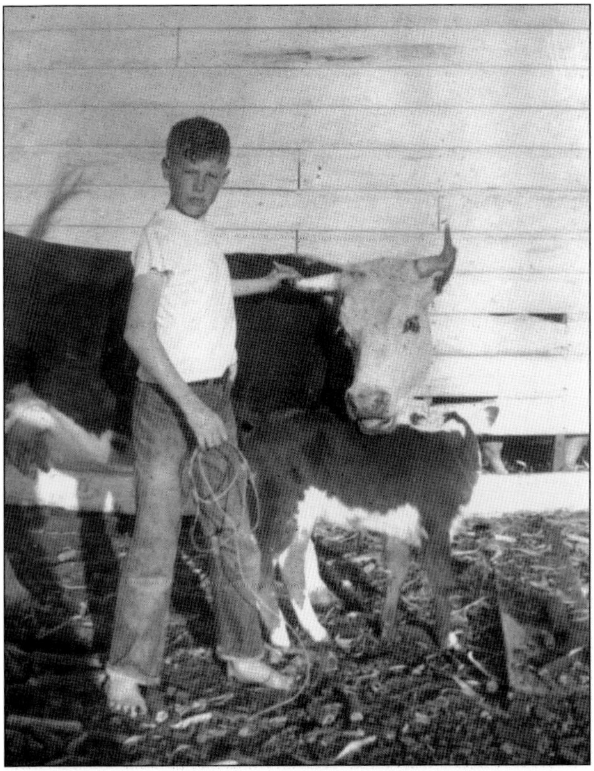

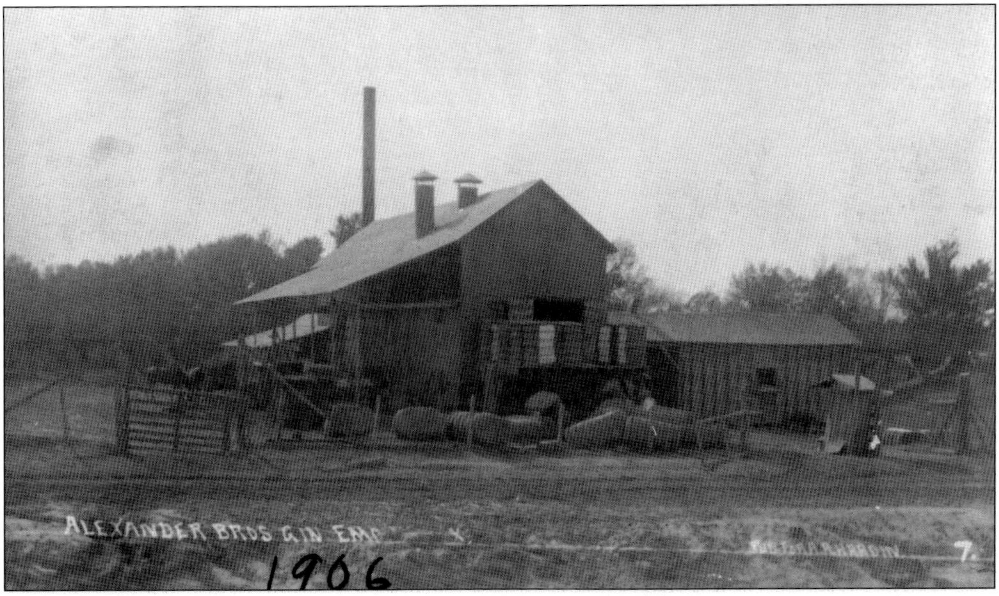


The Alexander Cotton Gin was passed from father to son during its existence. In the 1880s, Marshall Alexander built the first gin in Willow Springs Community, which was powered by mules using a screw-type press. His sons, Ed and George, moved the gin to Emory in 1901 and renamed it the Emory Gin. Power for the gin was supplied by two steam engines, which would eventually power a canning company and electric generator to provide the first electricity to residents of Emory. George Alexander and son Ivan operated the gin until closing it in 1953.

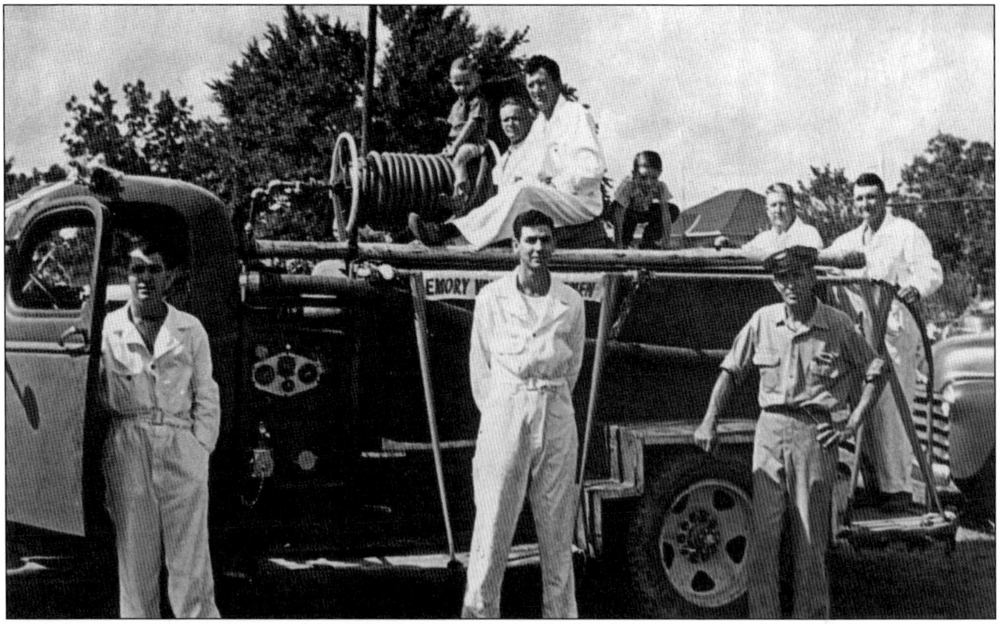

The Emory Volunteer Fire Department was formed in June 1948. Volunteers in the 1950s shown are, from left to right, (first row) Robert Holley, Jerry Lucy, County Agent, and Doc Vincent; (second row) Robert Chastain, unidentified, Joe Bob Chastain, El Holley, Charlie Walker, Frank S. Alexander, and Mr. Rylant.

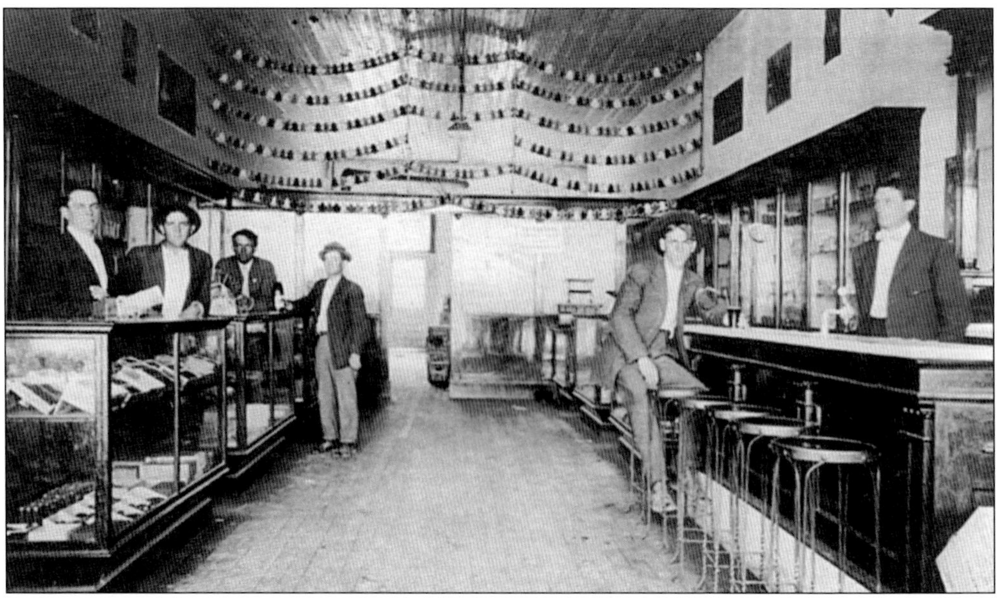

Robert Thurman "Mr. Bob" Pearson (1886–1956) moved to Rains County in 1909. He bought a share in the A.A. Hardin Drug Store in Emory, where he was the pharmacist for a few years. In 1911, he began a 41-year career as a rural mail carrier. When finished with his daily mail route, Pearson would work as pharmacist at the Reeves Drug Store. In 1908, standing left to right, are Al Reeves, Tom W. Hill, Robert Thurman Pearson, Ive Holderness, J. Will Stuart (seated), and Doug Pearson (behind soda fountain). A soda fountain was added between 1906 and 1908. (Courtesy of Jo Ann Stuart Turman.)

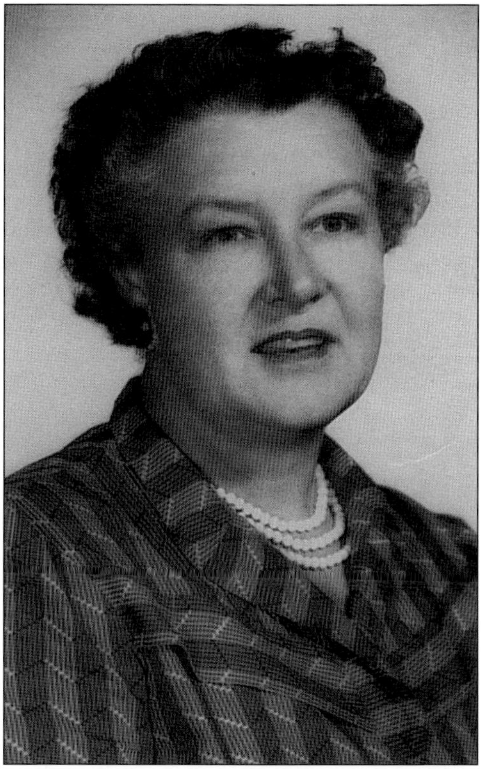

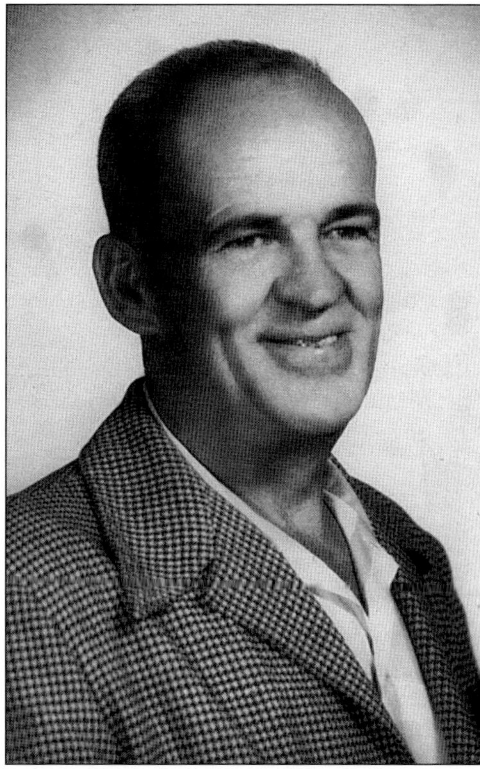

Alba and George Humphrey Sr. owned the City Café in Emory, which was originally located at the very end of the row of Alexander buildings in the 1940s. The café burned, and they reopened the business in 1950 in a structure behind the Henry building, facing Quitman Street and the drugstore. (Courtesy of Jeri McAree Humphrey.)

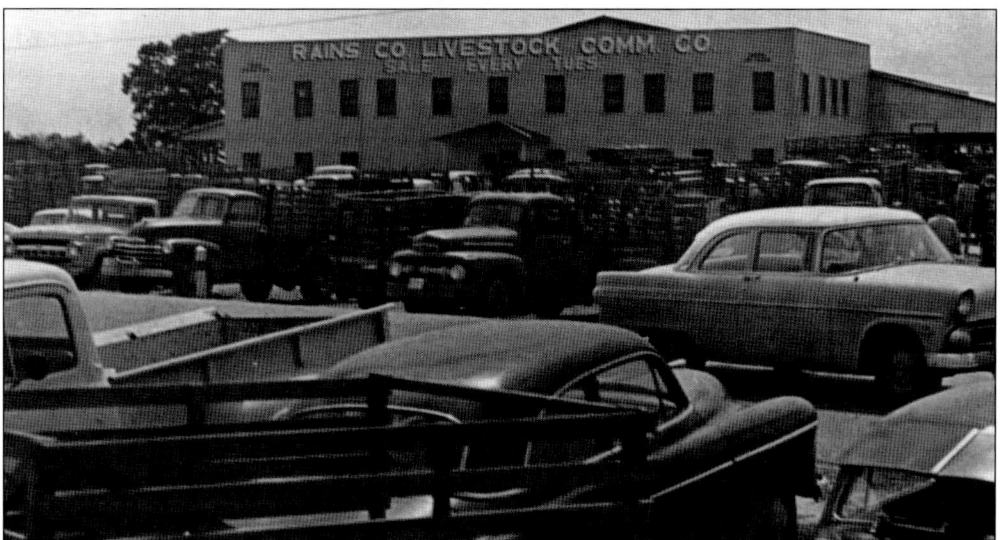


The Emory Livestock barn has served ranchers and farmers from far and wide. Auction day is Tuesdays of each week. Inside the building is also a restaurant. People go just to watch the auctions and to enjoy the companionship of others. The business was owned originally by J.W. Young.

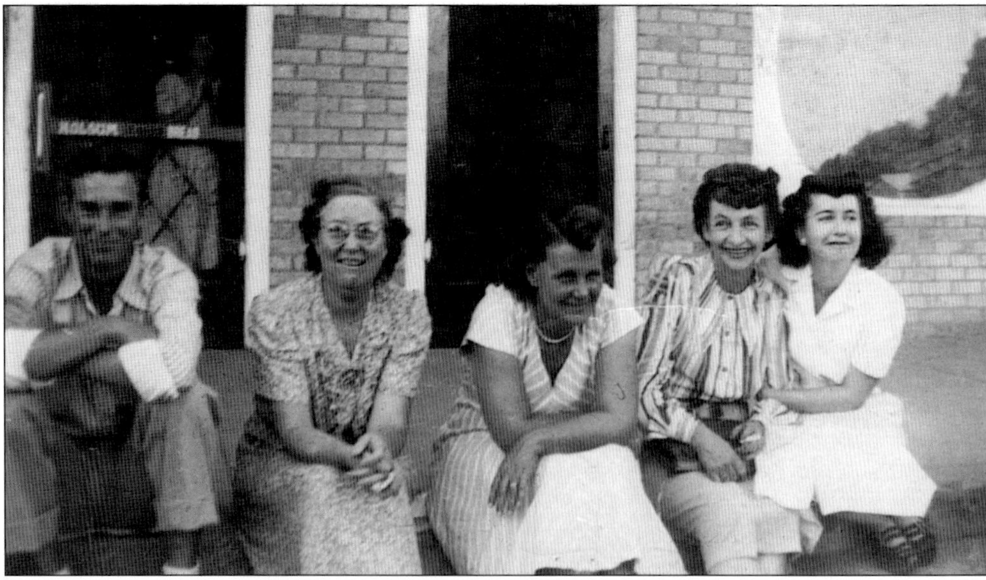

Above are employees enjoying the fresh air and each other's company on the sidewalk outside the Deluxe Café in 1949. They are, from left to right, Bobby Hazelwood, Georgia Hazelwood, Clara Armstrong, Ada Kerr, and Lola ?. Mary Alice Cain White can be seen inside the door. Ada Cain worked for many years as a waitress at the café after her husband's death. Coffee and tea cost 5¢, a good hamburger cost 15¢, and a bowl of steaming hot soup or chili cost 30¢. (Courtesy of Mary A. Cain White.)

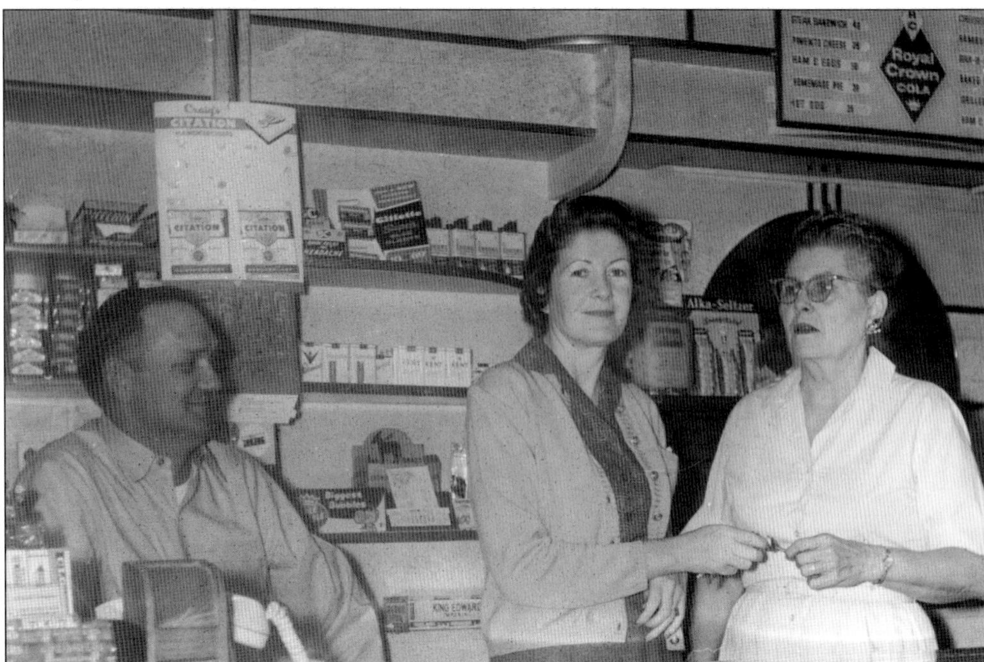


Dwain and Jewell Cooper purchased the Deluxe Café from Opal Phillips in the 1950s. It was in a building at the end of the strip of businesses on the west side of the square and was a very popular place to go when in town.

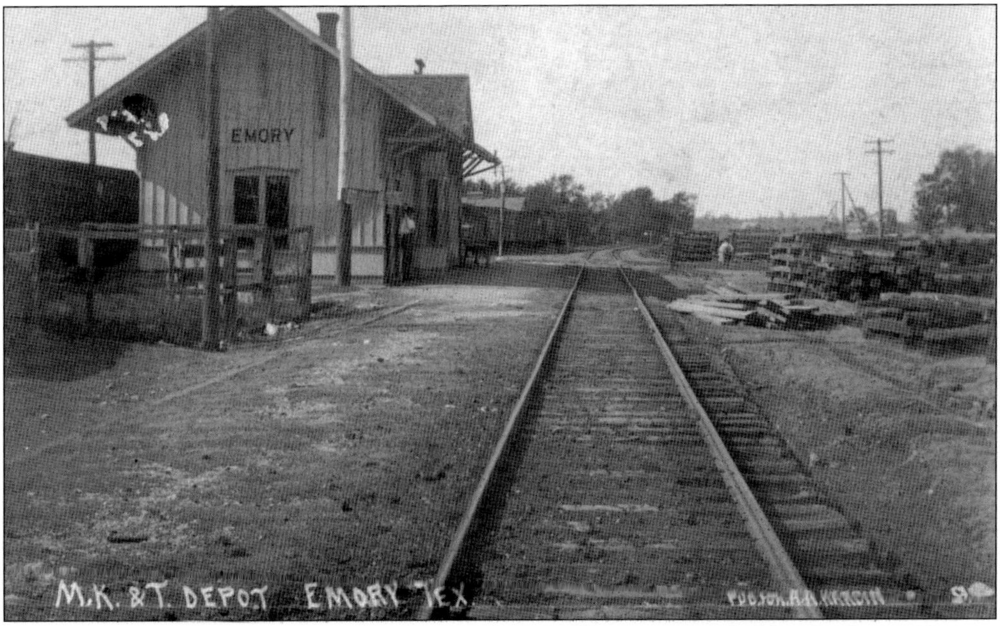


This postcard image that appeared in *Rains County History*, compiled by the Rains County Historical Commission in 1980, shows the Missouri-Kansas-Texas Railroad, better known as the M-K-T or Katy, which was built through Rains County in 1881, going from Greenville to Mineola. William R. Ratcliff recalled in the 1939 Pioneer Edition of the *Rains County Leader* that when Emory Rains saw his first train, "he looked at the engine from top to bottom. So I just asked him how he liked it. He said it was a good piece of work, and he thought it was a fine horse. . . . It was a great day when the first train came thru; people from miles around came to see the 'Iron Horse.' There was no depot—only a "flag station." The Katy charged 75¢ per meal in the dining car. On December 7, 1966, the railroad was officially abandoned after serving the county for over 76 years.

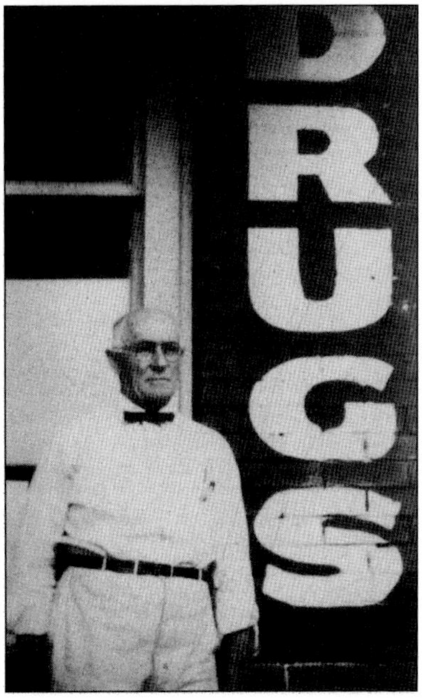


Doc Peoples stands in front of his drugstore. The business went through several ownerships between J.H. Foster and D.S. Peoples. Peoples's 1949 *Autobiography & Other Writings* says, "We don't really understand how we have kept our head above the tide, but we feel that the Good Lord has been with us or we would have gone down, having withstood part of one war and all of two World Wars, and six recessions and depressions in our business experience of these forty-nine years."

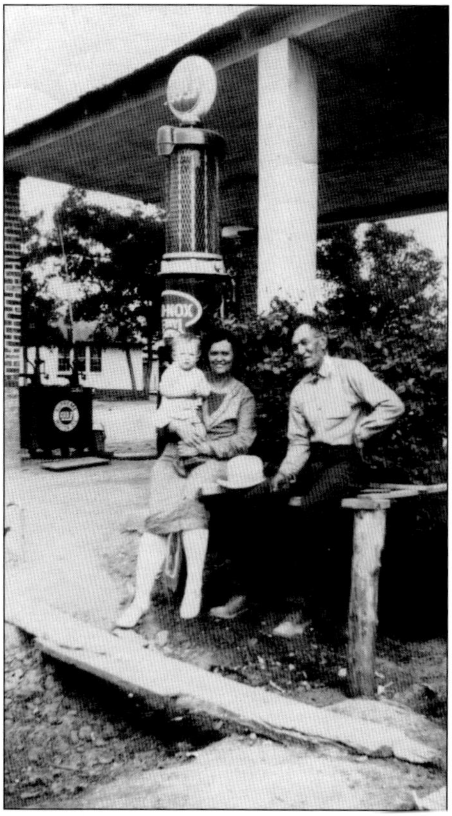


The Albert N. Betts store was located in the Bright Star community. The house in the background was the home of Minnie Betts Glass for many years.

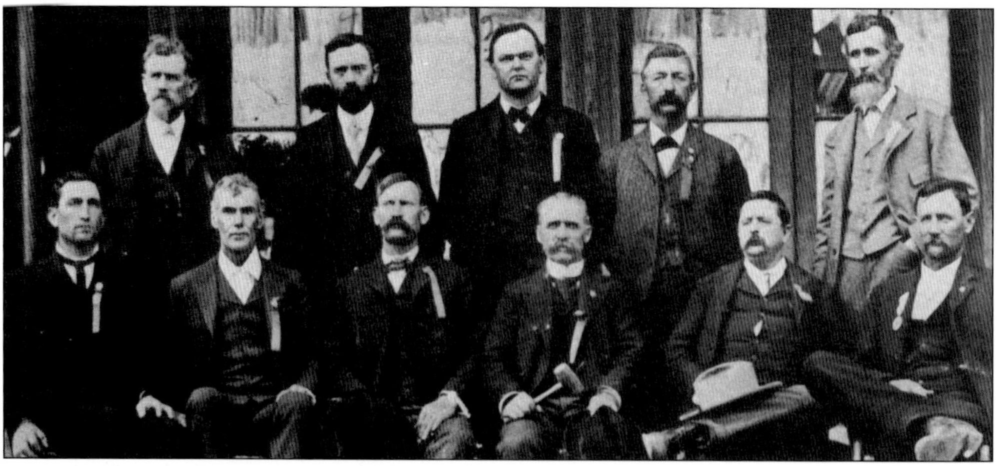

In 1902, a group of 10 men met secretly at Newt Gresham's barn near Point. A lantern provided light, bales of hay served as seating, and a five-cent writing tablet was used to record the bylaws. The Local No. 1 organized on September 2, 1902 at the Smyrna schoolhouse. Membership fee was $1. A local charter was submitted to the Texas secretary of state September 17, 1902. By 1905, the National Farmers Union became a national organization. Shown below are the organization's original organizers. They are, from left to right, (first row) William S. Sisk, J.B. Morris, Dr. Lee Seamster, Newt Gresham, and Oney Hervey Rodes; (second row) W.O. Butran, J.S. Turner, Jesse Adams, W.T. Cochran, and Thomas J. Pound. W.O. Butran stood in the absence of Tom Donaldson, one of the original founders.

# *Two*

# Home Is Where the Heart Is

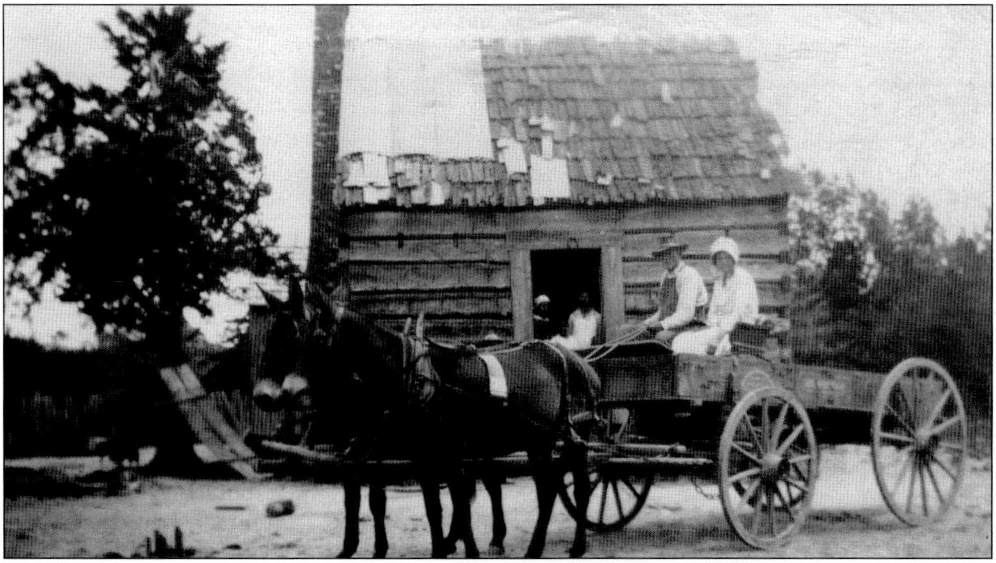

The family home is where family members find safety, comfort, and shelter. Families gather in their residences, whether small or large, cabin or house, to enjoy the company of relatives and family members. When men left for war or hunting, they longed to return home, just as their families longed to see them coming down the road to the home place. In his 1917 book *Early Days in Texas and Rains County*, W.O. Hebisen wrote, "How much better is a plain, quiet home, where all is peace and cordiality, the neighbors heartily welcome to come and go at will, and freed from the pestering, senseless conventionalities of fashionable life."

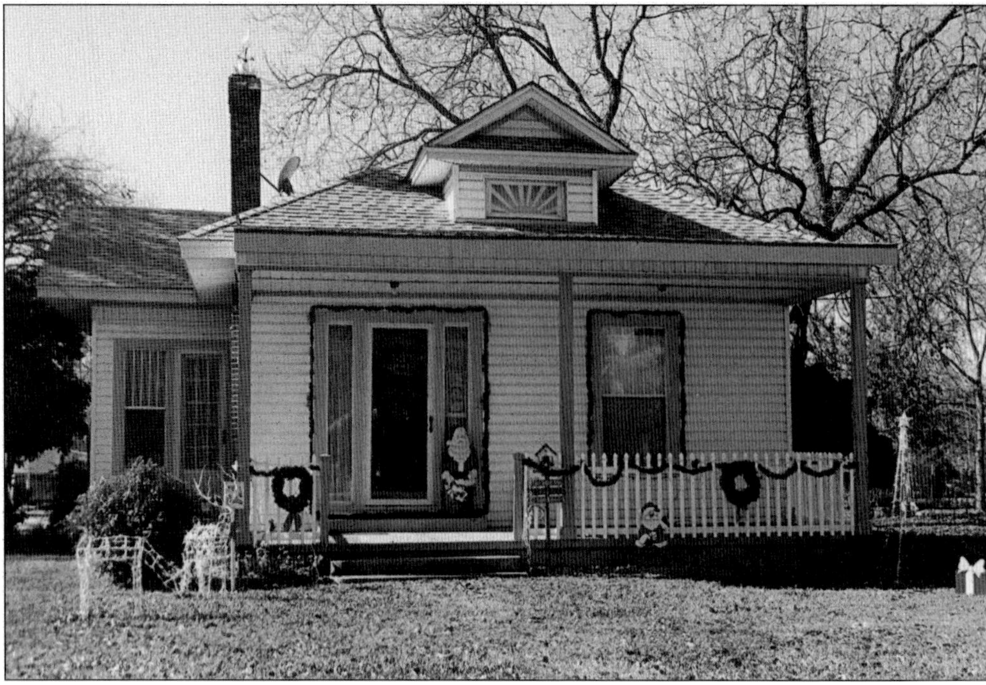

The R.B. "Doe" Bellah (1903–1987) home is located in Point, Texas. Bellah's family lived in the Lone Star community before the formation of Point. They were large landowners and a well-known family. (Courtesy of Elaine Nall Bay.)

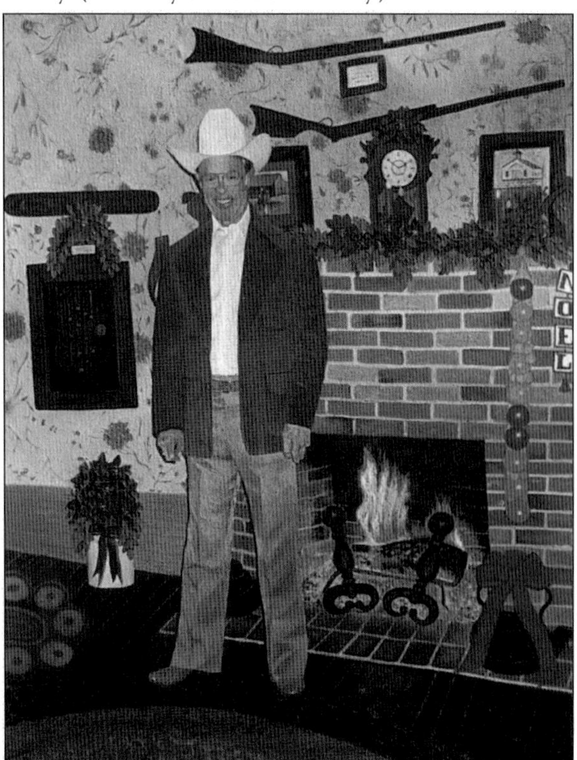

In this oil painting, Henry Potts, grandson of Henry and Ida Dougherty, is standing in front of the fireplace in the historic Dougherty home that is decorated by the family each Christmas. In the background are guns that belonged to Henry and Ida Dougherty. (Courtesy of Brenda Knight Styron.)

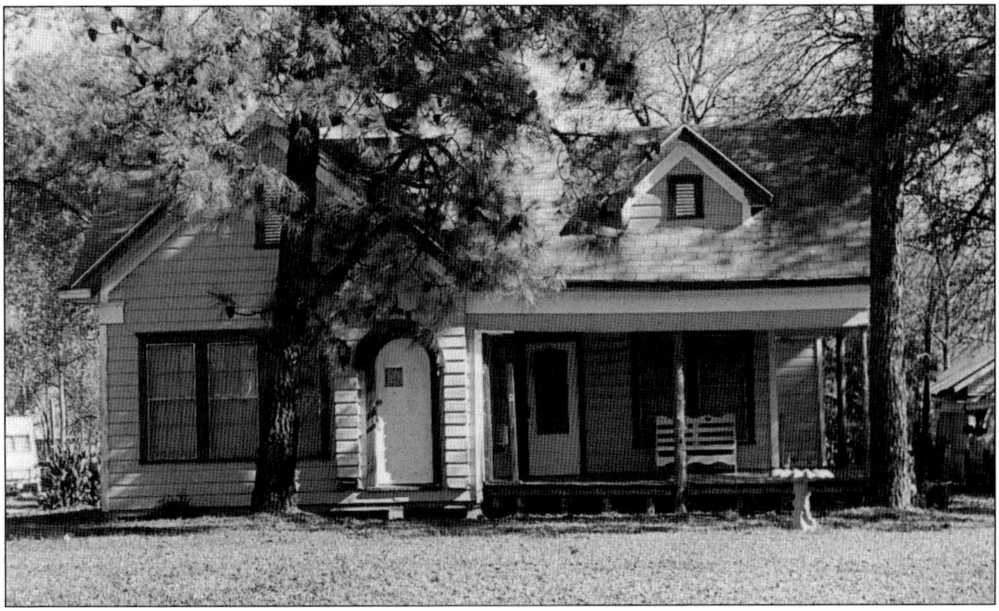

This home belonged to Mr. and Mrs. Bond Sparks of Point, Texas. Mattie Virginia was a beloved lady who loved children. Halloween was a favorite holiday because of children coming by to trick-or-treat. (Courtesy of Elaine Nall Bay.)

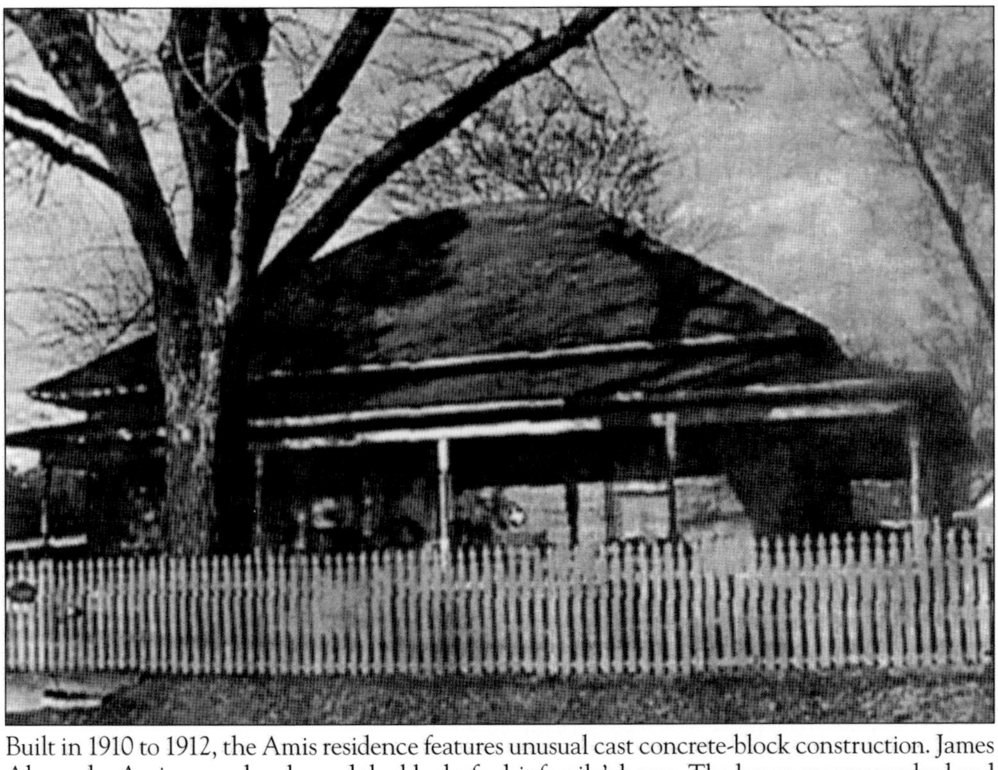

Built in 1910 to 1912, the Amis residence features unusual cast concrete-block construction. James Alexander Amis poured and cured the blocks for his family's home. The house was researched and restored by Aletha Amis Ashworth, daughter of James Alexander (1872–1929) and Carrie Etta Roan Amis (1875–1959). The Amis home received a Texas Historic Landmark marker in 1985.

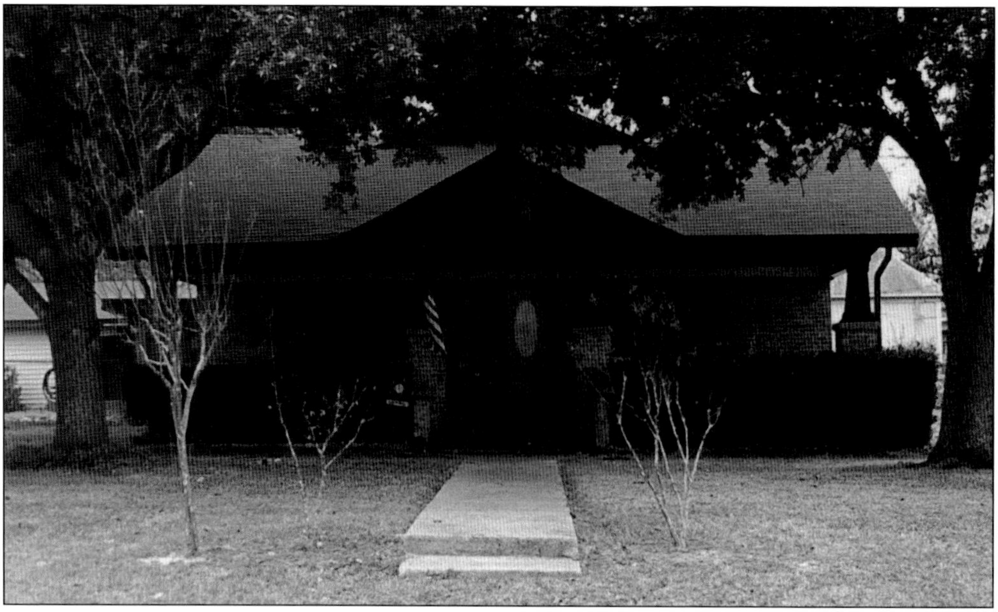

The oldest house remaining in Emory today is estimated to have been built in the 1880s by Capt. Tom Cain. Still standing on North Ravine Street behind the First Baptist Church, the house has halls, a parlor, and other rooms typical of the 1880s. After Captain Cain's death, his daughter and son-in-law, Lela and J.W. Bellew, occupied the home. Their daughter, Zula, visited the Washington Monument in Washington, DC, and brought back a cutting of ivy from the monument area, which was planted in the yard of the Cain house. According to stories regarding the Washington Monument, the original cutting of the ivy Zula brought home came from Lafayette's grave in Paris, France. (Courtesy of Elaine Nall Bay.)

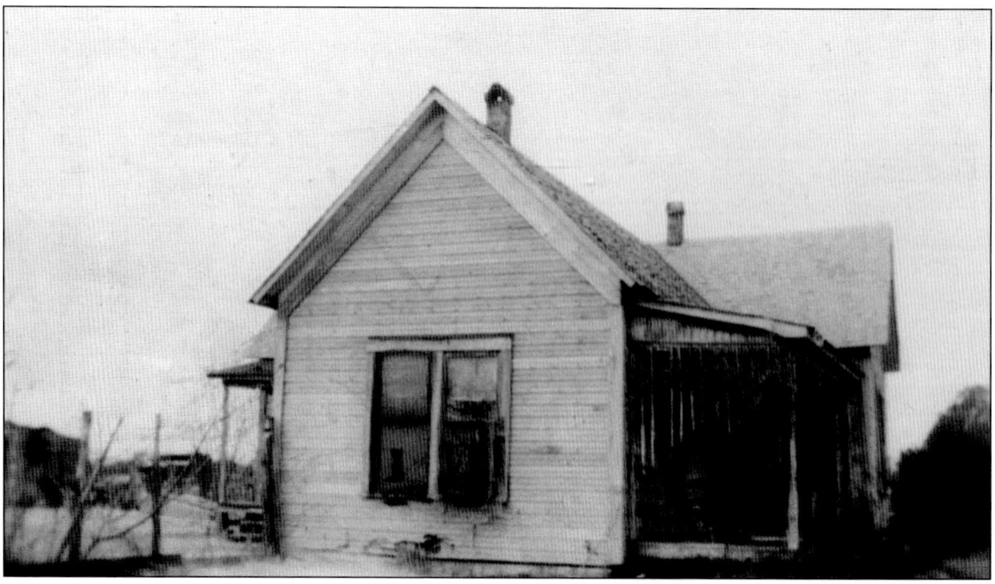

This is the home of the James D. Cain (1890–1943) and Ada Kerr Cain (1899–1985) family in 1934. It was located on Capt. Thomas Cain's land and stood on the south side of Highway 69 where James and Ada's daughter, Mary A. Cain White, built a restaurant. Mary and her three brothers were born in the house. (Courtesy of Ernest Cain.)

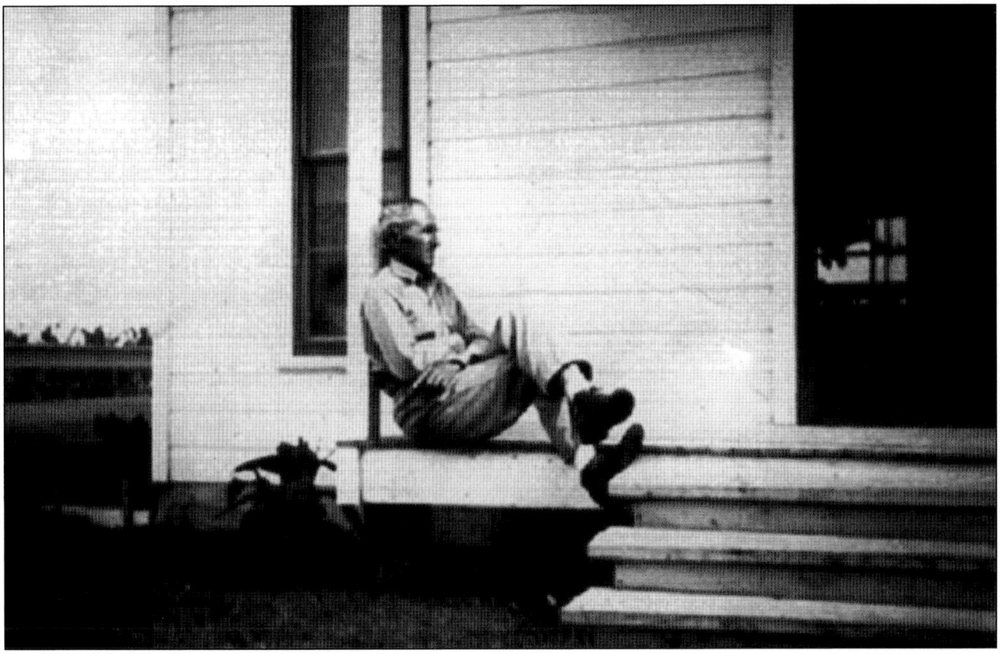

Marvin Cunningham (1899–1975) rests on the front porch of his home outside of Point. A cotton farmer, he married Connie Mae Weatherford (1900-1988). Marvin was the son of John Robert and Sarah Jemima Porter Cunningham and grandson of Pinckney "P.C." Columbus and Margaret White Porter. (Courtesy of Cindy Cunningham Watson.)

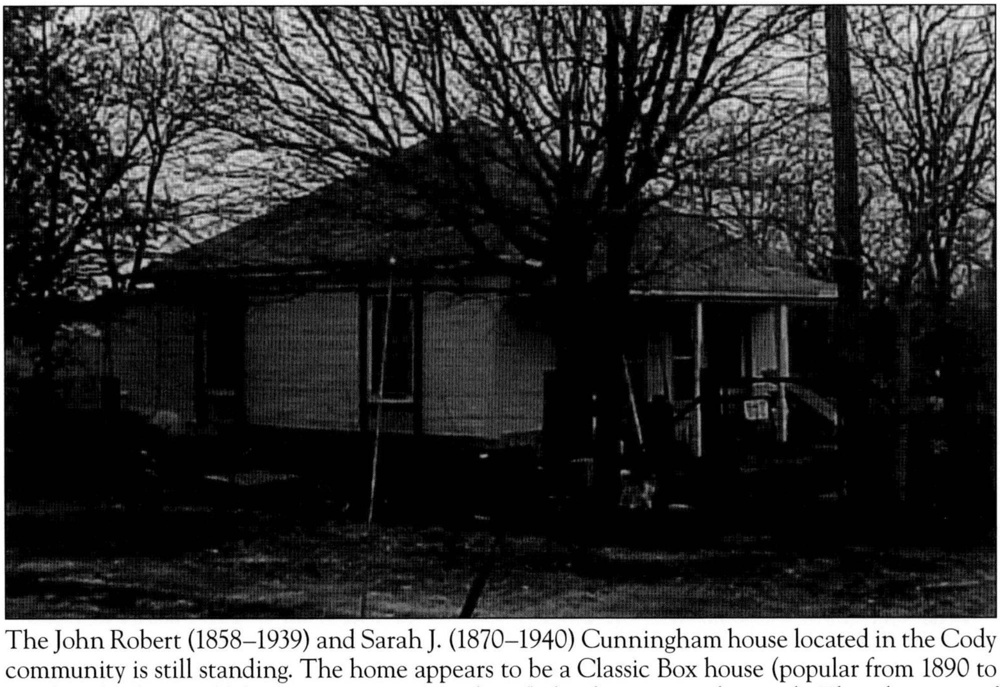

The John Robert (1858–1939) and Sarah J. (1870–1940) Cunningham house located in the Cody community is still standing. The home appears to be a Classic Box house (popular from 1890 to 1910) with a hip roof (also known as a pyramid roof) that hangs over the porch. The advantage of a hip roof is that the house is surrounded by eaves, which protect the walls from the weather and help shade both walls and windows from the sun. (Courtesy of Cindy Cunningham Watson.)

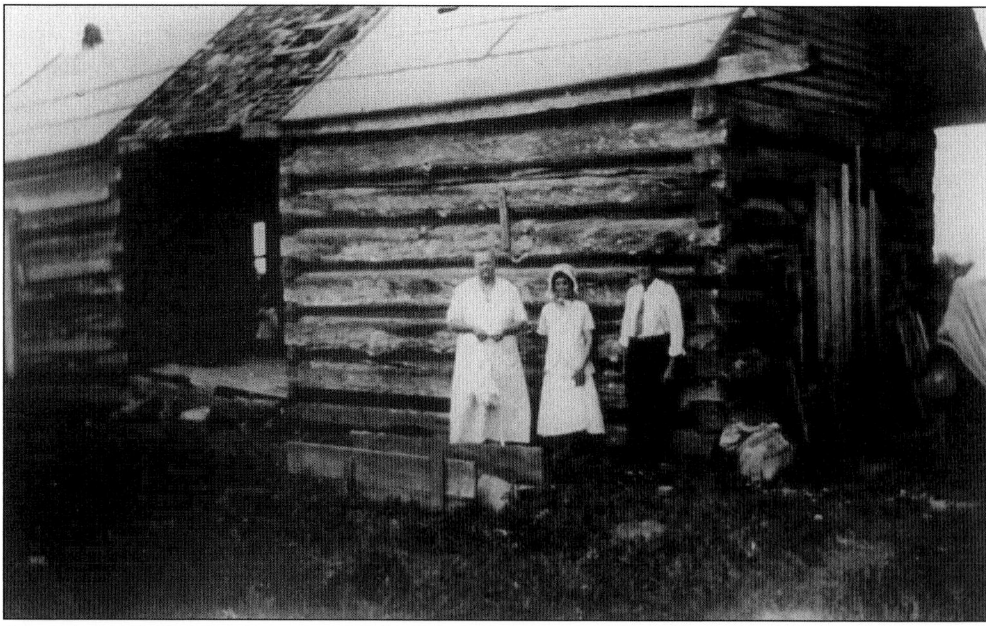

Samuel Gee (1794–1877) served in the War of 1812. He obtained a veterans land grant in the Pilgrim Rest community. Gee and his family were in the area by 1852 and built a three-room cabin, where he lived until his death. O.C. "Pat" Vincent (1867–1943) recalled for the editor of the *Rains County Leader* that the first school teacher in Pilgrim Rest community was Squire Gee—his grandfather. Among the first doctors in the county was his uncle, Dr. Alonzo Gee. Standing in front of the cabin about 1900 are Chloe Gee Horsley (center) with relatives Mr. and Mrs. Vincent. The cabin stood until 1973.

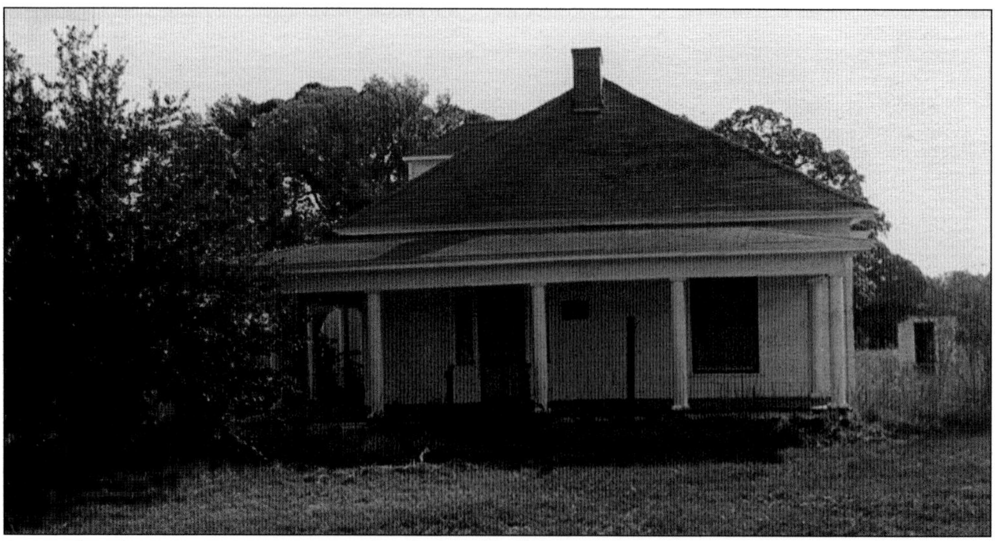

Located in the Prospect community, the George W. (1864–1942) and Florence Woodson (1884–1979) Luckett home was built in 1912. Their daughter Mattie was the first child born in the house. The residence has a front parlor, three bedrooms, and a kitchen in the back plus a large dining area. Interior stairs lead to the attic where the Luckett boys slept. The house was donated to the Rains County Historical Society by the Luckett descendants and sits in the Rains County Historical Park. (Courtesy of Elaine Nall Bay.)

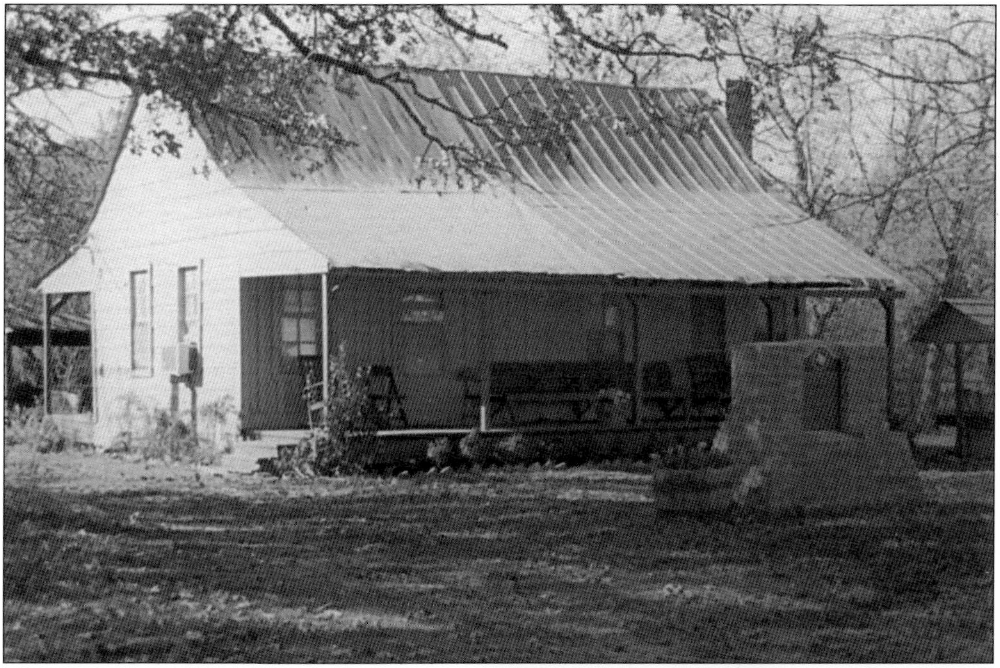

The Dougherty home place and farm is designated as a Texas Century Farm and a Designated Family Land Heritage Property by the Texas Department of Agriculture. In addition, there is also a Texas Historical Marker dated 1983 placed by the Texas Historical Commission. Robert Newberry Dougherty (1825–1909) assumed management of his father's farm in the 1860s and was the sole owner of the family's land by 1870. In the years 1880–1881, Robert Dougherty constructed a one-room house. Over the years, additions have been made to the original structure. At one time, the Dougherty home served as the headquarters for the Dougherty rural telephone company. (Courtesy of Elaine Nall Bay.)

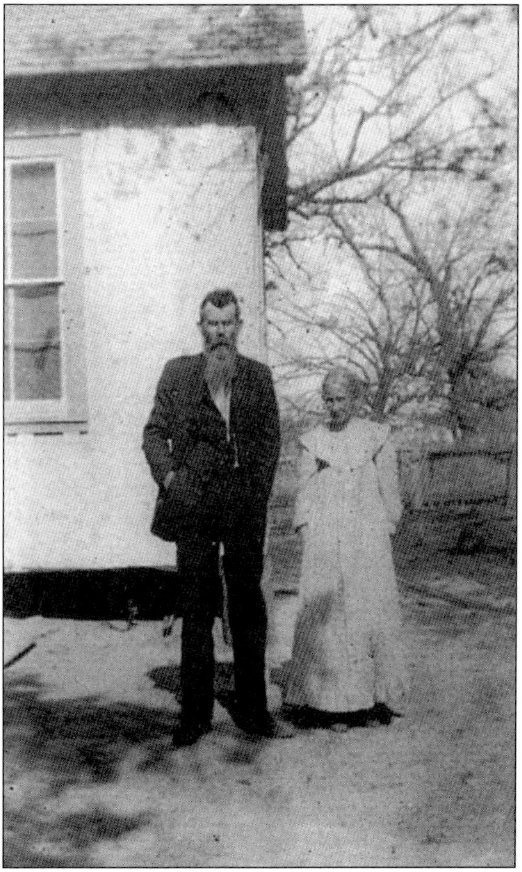

Stephen James "S.J." Stuart (1846–1919) and his wife, Sarah Jane "Janie" Forbis Stuart (1859–1935), are standing in front of their first home in Rains County. Their land was at the end of Planters Street, where there is now just an open pasture. (Courtesy of Jo Ann Stuart Turman.)

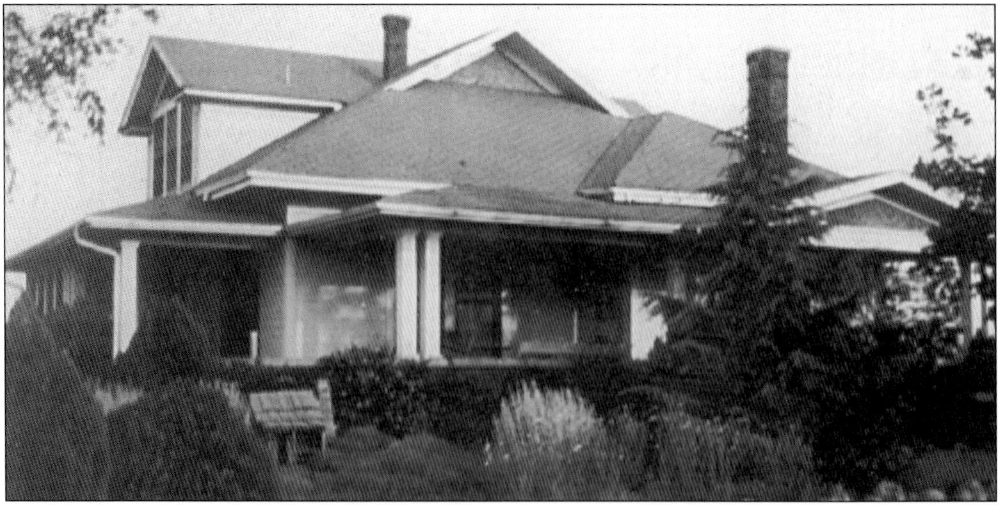

Baud Montgomery, grandson of Emory Rains and twin brother of Julia, built his business and home in Point. While the brick home was being constructed, the Montgomery family lived in a frame house on the adjacent lot. One night, Baud sensed that something was wrong so he went next door to check on the unfinished home. On the bottom step was a can with kerosene and a rag in it. If Baud had not followed his instinct, the new brick house would have burned. When the steps to the house were being finished, he insisted that the burn mark from the can be left on the bottom entrance step. (Image courtesy of Philip Kerr; information provided by Cay Frances B. House.)

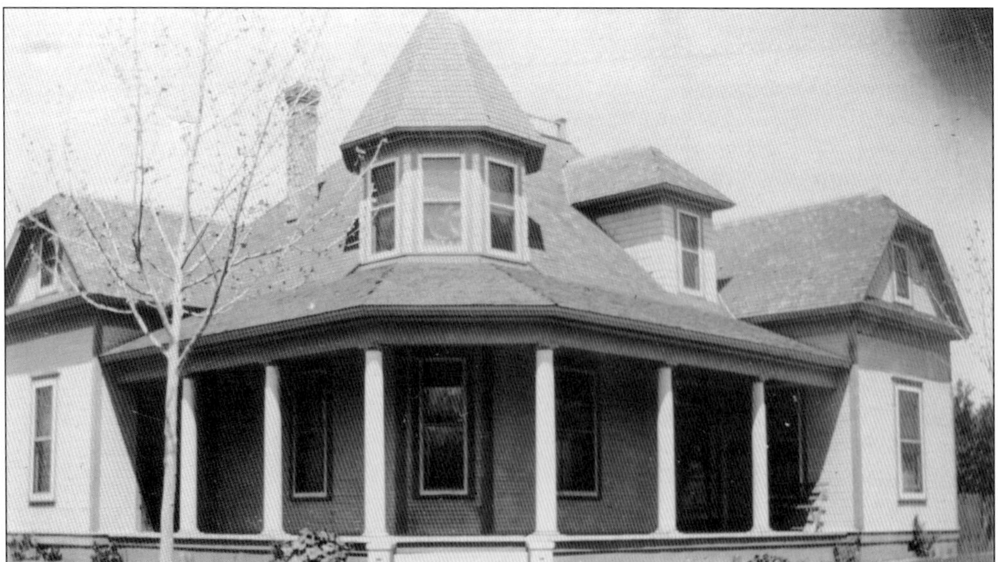

This Emory home was occupied by Ada Cain (1865–1944) and Dr. W.A. Duffey (1857–1906). Ada was the daughter of Capt. Thomas Cain. On June 1916, "The following pleasure seekers enjoyed a midnight lunch Monday night at the Mrs. Duffey pool southwest of Emory: Misses Jessie McCrum of Lone Oak, Zula Ballew, Maude and Lillie Ivie, Mary and Josie Henry, Gladys Robinson, Elizabeth Romine of Brashear, Mesdames Lois Galt of Dallas, Hallie Stuart and Emma Henry; Messrs. Ben Mercer, Dee Mercer and Jack Hull of Cumby, Dr. Warsham of Brashear, Leo Allen, Jesse Woosley and Jack Blount," the *Rains County Leader* reported. (Courtesy of Mary A. Cain White.)

# *Three*

# Jesus Loves Me, This I Know

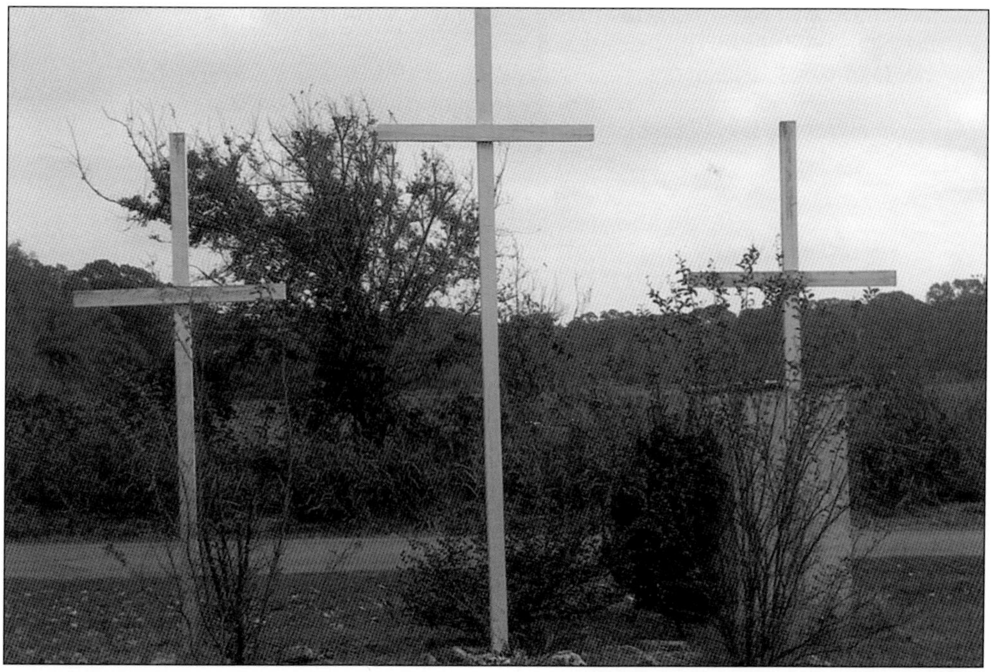

"For where two or three are gathered together in my name, there am I with them" (Matthew 10:20 KJV). Early settlers met in homes to read the Bible and pray together. When a church building was constructed, the different denominations would rotate, each given one Sunday of the month to have services. This was the era of the traveling preacher. Churches established in Rains County in the early 1900s were Protestant denominations: Methodist, Baptist, Christian, Presbyterian, and Church of Christ. (Courtesy of Elaine Nall Bay.)

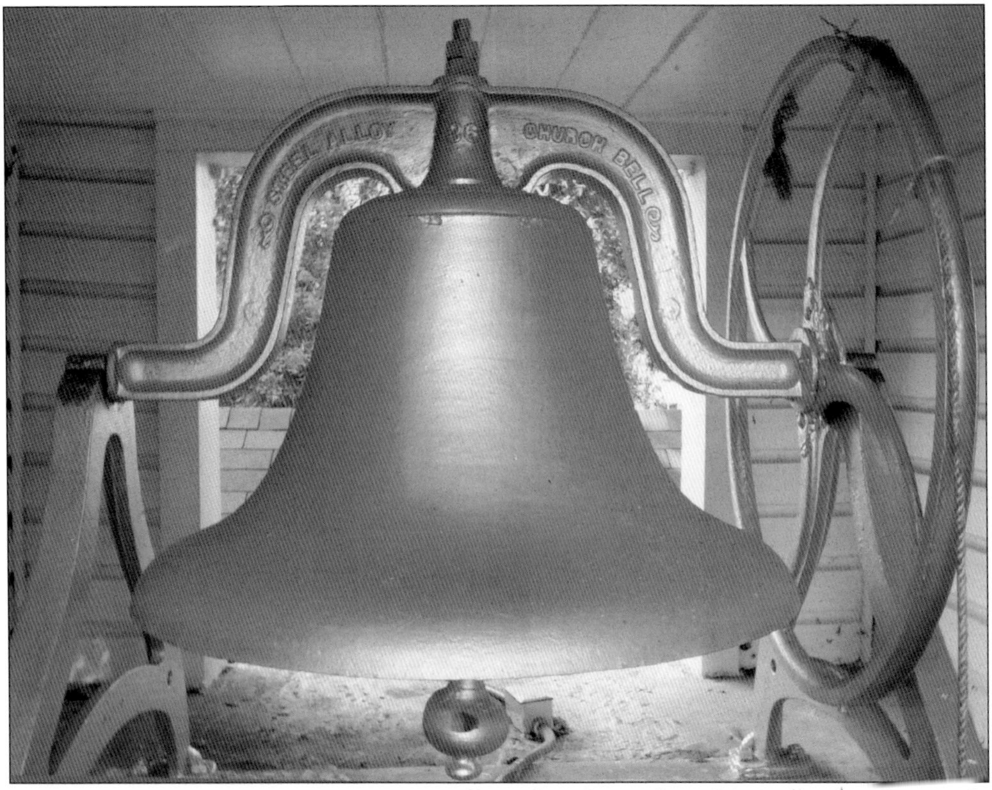


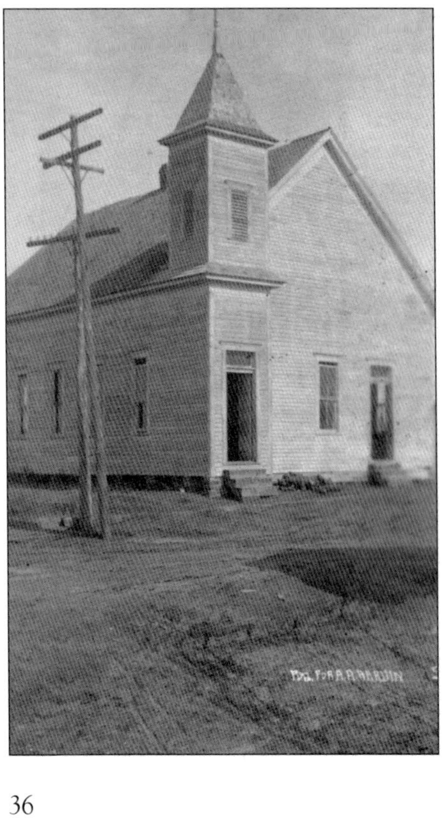

Records indicate that a Methodist church existed as early as 1867 in Springville, Wood County. At first, the congregation met in the Masonic Hall on the town square. In July 1891, F.T. Beaird sold a tract of land in Emory for $5 to the First Methodist Episcopal Church of Emory trustees Thomas M. Cain, George R. Kimbrough, and Felix P. Hardin. In February 1893, the Emory Methodist Episcopal Church South requested financial help from the North Texas Annual Conference in order to build a house of worship; the church was granted aid in the amount of $150. In 1889, a house of worship, located a block west of the town square, was completed in time for Easter services. The 1894 tornado destroyed the church and contents. "I remember one thing," affirms Lela Ballew, "we had just bought a new organ Friday afternoon; the cyclone struck Saturday night. Monday I had to send a $115 check to pay for it." The only item saved was the bell that had hung in its belfry. The 1904 Methodist church building was a wooden structure furnished with wooden pews and located west of Emory's town square; it was moved several years later to its present site on North Texas Street. (Courtesy of Jeri McAree Humphrey.)

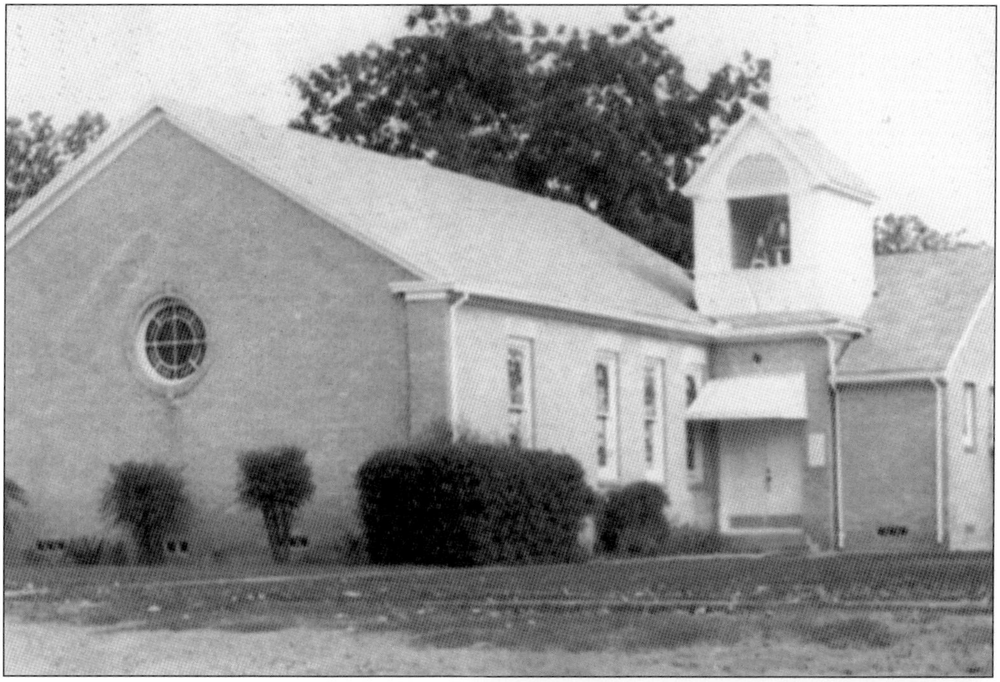

In 1944, a brick structure was built due to weather damage to the 1904 building. Good lumber from the old frame church plus a campaign that raised $10,000 helped construct the new, debt-free church building dedicated to God's work in September 1945. The grandchildren of David M. and Anna Elizabeth Rodes donated new pulpit furniture. After the services, a dinner was held on the grounds for the congregation and many friends in the community. Beautiful stained glass windows are inscribed with the names of some of the founders and sustainers of the church. The Gethsemane window was dedicated to Mr. and Mrs. W.D. Shaw, the parents of "Miss Essie" Jenkins. (Courtesy of Jeri McAree Humphrey.)

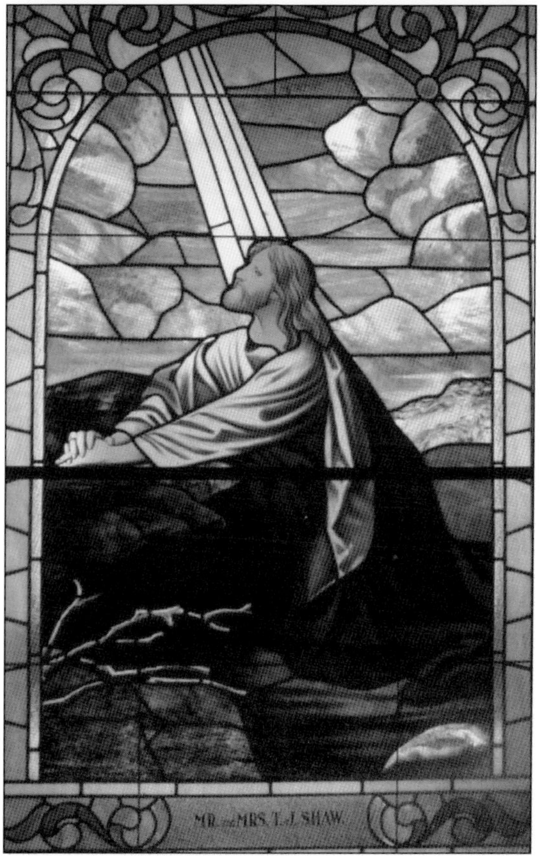

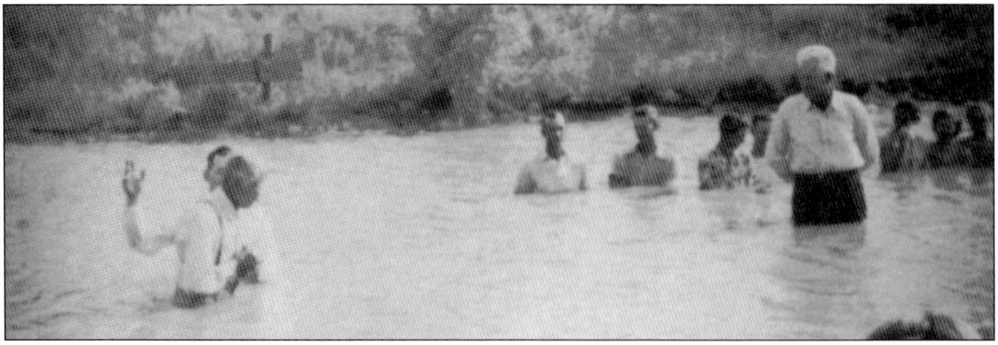

In his *Autobiography & Other Writings*, D.S. Peoples shared a photograph of baptismal services held at Ray Pilton pool. Ray is in pictured the background, and T.J. Nelson is the candidate.

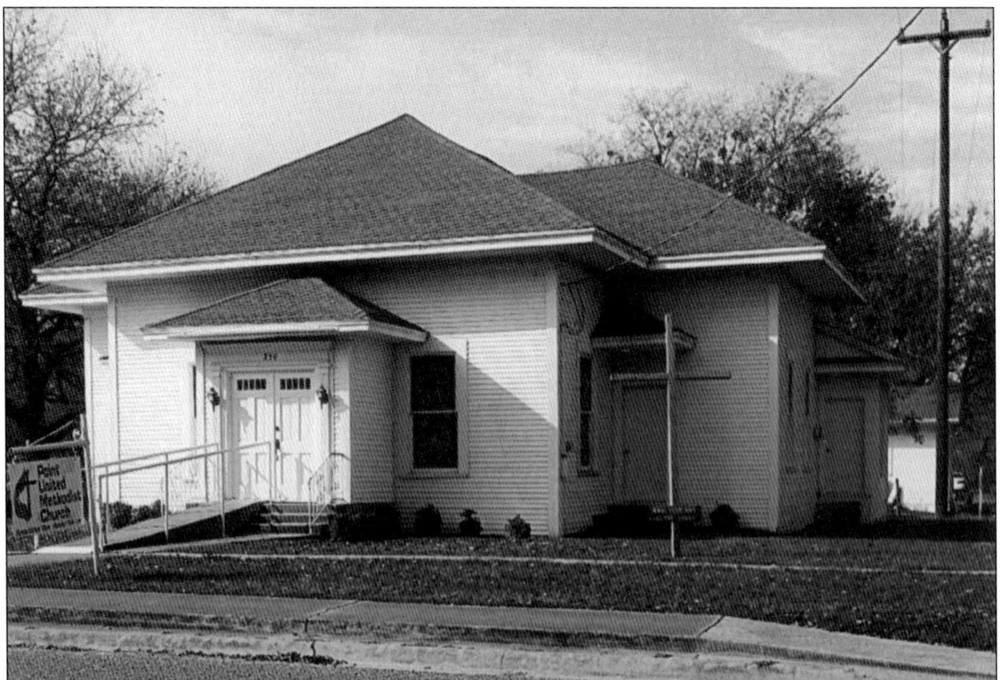


It was announced in the January 24, 1913, *Rains County Leader* that "the new Methodist church is under construction by Messrs. Ernest McFadden of Point and Clarence McKnight of Greenville. We hope to have it completed in the near future. . . . Rev. Edwards, the pastor of the M.E. church at Point, tells us that they have ordered seats for their church, which cost them $465. They are individual seats. . . . The size of the main building is 42 feet long and 32 feet wide, but it has two wings 8 feet wide and 16 feet long . . . The building will cost about $2,500 when completed." (Courtesy of Elaine Nall Bay.)

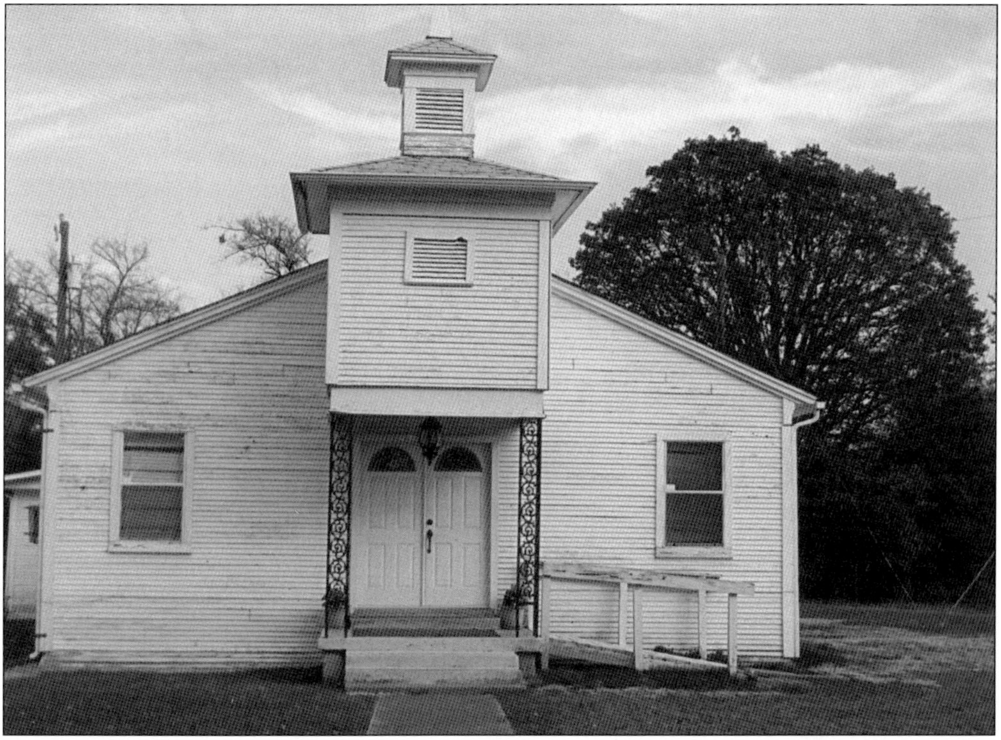

The Richland Baptist Church is located in the Richland community in the northwestern part of Rains County and serves African American residents of the community. The building was built in the early 1900s. (Courtesy of Elaine Nall Bay.)

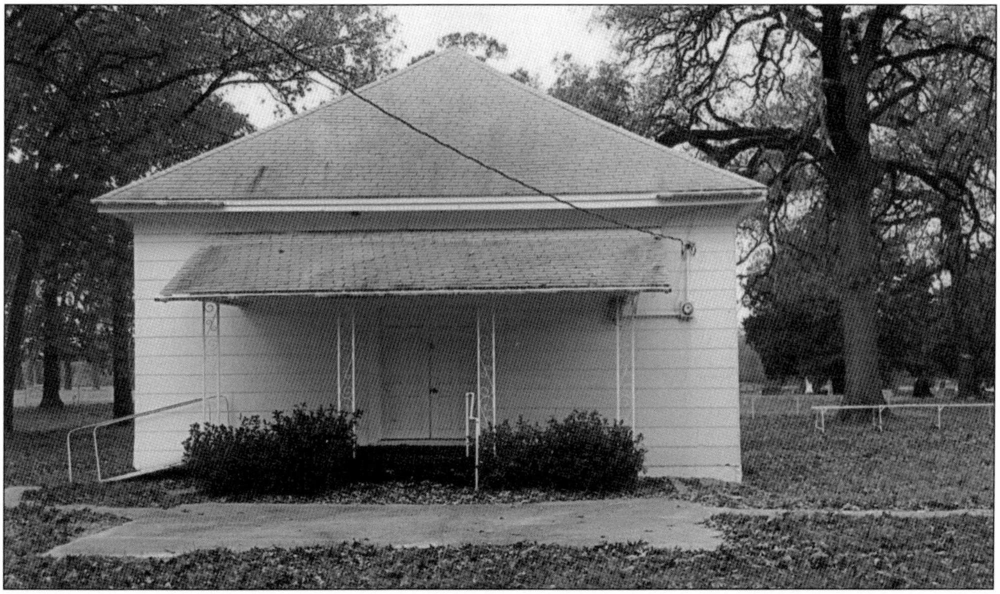

The Colony Church of Christ was built in 1912 to be used as both a church and a school. Some of the early settlers in the Colony community were the Powers, Case, Gilley, McGahey, McAree, Parker, Milliron, Butler, Moody, Horne, Cause, Poston, Reader, Eads, Walker, Hutchins, and Thornhill families. (Courtesy of Elaine Nall Bay.)

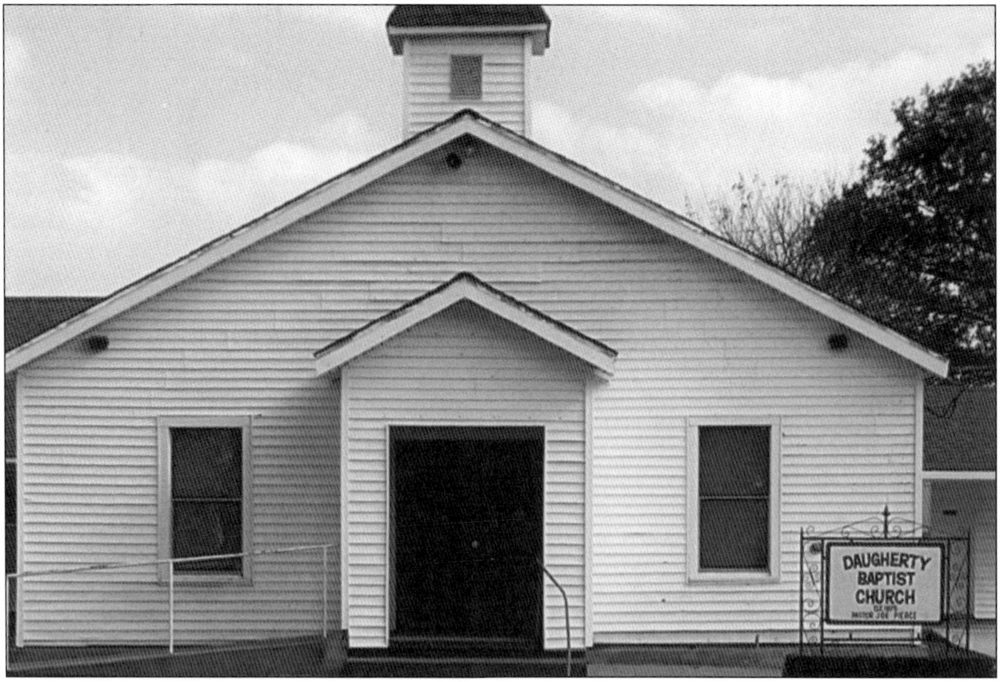


Jim Garrett donated land for a school. In 1909, the church organized into the Daugherty Baptist Church of Christ. In December 1922, a building with seating for 200 was erected on the south portion of the school land. A third church building was dedicated in 1924 but was damaged by a storm in 1953. Rather than repair the old building, members made a decision to build a new one. (Courtesy of Elaine Nall Bay.)

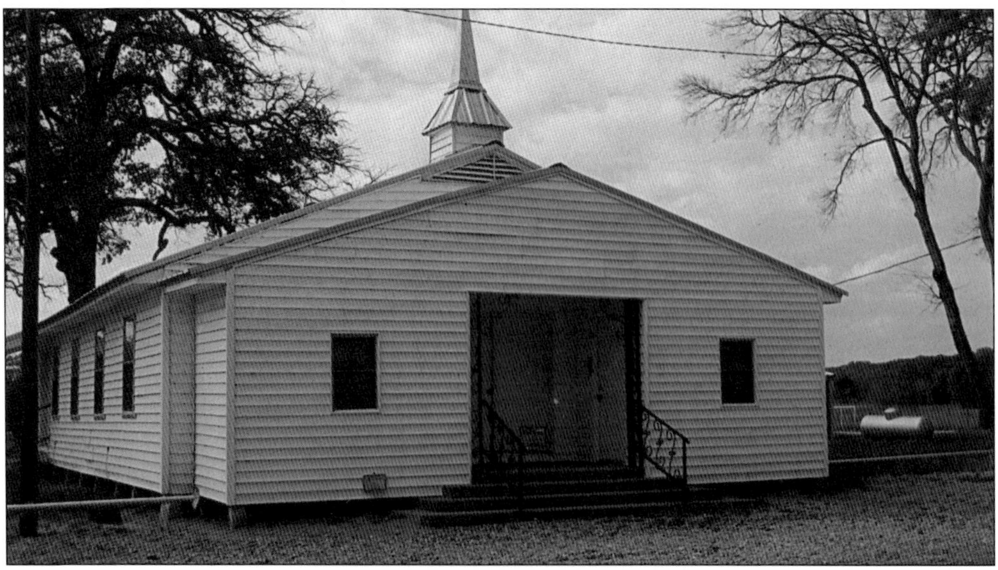

Used for school and church purposes, the original Smyrna building burned in 1902. A new two-story structure with a belfry replaced the first church, and the bell in the belfry was rung to announce community happenings. The top room was used for lodge meetings, and the lower room for preaching and other activities. The building was remodeled by removing the top floor. In the late 1950s, a new brick building replaced this structure. (Courtesy of Joanna Robertson Pound.)

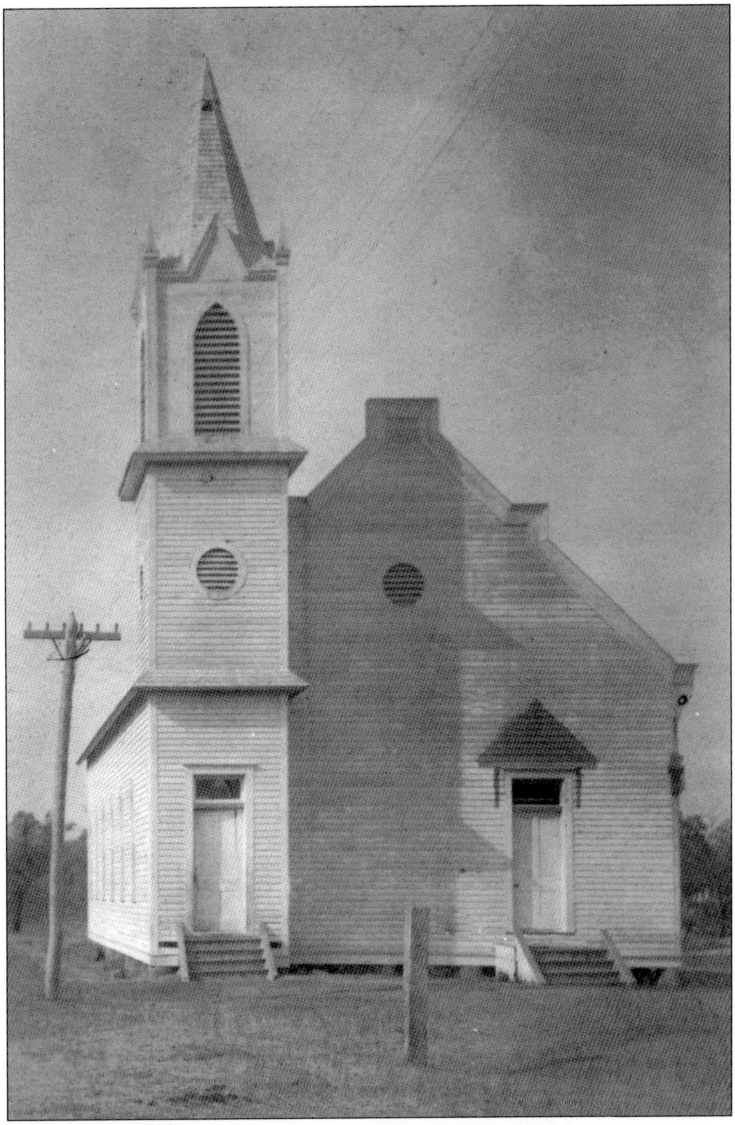

The current Emory Baptist Church was known as Salem Baptist Church and First Baptist Church of Emory before Rains County was formed. In 1880, Emory Baptist Church was located in front of the M.S. Pierson residence. That church was destroyed by the 1894 tornado that passed through Emory. The church building shown on the right is dated about 1906. In 1915, the Emory Baptist Church was organized with 40 members present. In 1932, a brick building was constructed, pictured below. (Courtesy of Jeri McAree Humphrey.)

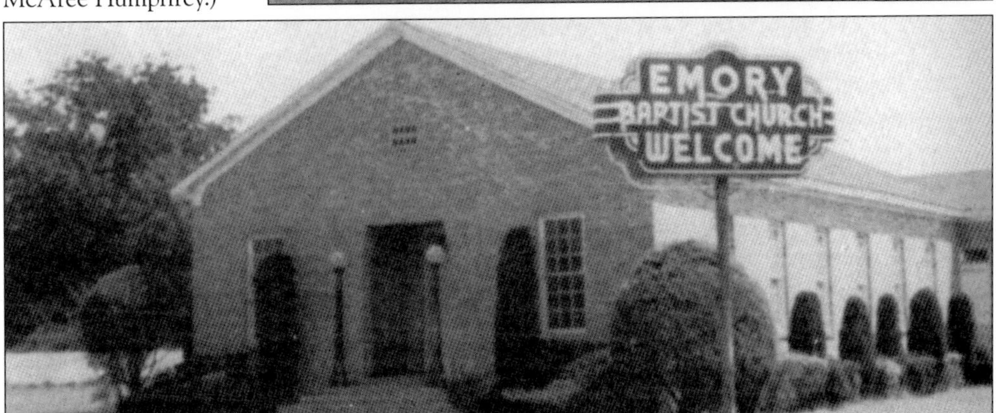

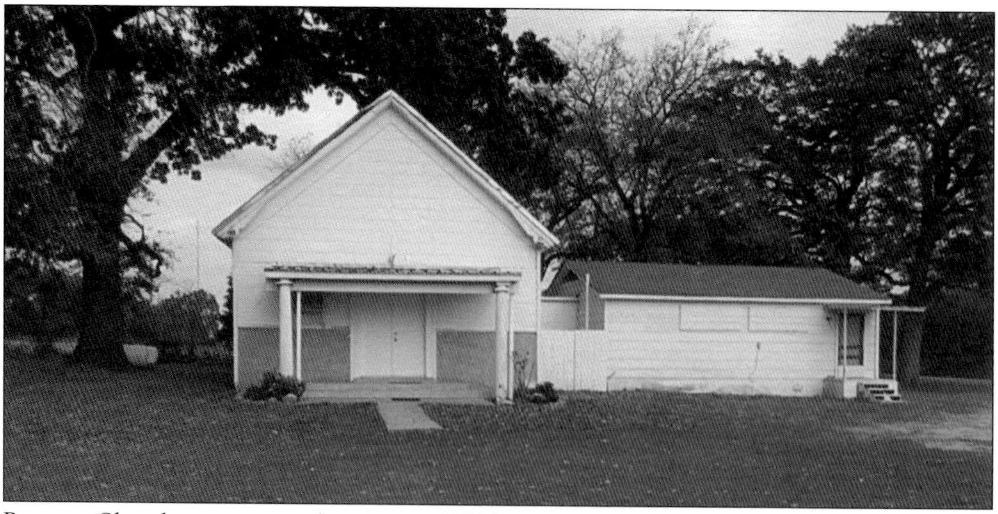

Prospect Church was organized in August 1878 by Rev. A.C. McKay during a brush arbor revival meeting. Twelve families were charter members. Baptisms were held at the Dyer or Yandell gin pools. Land was donated by A.R. and Molly Cornelius in 1881, W.R. and Julia M. Shultz in 1895, and Lillian L. Dyer in 1954. A new building was completed in 1971. (Courtesy of Elaine Nall Bay.)

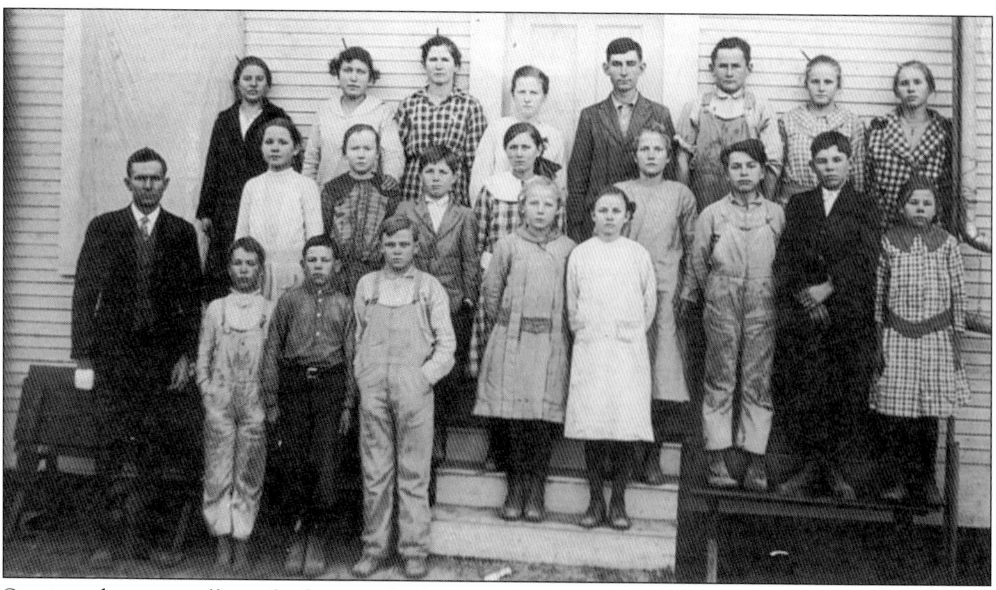

Singing classes usually took place in the late summer after the crops were planted and gathered. The above group attended a singing class at Freedom church (today's Freedom Church of God). The Freedom community is located in western Rains County near the Rains and Hopkins county line. (Courtesy of Mike Freiberger.)

The Emory Church of Christ originated in the Willow Springs community around 1860. In 1904, the congregation moved to Emory and met in a brush arbor. A frame building was built that served until 1949, when the members built a new rock building. As the congregation grew, a new brick facility was built west of Highway 69 in 1970. (Courtesy of Elaine Nall Bay.)

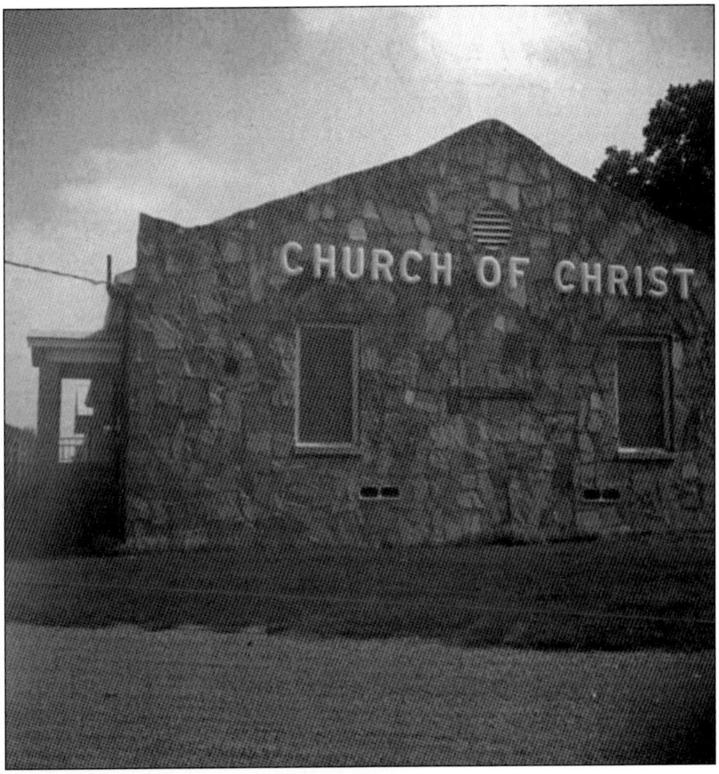


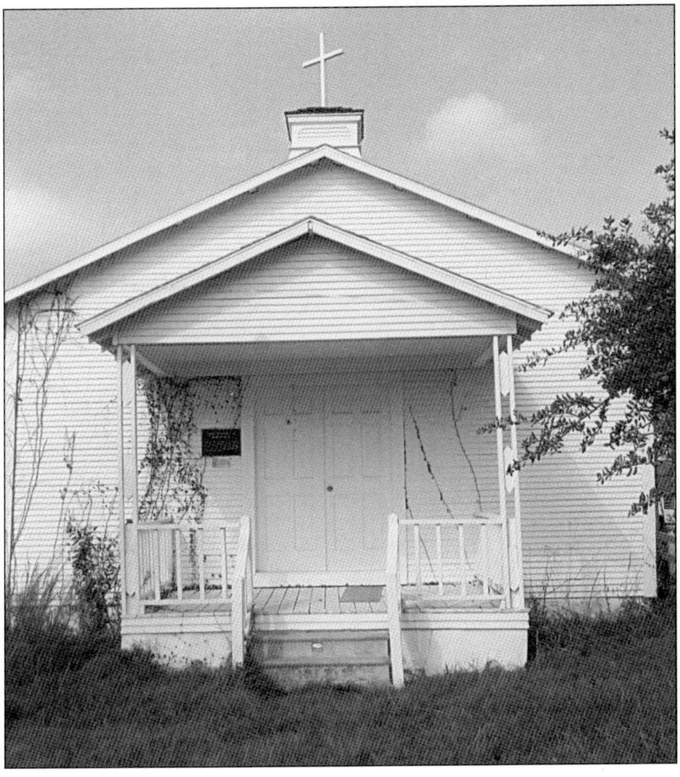

The Shady Grove Missionary Baptist Church was founded in 1930. This building served its members until 1997. It was constructed by members and friends in the era of hand-planed lumber and is typical of early Texas rural churches. The structure was donated by the membership of Shady Grove Missionary Baptist Church to the Rains County Historical Park. (Courtesy of Elaine Nall Bay.)

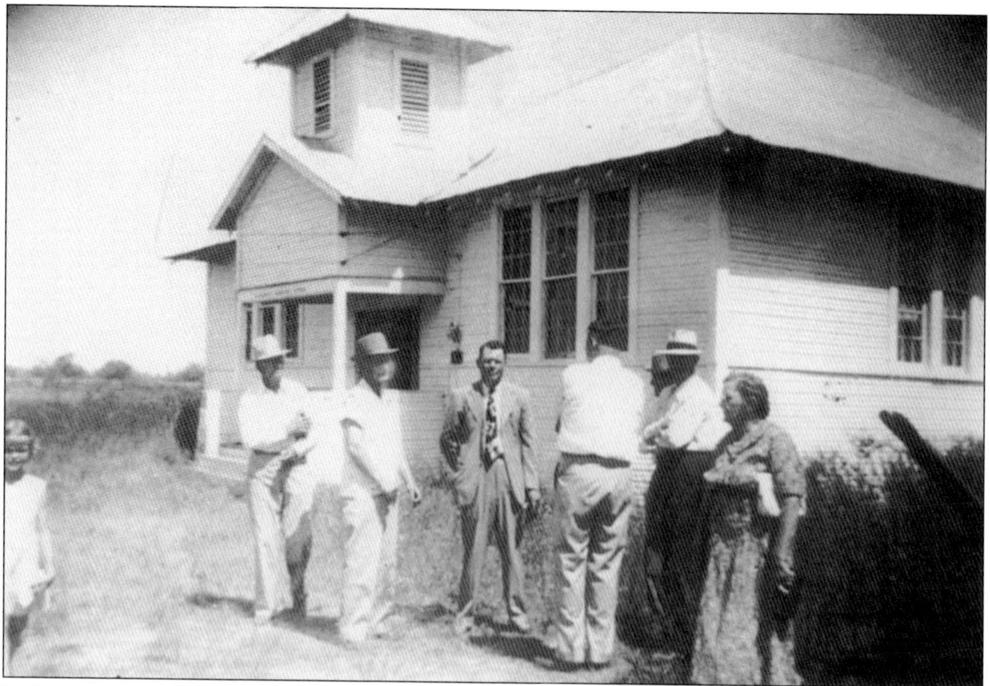

In January 1952, the Rains County Board of Trustees deeded the land and buildings that were once part of Daughtery School District No. 15, established in 1899, to the Dougherty community trustees (Guy Holman, Fred Blanton, and Charlie Sparks) for religious and community purposes. (Courtesy of Gwen Freiberger Holman.)

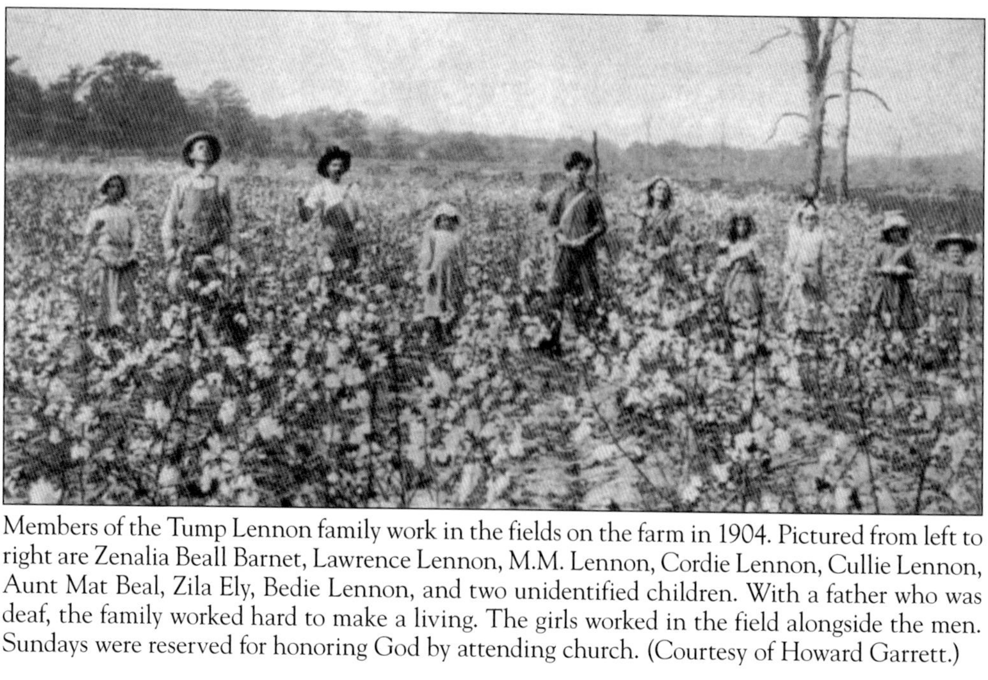

Members of the Tump Lennon family work in the fields on the farm in 1904. Pictured from left to right are Zenalia Beall Barnet, Lawrence Lennon, M.M. Lennon, Cordie Lennon, Cullie Lennon, Aunt Mat Beal, Zila Ely, Bedie Lennon, and two unidentified children. With a father who was deaf, the family worked hard to make a living. The girls worked in the field alongside the men. Sundays were reserved for honoring God by attending church. (Courtesy of Howard Garrett.)

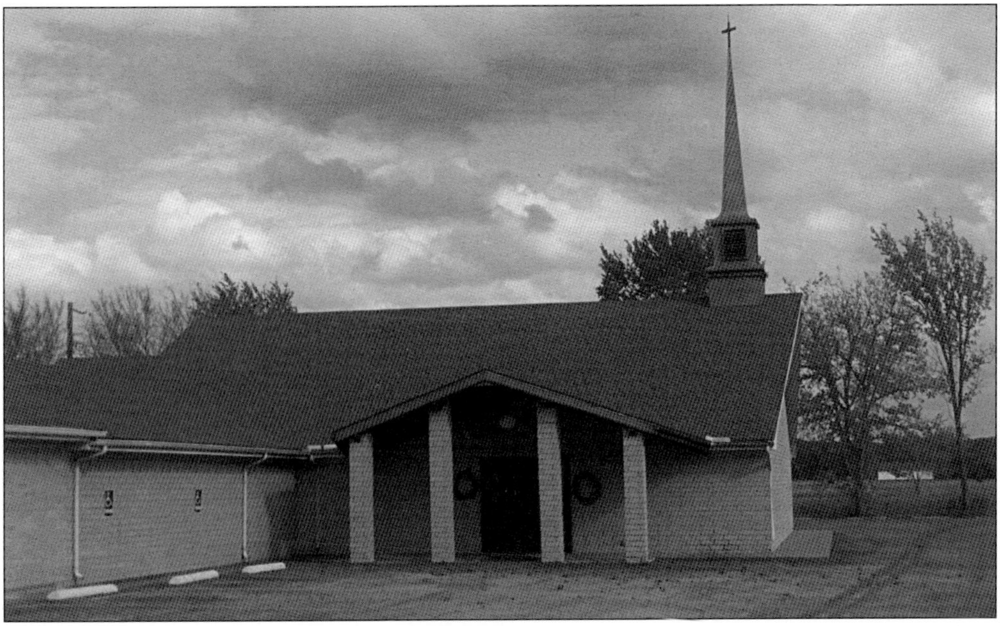

In 1916, several families moved from Tennessee to Flats community in Rains County, where the Church of God was nonexistent. After a revival in 1916, a Church of God was organized on August 12, 1917 with 21 members. Land for the church was donated by Robert Rabe, and a small frame building with dirt floors was erected. Above is the current building. (Courtesy of Elaine Nall Bay.)

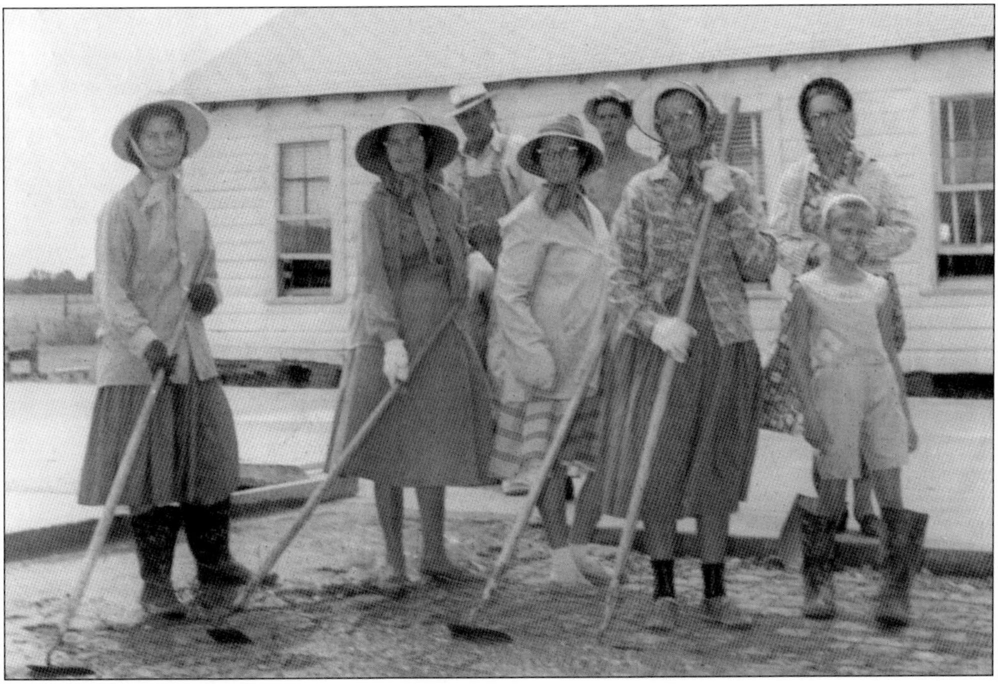

"If you think the wimmin' folks can't build a church, just come to Flats, Texas." The ladies pictured are Edith Carter Trimble, Vera Rabe, Maggie Cason, Lota Cason, Sister McBride, and Glenda Carter. The third red brick building for Clark's Chapel was built in 1967.

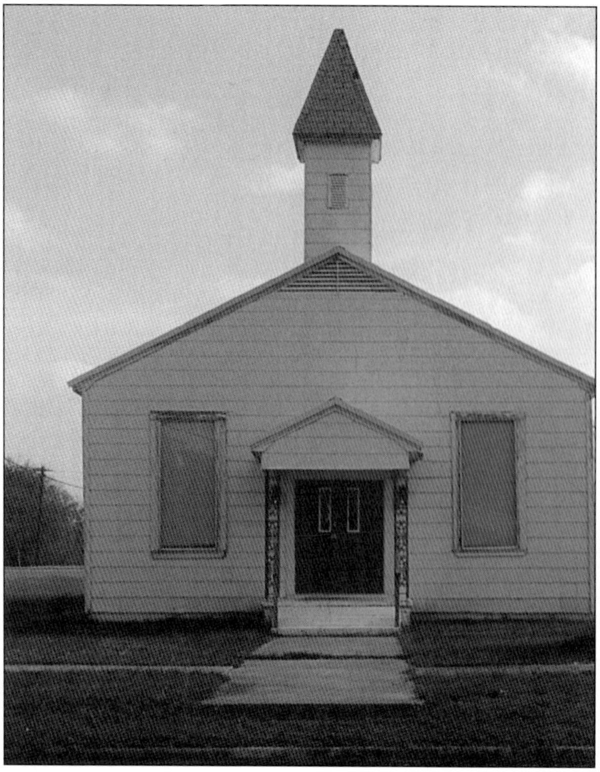

The First Baptist Church of Point was organized about 1894 in the Point Union Church, which was used by Presbyterian, Baptist, Christian, and Methodist congregations. The First Baptist Church building erected in 1949 still exists but has been replaced by a modern, brick structure about a mile west of the original. (Courtesy of Elaine Nall Bay.)

The quaint Willow Springs Church sits vacant on land near the entrance to the Floyd Greene ranch. It is now used for weddings because of its scenic setting. (Courtesy of Elaine Nall Bay.)

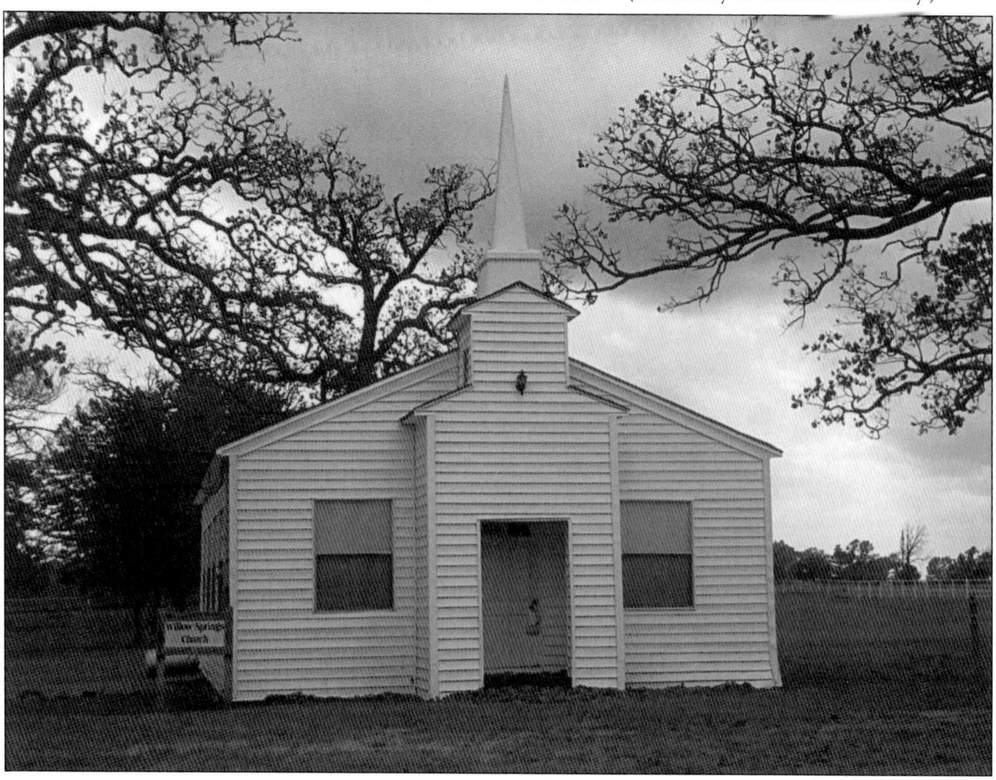

# *Four*

# Ashes to Ashes, Dust to Dust

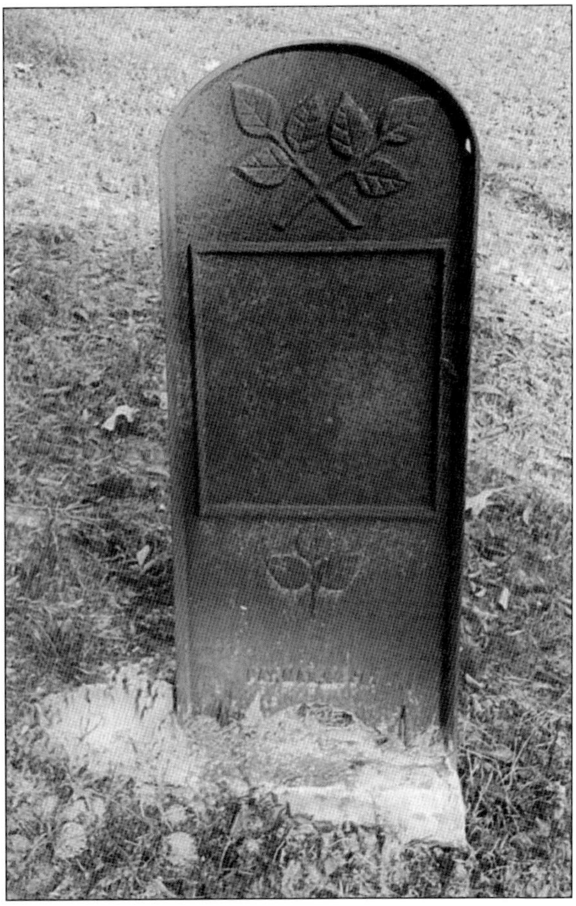

"Ashes to ashes, dust to dust" is often quoted at funeral services. Typically, in the settlement days of Rains County, a loved one was buried on a plot of land on the family farm that evolved into a family cemetery. Graveyards are also found near churches in some of the communities. The local cemetery evolved from a land donation to which additional land was added from time to time and designated as a public burial ground. Cemeteries, many of which are neglected, are records of Rains County's past. They are resources of vital records and may reveal details of citizens' ancestors' lives and deaths. (Courtesy of Elaine Nall Bay.)

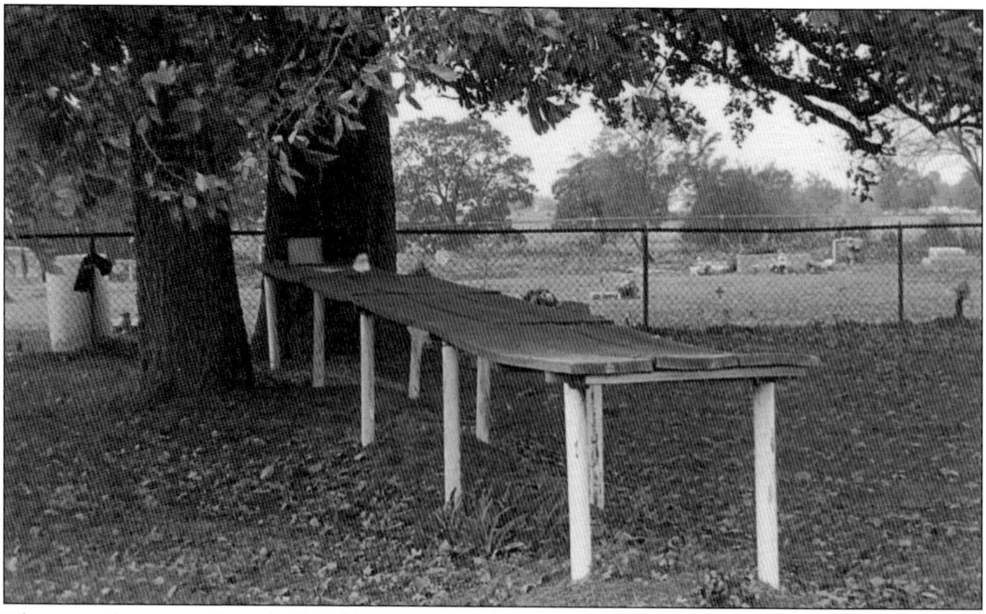

These outdoor, wooden plank tables are a reminder of the many church dinners and cemetery memorial days from years past. They are on the grounds at Prospect Cemetery and Church and are located under a group of trees near the Prospect Cemetery fence. Many have gathered around these tables and similar tables at the other Rains County rural cemeteries to eat and fellowship at cemetery memorial days or to take a break from cleaning up the cemetery. (Courtesy of Elaine Nall Bay.)

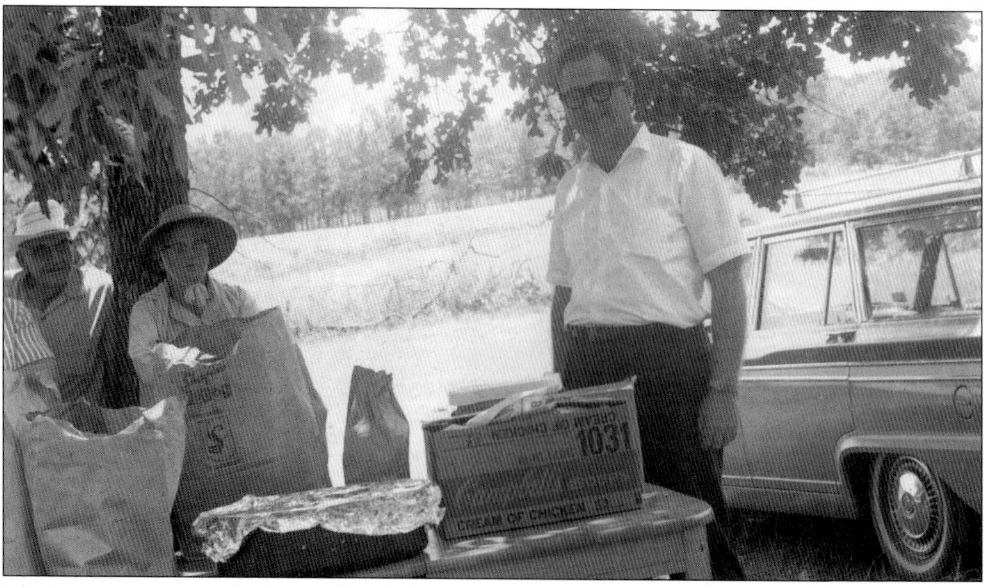


The *Rains County Leader* frequently published notices of graveyard workings. "Graveyard Working: There will be a grave yard working at Henrys Chapel graveyard next Friday. Those who are interested are requested to attend, bring their dinner and stay all day." Today, a caretaker maintains most cemeteries. Many hold memorial days with dinner on the grounds following the cemetery association meeting. In this photograph are, from left to right, Elbert Herring, unidentified, and Ivan Alexander.

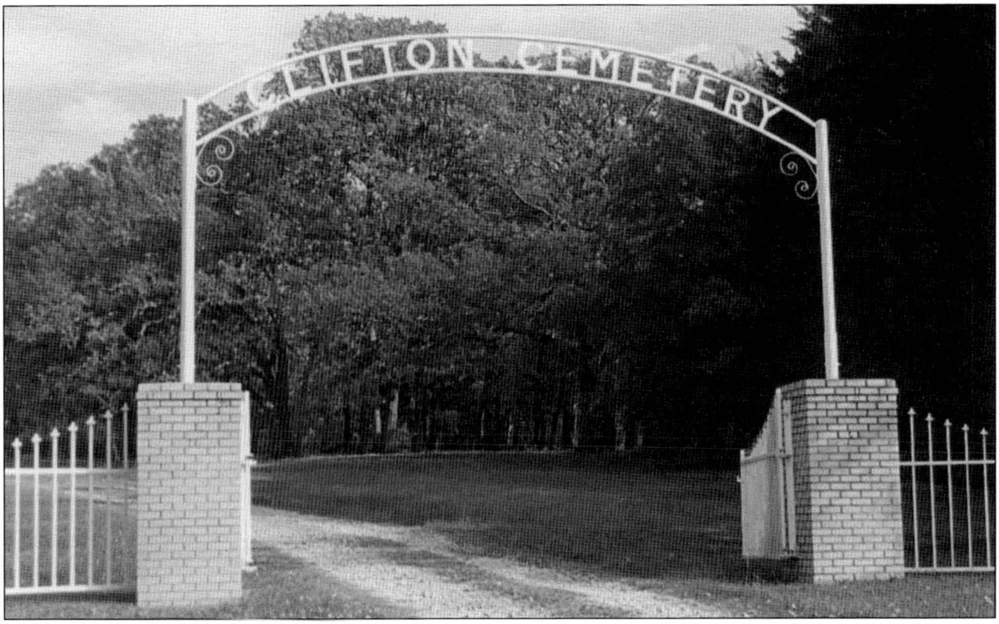


The first burial in the Clifton Cemetery was that of William Marion Clifton (1834–1877). The burial ground is located on his family farm. (Courtesy of Elaine Nall Bay.)

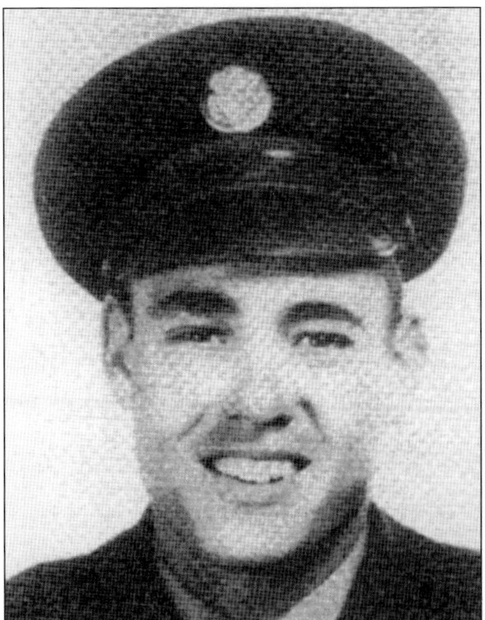

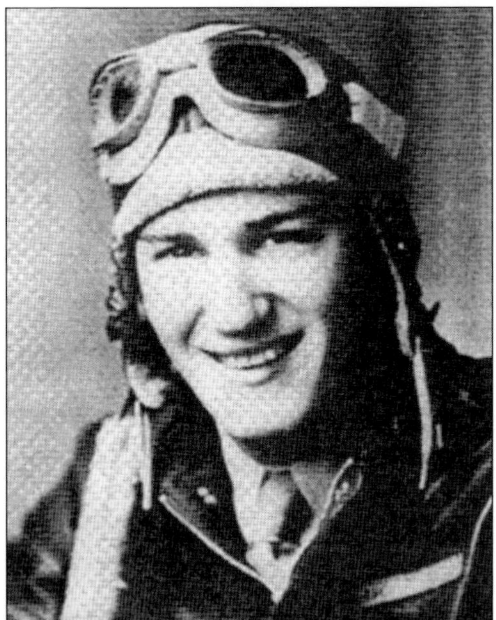

Two sons of Basil Barney and Daisy Morris Rabb, Robert (1928–1950) and Harold (1924–1943), gave their lives for their country. Harold's B-24 bomber was shot down over Germany in 1944, and in 1948 the parents received the telegram declaring their son dead. Harold is buried in a military cemetery in Belgium. Robert was killed when his Jeep hit a land mine while he was laying communication cables behind enemy lines in Korea. His body was returned to the United States, The family erected a double memorial tombstone in the Lone Star Cemetery a couple of miles north of Point, in honor of their sons. (Courtesy of Mary Frances Anderson Rabb.)

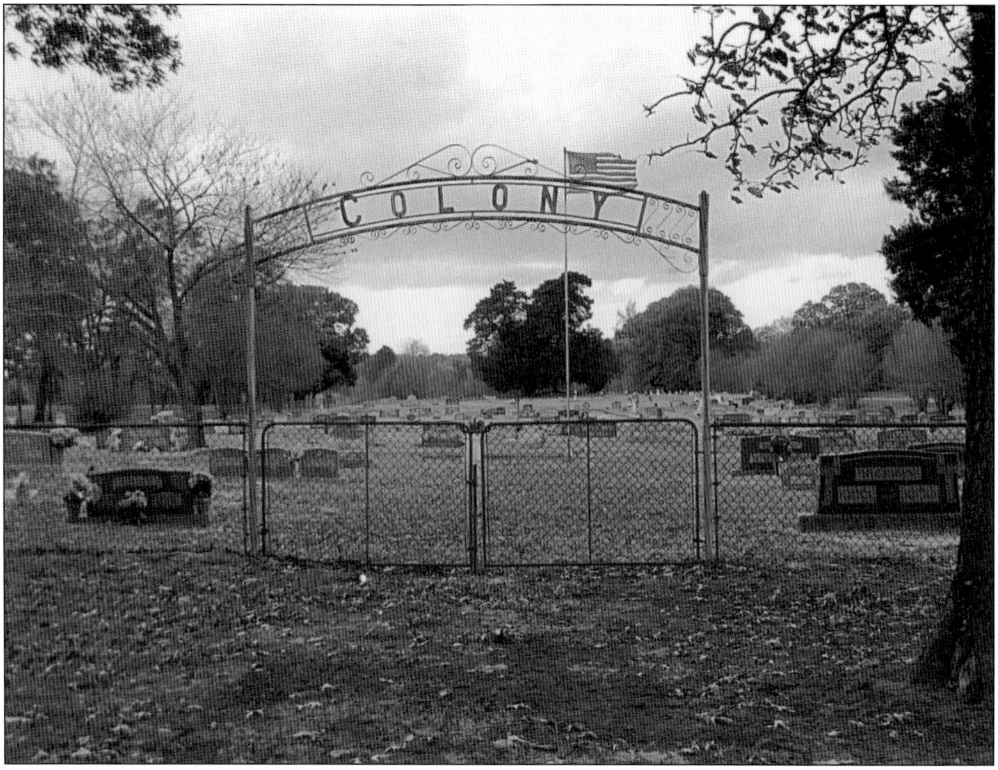


The Colony Cemetery is located behind the Colony Church, which is near the Wood County line. There are many unmarked graves, and others are marked with rocks. The cemetery expanded several years ago and took in the oldest burial ground in Rains County, a small plot for the Powers family (below) that consists of eight marked graves. (Courtesy of Elaine Nall Bay)

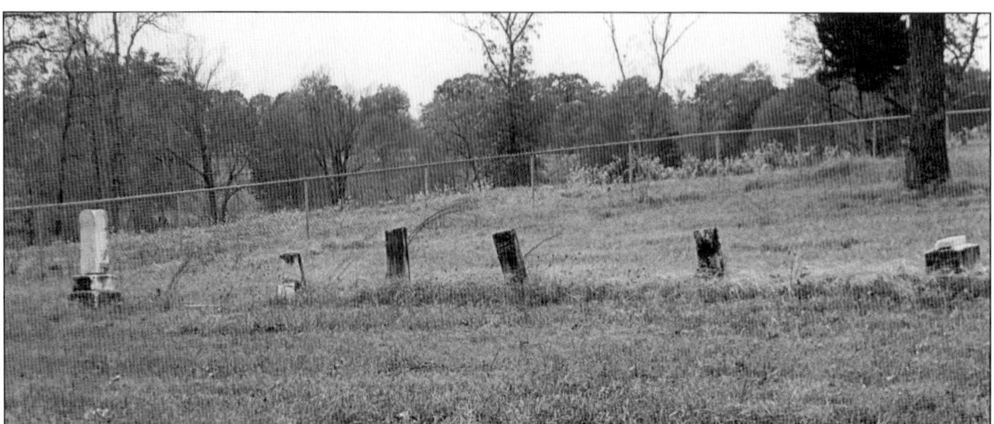

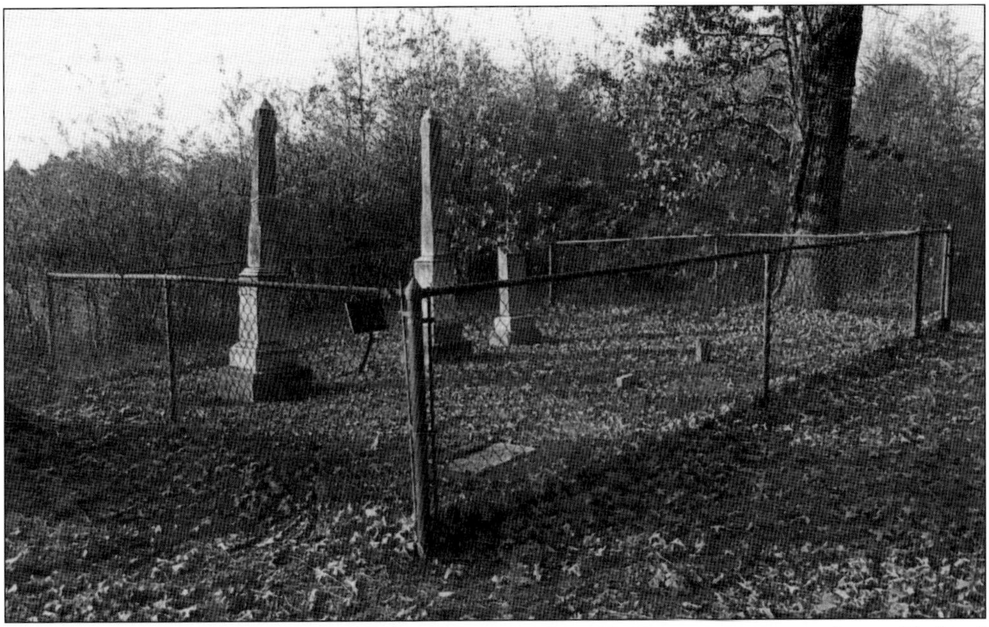

Ambrose Fitzgerald, early pioneer of Rains County, is buried in a private cemetery located behind the Hopewell Cemetery on land he purchased in the 1880s. Fitzgerald read his Bible and meditated under a huge post oak. He was laid to rest beneath this tree on June 15, 1893. Fitzgerald selected the burial site for himself, his wife, and their daughter because it was the largest tree seen from his front porch. (Courtesy of Elaine Nall Bay.)

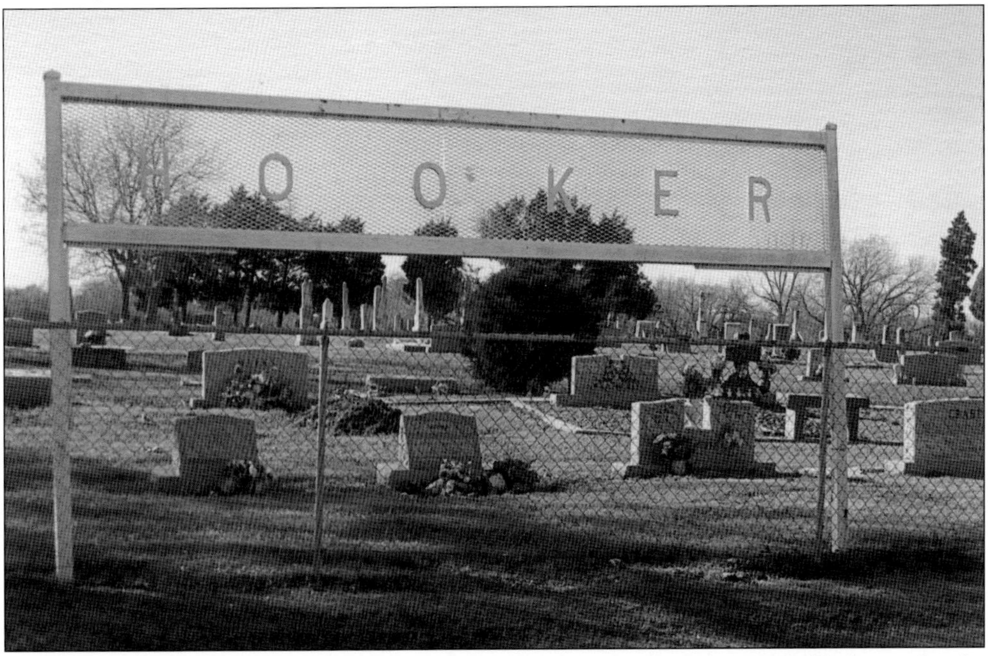


Hooker Cemetery began as a burial site on James Hooker's land. Nathan B. Rabb donated eight acres for the cemetery in the early 1900s. The first burial was of Ann R. Hooker (1821–1854). It is believed that slaves are buried in the original burial ground. The cemetery is located in Rains County, about half a mile from the Hunt County line. (Courtesy of Elaine Nall Bay.)

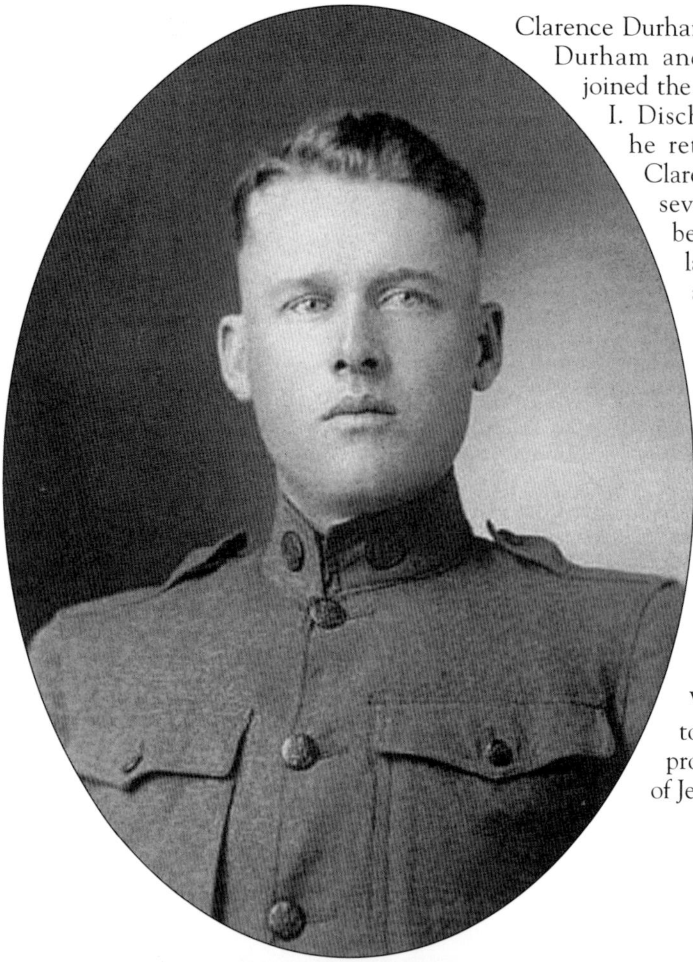

Clarence Durham (1892–1919), son of W.T. Durham and Tommy Jefferson Jack, joined the military during World War I. Discharged in February 1919, he returned to Rains County. Clarence and John Whittle had several fights, and Clarence beat him up. About a week later, Clarence was spending an October evening in front of the drugstore talking with friends. John Whittle rode up in the dark and started shooting. Everyone except Clarence ran into the darkness. Clarence received one shot that went through his throat and one shot that entered his kidney. He suffered six long days before passing away and was laid to rest in the City Cemetery. John Whittles's trial was moved to Greenville; he received a probated sentence. (Courtesy of Jeri McAree Humphrey.)

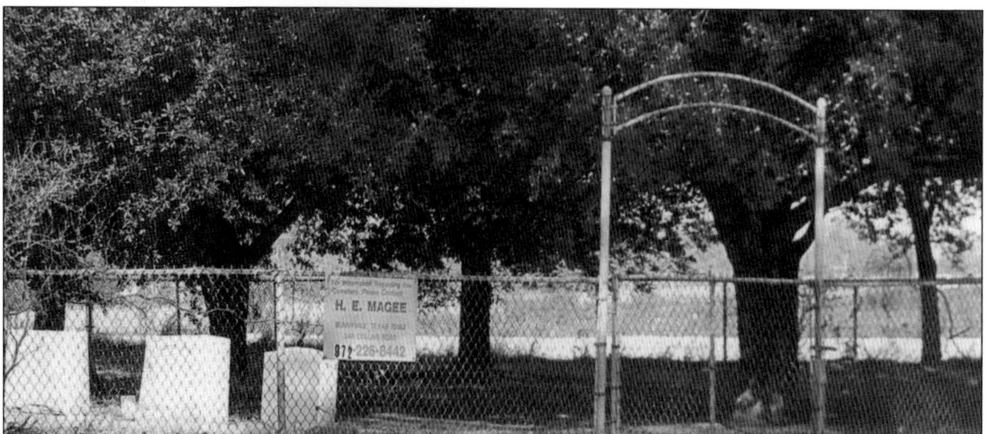


Magee-McCord Cemetery originated when a family passing through Rains County lost a family member near Eli Magee's land in eastern Rains County. Rainy weather prevented them from burying the body at Pilgrim Rest Cemetery. Eli Magee and Mr. McCord deeded land for the cemetery. (Courtesy of Elaine Nall Bay.)

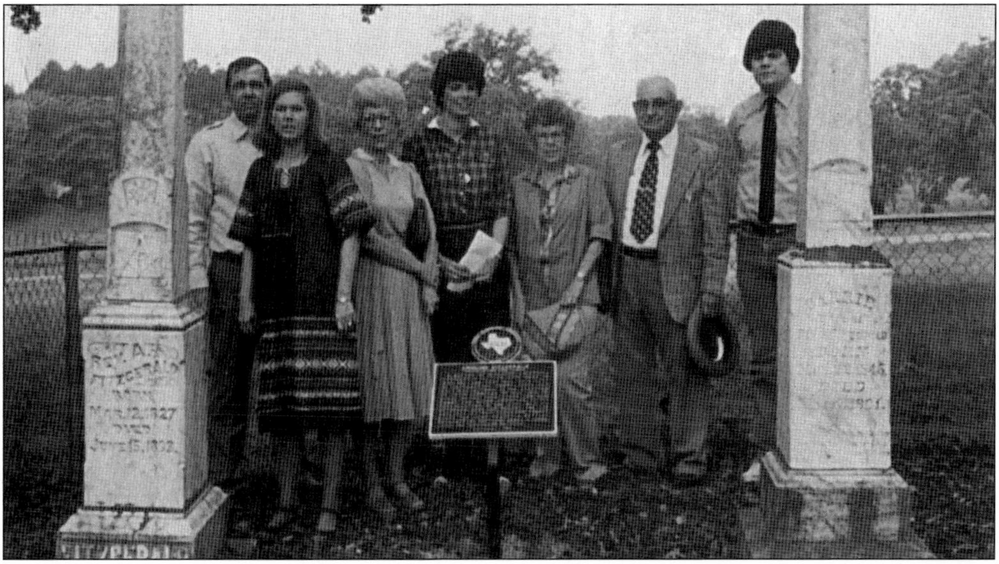

Members of the Rains County Historical Commission attend the dedication of the historical marker at the Ambrose Fitzgerald gravesite in 1983. Pictured from left to right are Jay Jenkins, Elaine Jenkins, Norma Lee Gowin, Maxanne Potts, Juandell Weddle, Edward Toles, and Phillip Kerr.

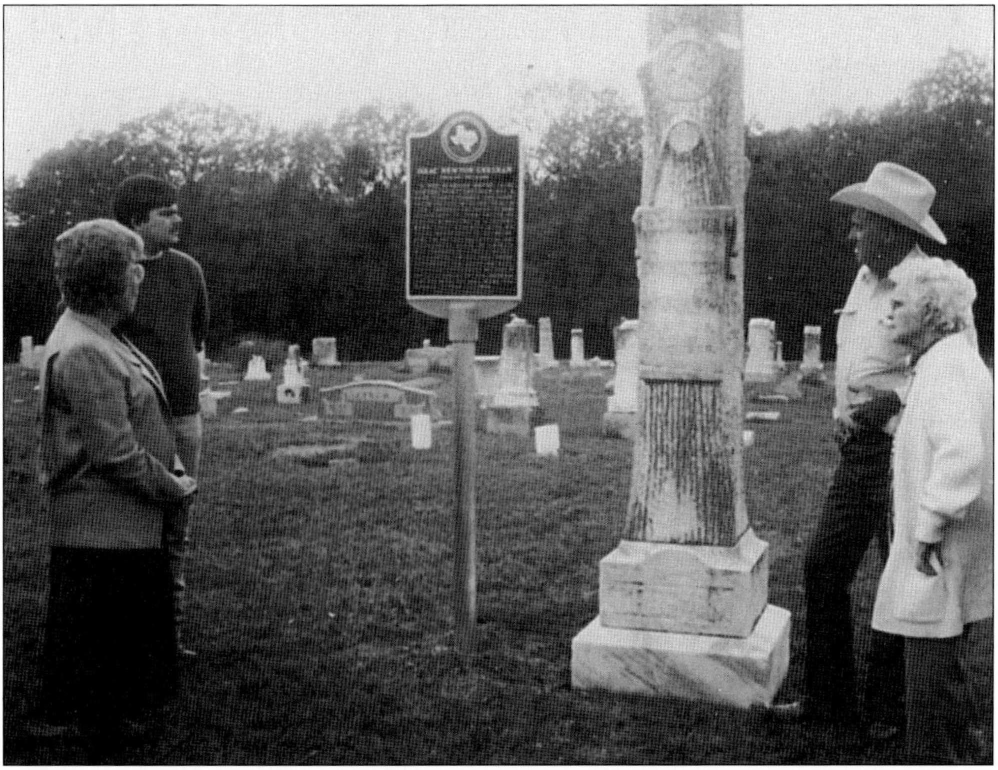

Members of the Rains County Historical Commission view another historical marker—that of Newt Gresham along with visitors attending the National Farmers Union centennial celebration. The grave is located in Lone Star Cemetery. From left to right are Philip Kerr, Juandell Weddle, and two unidentified visitors.

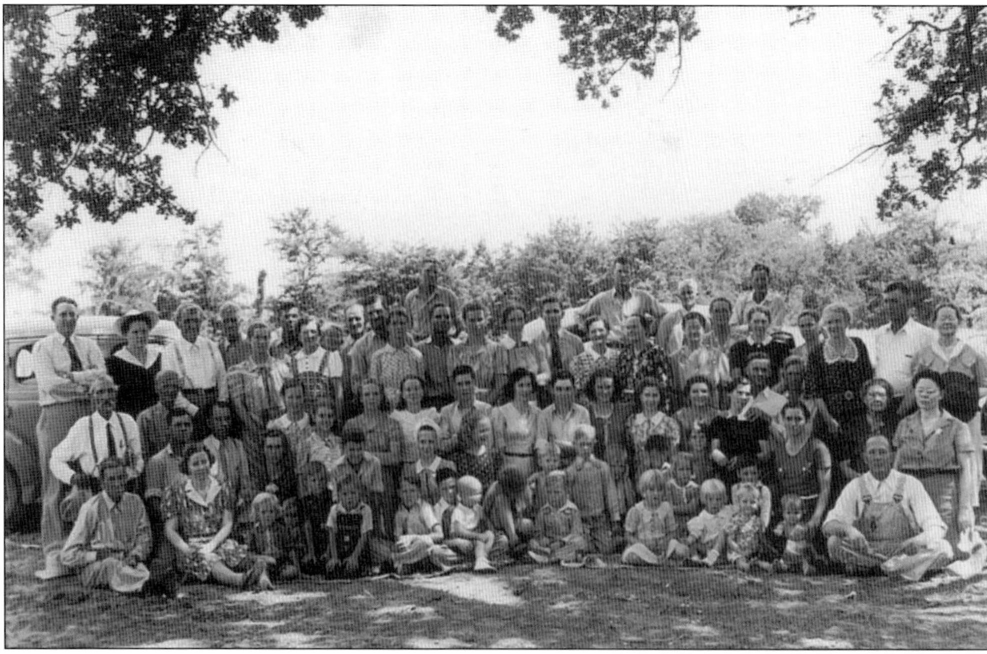

A group of people gathered at the Lynch Cemetery for a cemetery memorial day in the early 1940s. Lynch Cemetery was first called Pleasant Grove Cemetery in the 1890s and is located southwest of Point on the south side of the road, between Emory and East Tawakoni. (Courtesy of Helen Skaggs.)

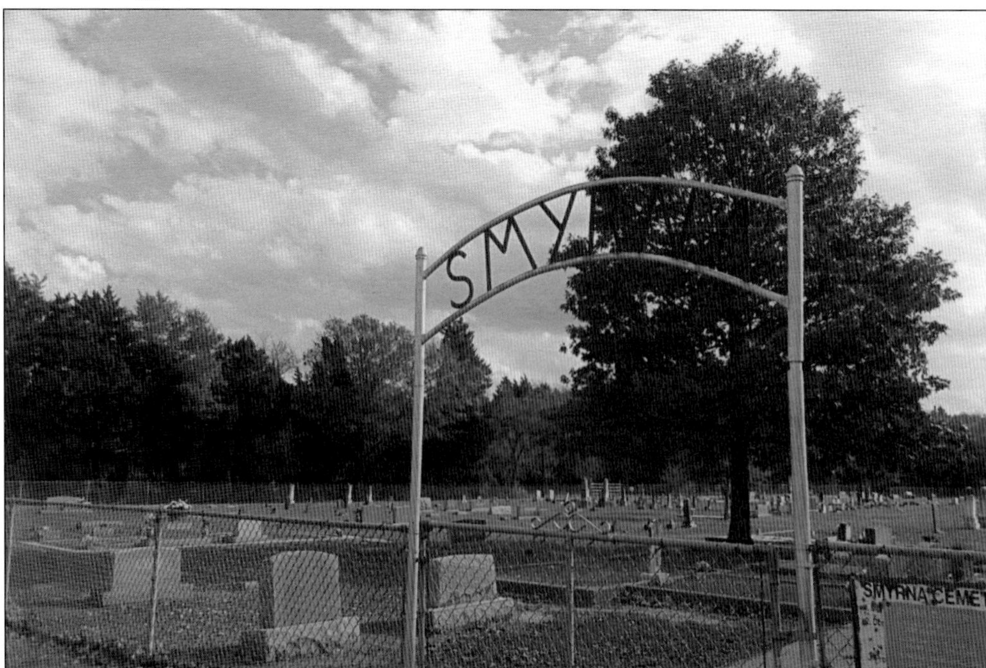


Judge O. H. Rhodes gave two acres of land on January 9, 1909. The deed specified that the land was to be used as a cemetery by all religious denominations. David Shiflet donated one acre of land to the Smyrna Cemetery in August 1985. (Courtesy of Elaine Nall Bay.)

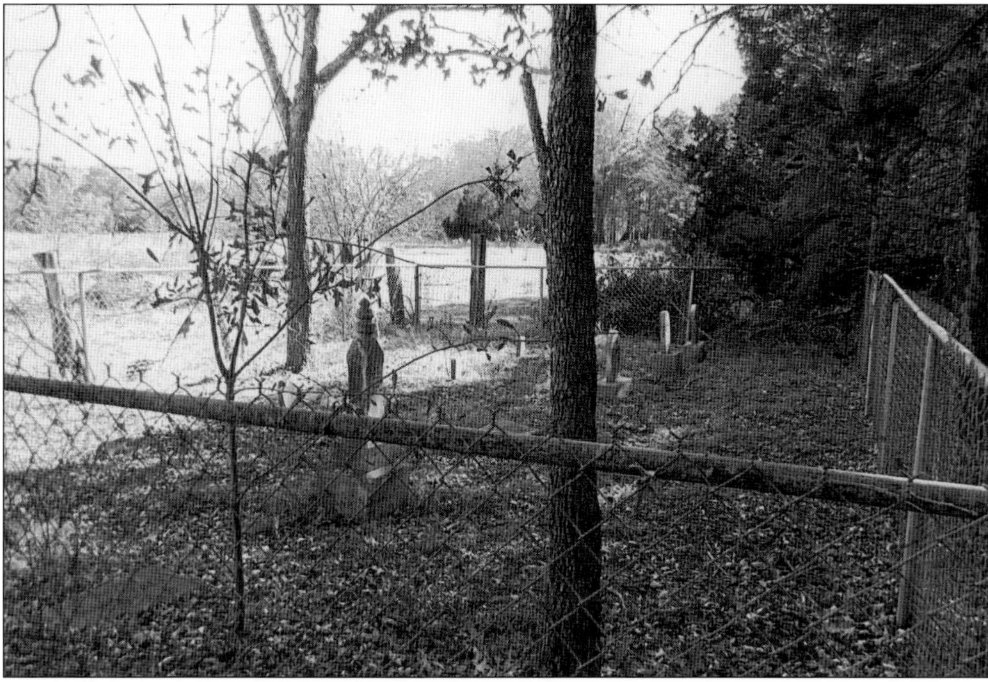

The Worcester-Cooper Family Cemetery is located on private property near Point. There are six known graves here, including the indication of one for the Ballew family. The earliest burial documented is Grandmother Cooper (1801–1870). (Courtesy of Elaine Nall Bay.)

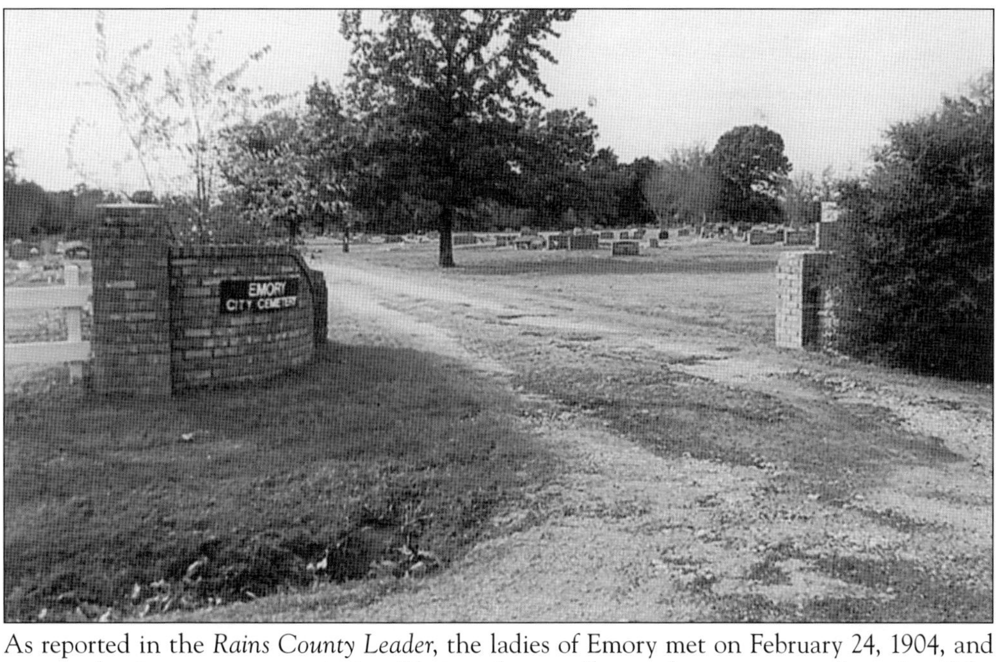


As reported in the *Rains County Leader*, the ladies of Emory met on February 24, 1904, and organized a city cemetery association. Their goal was to "better the appearance of our city of the dead." In 1904, workers arrived to clean the grounds. The fundraiser was an oyster supper. The Cemetery Association met and decided to sell the lots at $10 each for the most desirable sites and $5 each for others. (Courtesy of Elaine Nall Bay.)

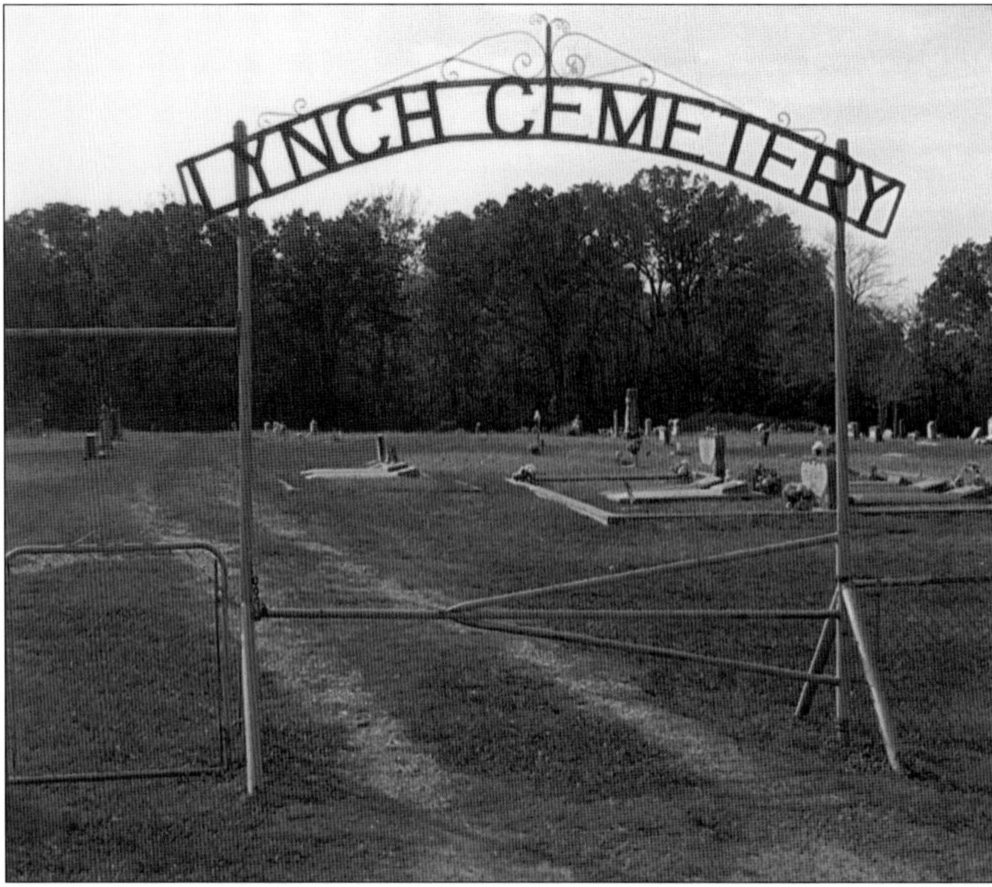


Lynch Cemetery is located in the Lynch community on the western side of the county. In the graveyard is a military marker for Civil War veteran Pinckney Columbus "P.C." Porter (1849–1923), who served in the Union army. P.C. married Margaret Olive White in 1867 in Alabama. (Courtesy of Elaine Nall Bay.)

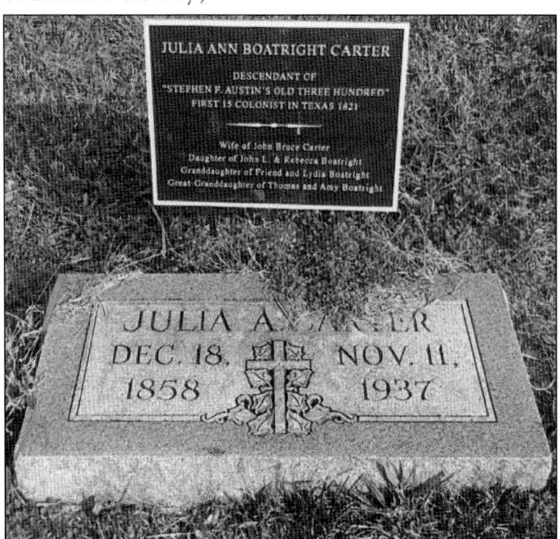


Julia Boatright Carter is a descendant of Austin's Old Three Hundred; her grandfather Thomas Boatright came with Stephen F. Austin to Texas and colonized the first colony in 1821; Thomas Boatright arrived and camped on New Year Creek, which they named as a remembrance of their arriving in Washington County, Texas, on January 1, 1822. Julia (1838–1937) lived the last years of her life in Rains County; she is buried in the Lone Star Cemetery, north of Point, Texas, and her grave is marked with a memorial that reflects her place in Texas history. (Courtesy of Elaine Nall Bay.)

On a drizzly Sunday in September 2002, family and friends gathered for the placing of a Union Civil War footstone on Pinckney Columbus Porter's grave at Lynch Cemetery. Dressed as Confederate soldiers, Don Majors (left) and Leland Carter (right) unveiled a Union footstone commemorating P.C.'s role in the Civil War. The two men also posted the US and Texas flags, and Gerald Porter, a descendant, posted the Alabama flag. Harold and Grady Cunningham placed a wreath on the footstone. A bag of Lauderdale County, Alabama, soil was sent to Cindy Cunningham Watson. For the special ceremony, the Alabama soil was placed in a brown bottle and was sprinkled onto the Texas soil atop P.C.'s grave. (Courtesy of Cindy Cunningham Watson.)

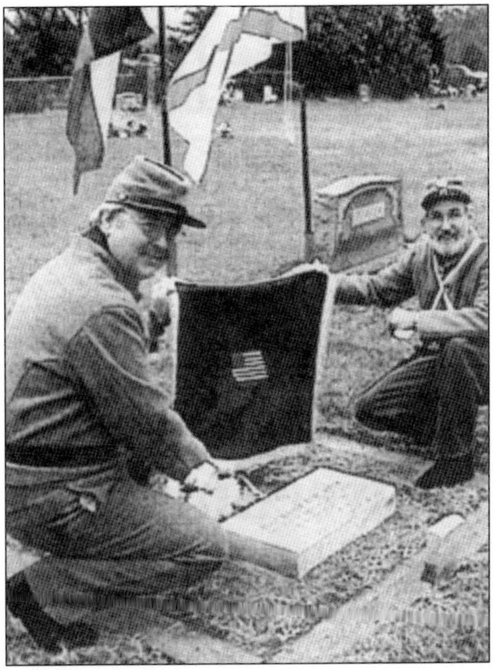

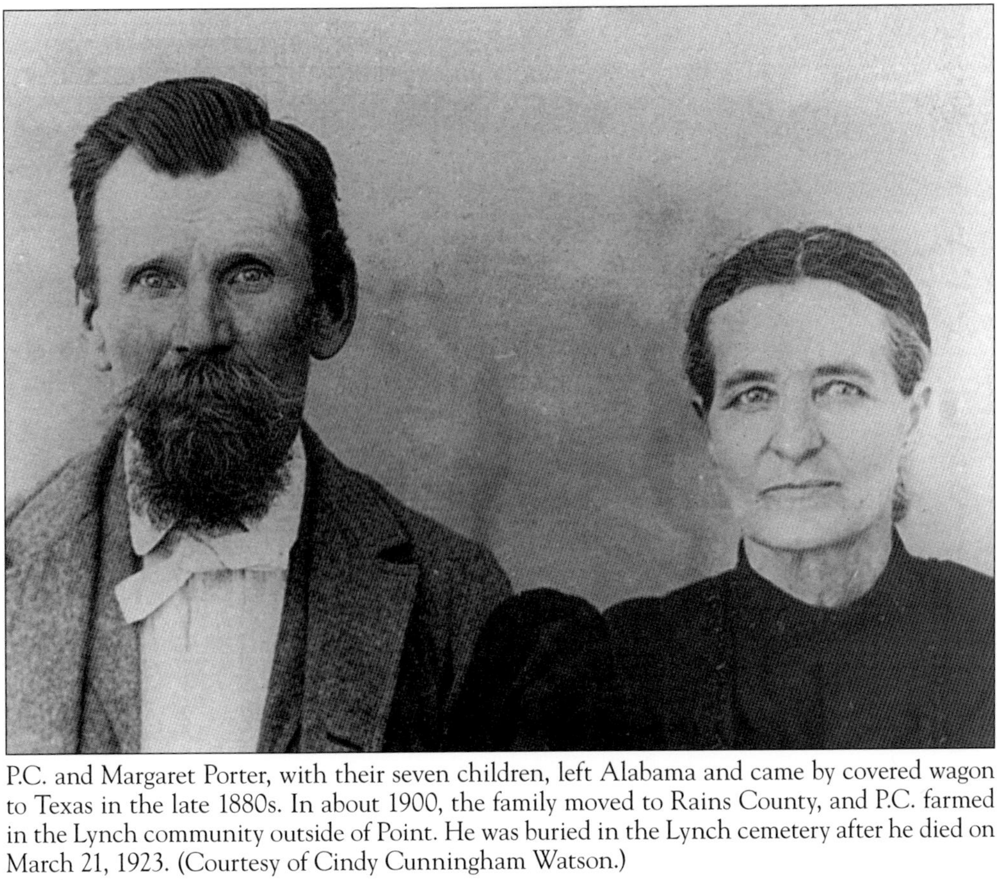

P.C. and Margaret Porter, with their seven children, left Alabama and came by covered wagon to Texas in the late 1880s. In about 1900, the family moved to Rains County, and P.C. farmed in the Lynch community outside of Point. He was buried in the Lynch cemetery after he died on March 21, 1923. (Courtesy of Cindy Cunningham Watson.)

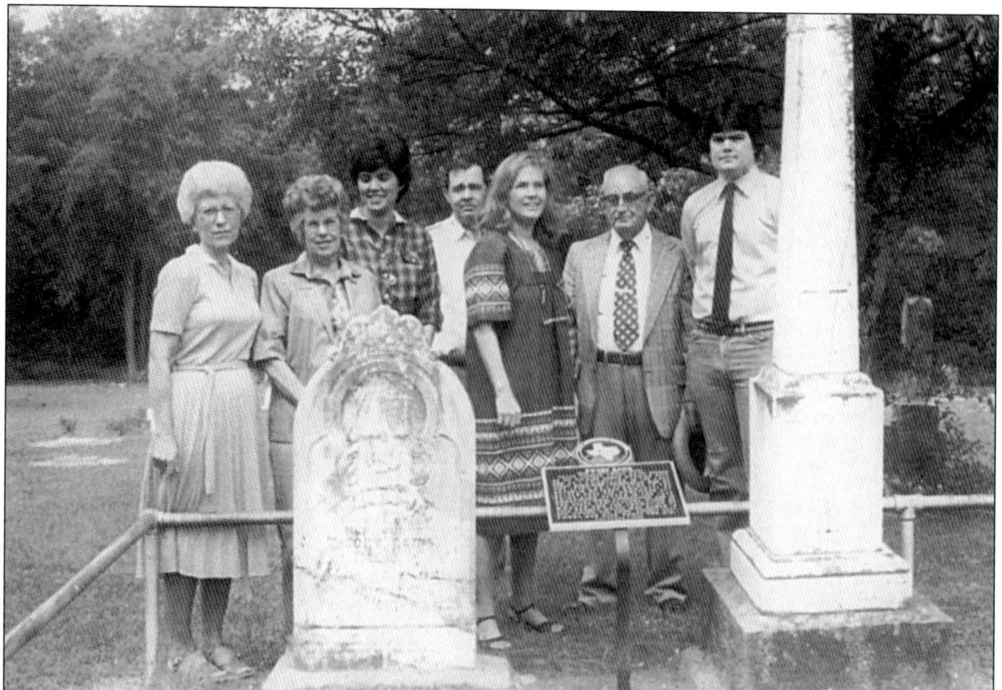

Members of the Rains County Historical Commission stand at the grave of Emory Rains in the Emory City Cemetery. The historical marker was placed in 1983. Standing from left to right are Norma Lee Gowin, Juandell Weddle, Maxanne Potts, Jay Jenkins, Elaine Jenkins, Edward Toles, and Phillip Kerr.

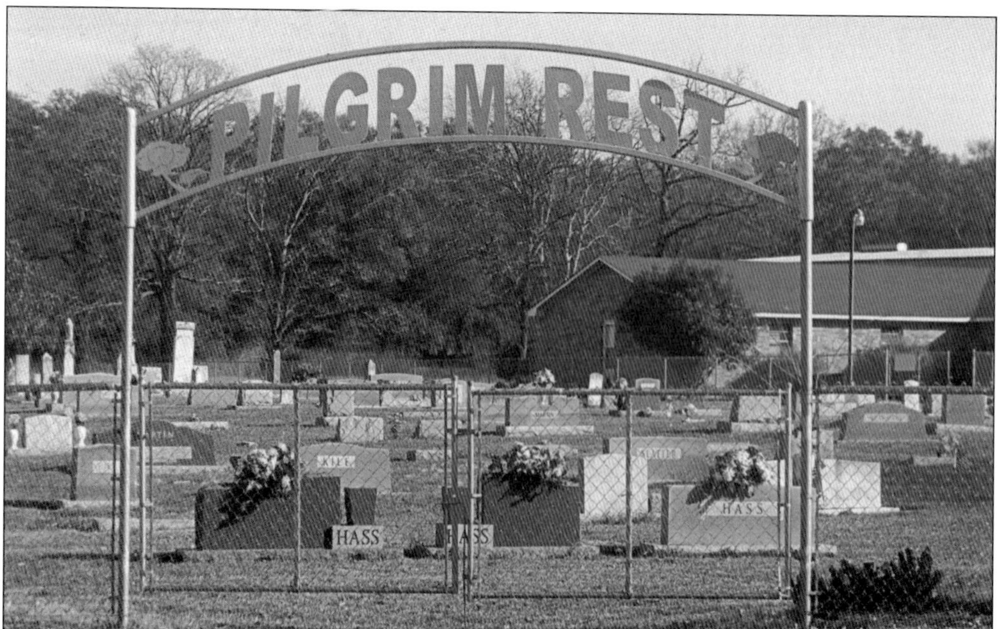


The name Pilgrim Rest is said to come from the fact that travelers en route to market at Marshall, Jefferson, and Shreveport used the area as a favorite camping place. The Pilgrim Rest Cemetery is located on the grounds of Pilgrim Rest Church. (Courtesy of Elaine Nall Bay.)

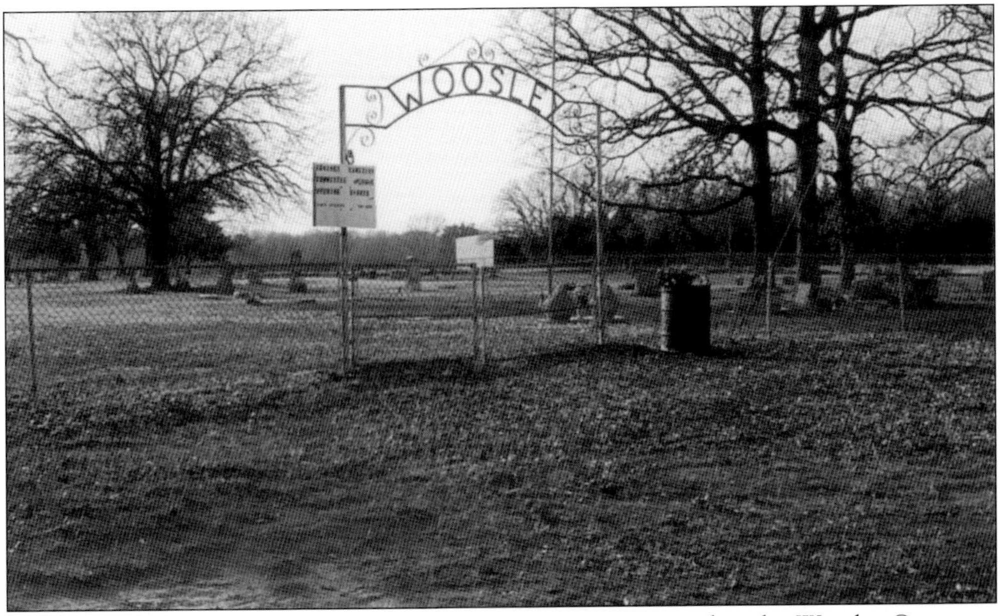


"In 1922 on Thanksgiving Day, a great yard working was arranged at the Woosley Cemetery. The program included a big stew, coffee, cake, pies and everyone was asked to bring something for the stew. Entertainment at the dinner hour was singing," reported the *Rains County Leader.* (Courtesy of Jeri McAree Humphrey.)

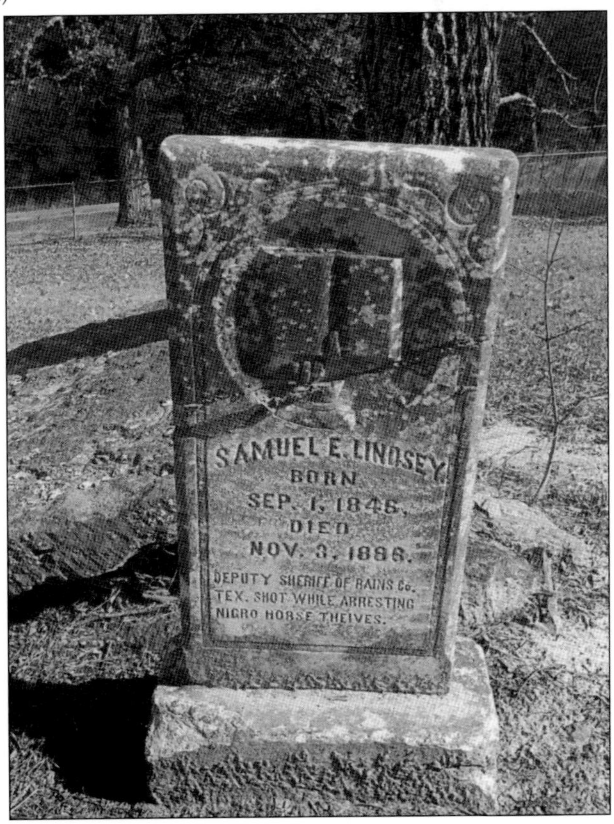


At the time of his death, Samuel E. "Sam" Lindsey was boarding with the M.J. Bradley family in Emory. On November 3, 1866, Dep. Sheriff Lindsey was killed in the line of duty. He was with a posse in pursuit of Joe Stroud, who was accused of horse theft and had escaped from Kaufman County Jail to Rains County, near Emory. As the officers and posse approached Stroud's camp, three shots were fired, one hitting and killing Deputy Lindsey instantly. Deputy Sheriff Lindsey was laid to rest under a tree in the Emory City Cemetery. His name has been placed on the National Law Enforcement Officers Memorial in Washington, DC, as well as on the Texas Peace Officers' Memorial in Austin. (Courtesy of Elaine Nall Bay.)

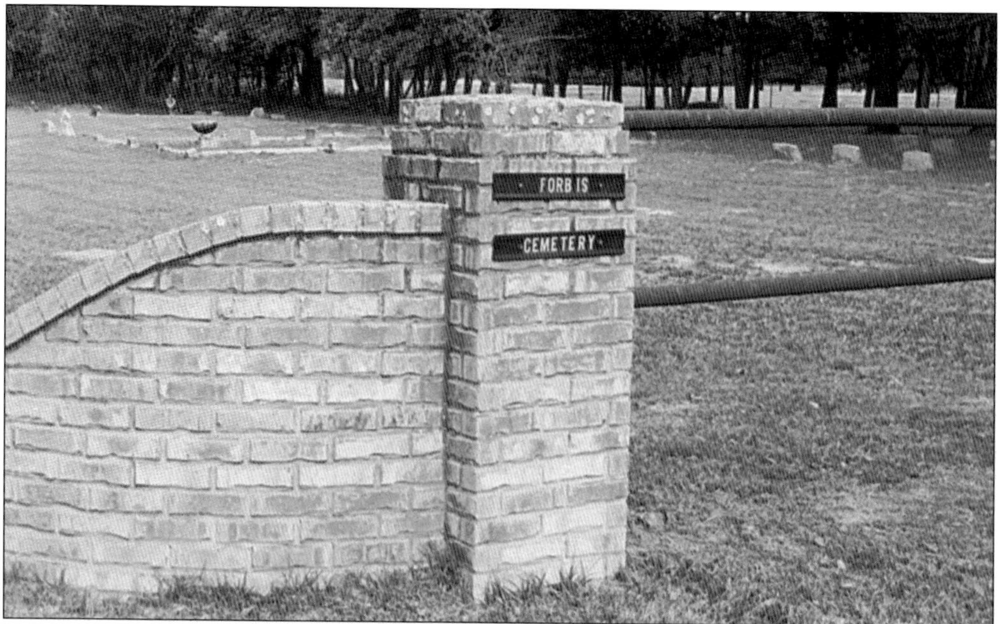

Forbis Cemetery is about two miles from the Emory City Cemetery; the Cemetery Association cares for both cemeteries. In 1880, it is reported that O.S. Forbis and Capt. Tom Cain owned most all of the land in and around the north part of Emory. O.S. Forbis gave the land to the city of Emory. His daughter Sarah Jane married Steve Stuart, and they are buried in the cemetery surrounded by a host of friends. (Courtesy of Elaine Nall Bay.)

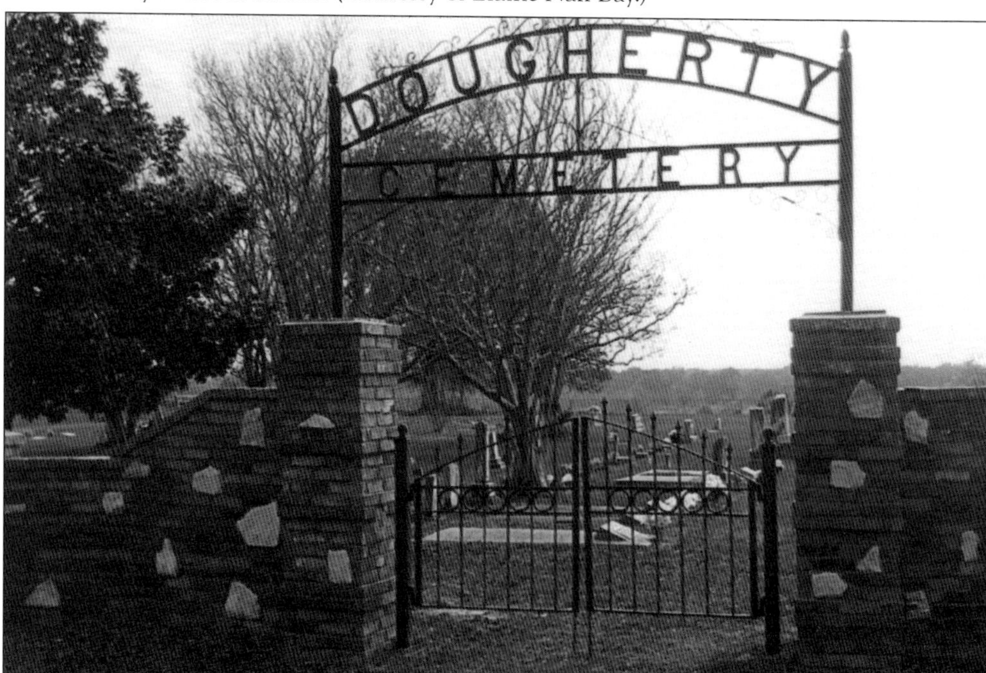

The Dougherty Cemetery is on land donated by Robert N. Doughtery in 1877 for a community burial ground. The gate entry is dedicated to Frances Dougherty Potts, granddaughter of Robert N. Doughtery. (Courtesy of Elaine Nall Bay.)

# *Five*

# Paint the Town Red

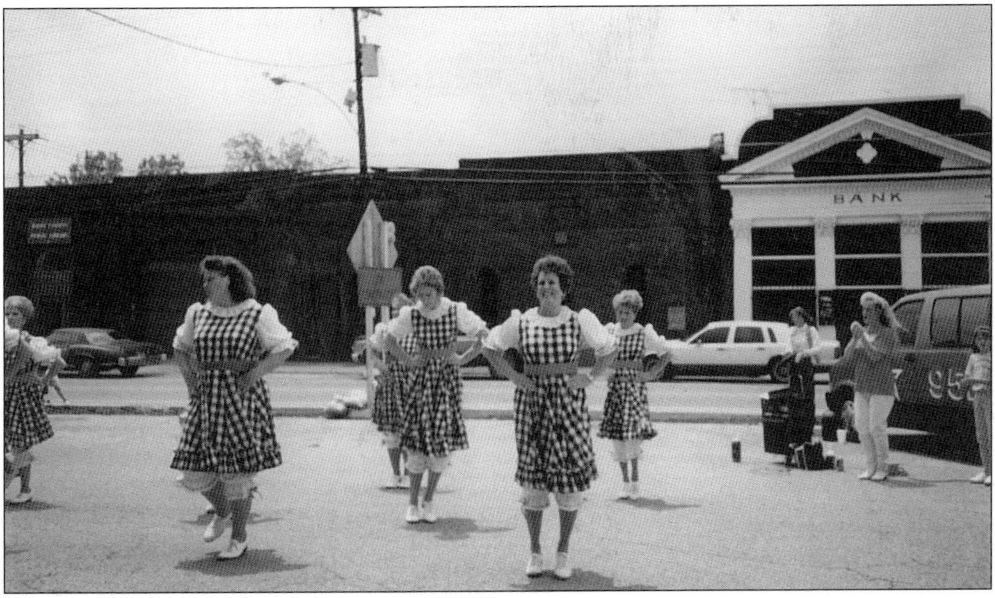


In the epigraph to *The Enormous Room*, E.E. Cummings writes, "looking forward into the past or looking / backward into the future I / walk on the highest / hills and / I laugh / about / it / all / the / way." The ancestors of Rains County citizens did thrive and enjoy life and had their fun and pastimes. Entertainment during the 1870 to 1950 era in Rains revolved around social gatherings. Churches provided singings and suppers on the grounds. Schools would have plays and refreshments on the closing day of the term. The entire town enjoyed Saturdays on the square, county fairs, cemetery clean-up days, and sports competitions between the different school districts. (Courtesy of Elaine Nall Bay.)

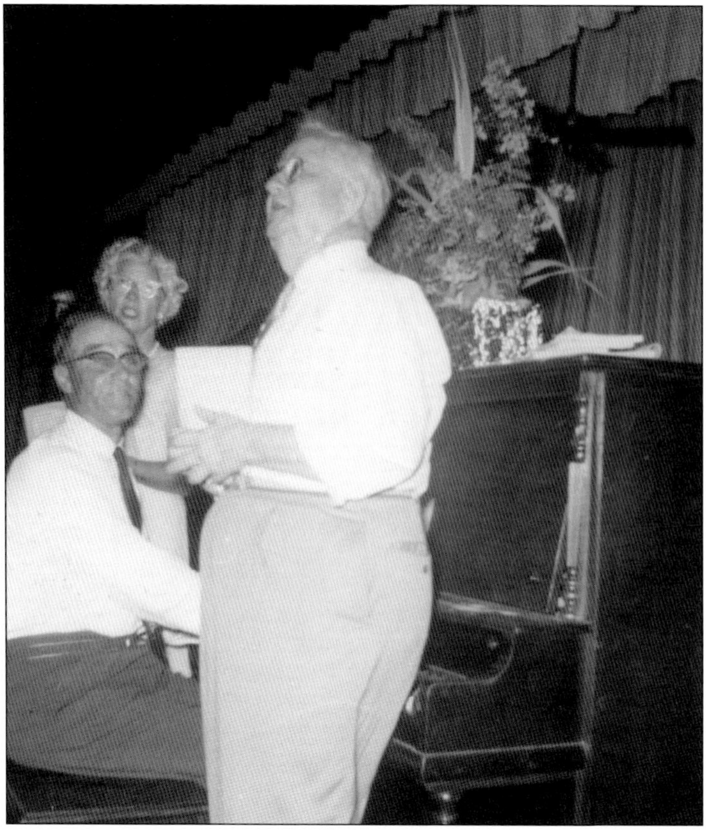

Robert Edward "Buck" Watts (1895–1969) settled five miles northeast of Point in Wattsville. Buck taught himself to play a piano. He loved Gospel music and taught singing schools after crops were laid by. There was nothing Buck enjoyed more than a Sunday afternoon singing or county singing conventions. Pictured Mrs. Lynch, Mr. Lynch (sitting at piano), and Buck Watts. Hebisen wrote in his *Early Days in Texas and Rains County* in 1917, "The old-time 'sings' at the church and school houses and in the home . . . a recollection that many a person cherishes today."

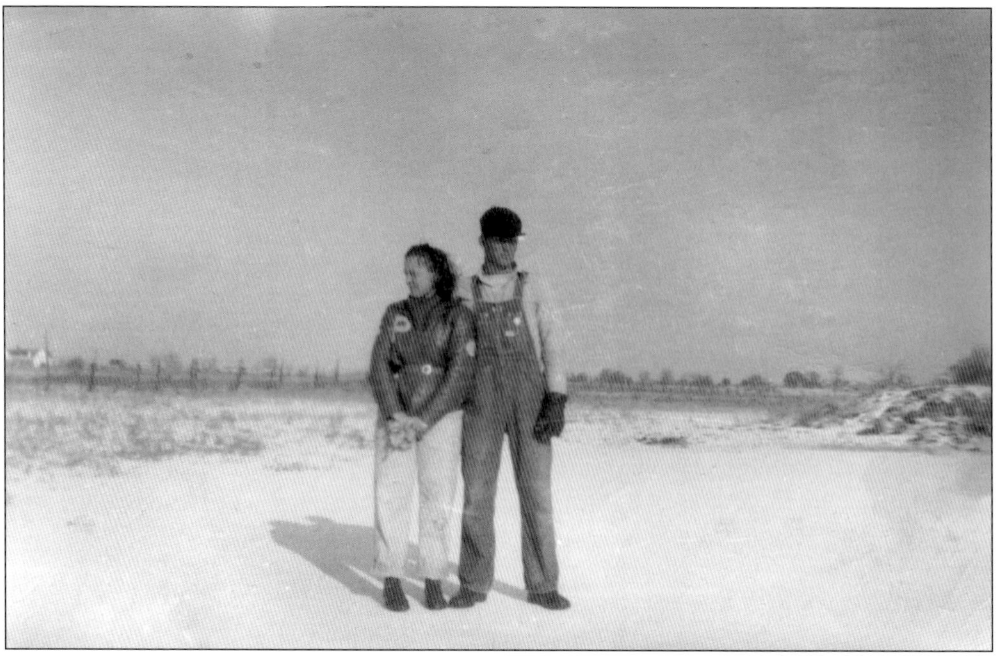

Averal and Ola V. Fenter, standing on a frozen pond in the Cody community in 1948, had just recently married. Ola V. has on her sister's Point High School jacket. (Courtesy of Ronnie M. Fenter)

Emily Nell Hamilton is pictured in August 1940, when a tent skating rink came to Emory in the summer. (Courtesy of Emily Hamilton Adams.)

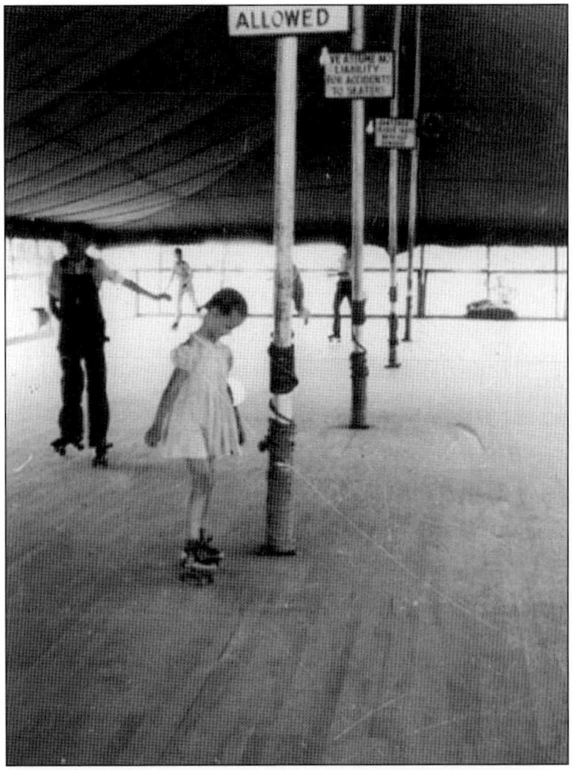


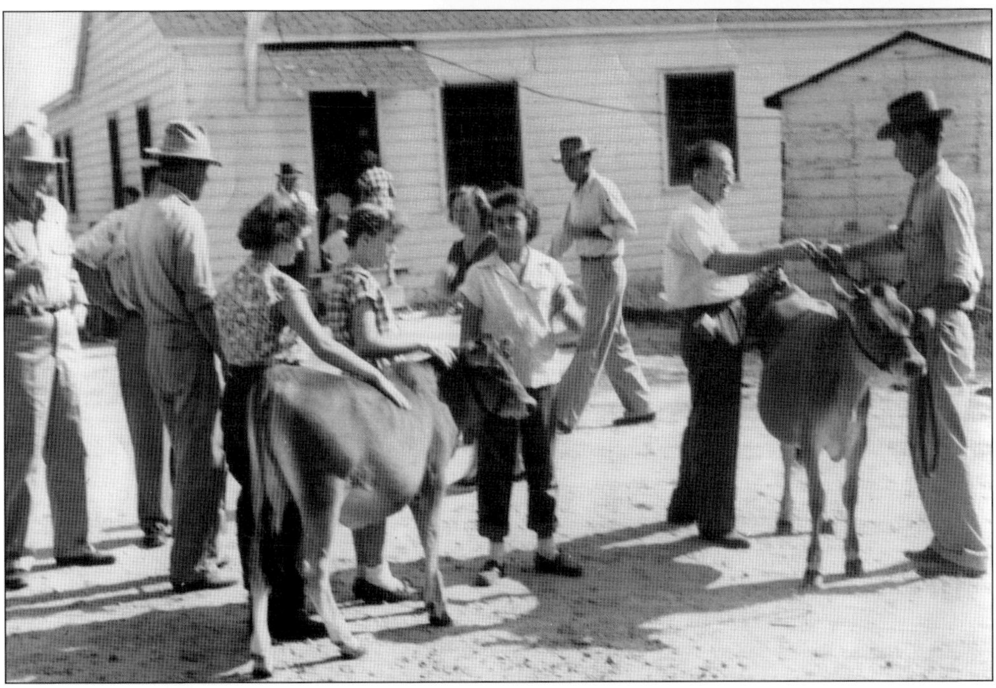

People come to the Rains County Fair to visit neighbors and friends, ride the rides, eat the aromatic food, watch the beauty contests, enjoy the country-and-western dancing, and listen to music; but the most important part of the fair for many is the livestock show and sale.

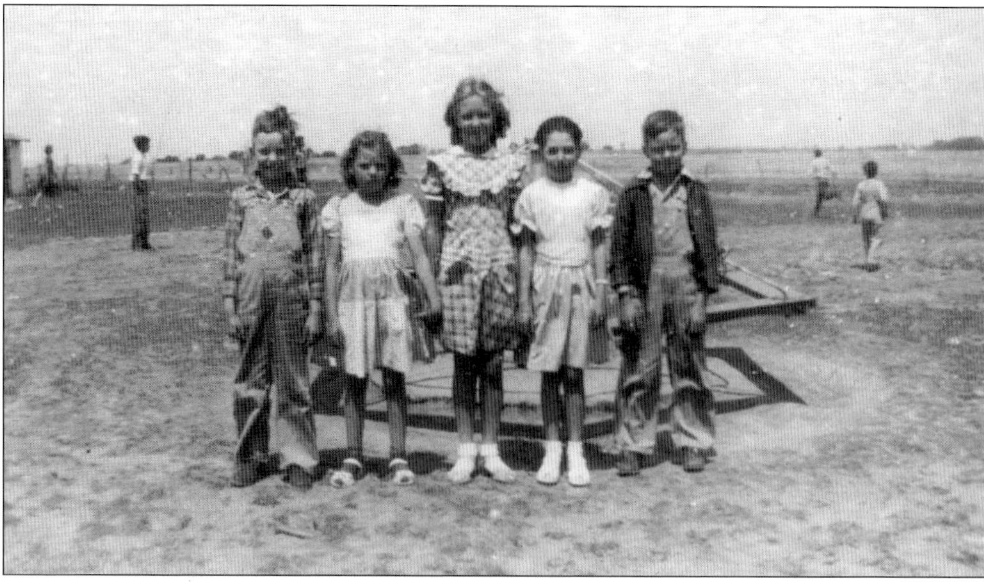

The playground of the Lynch School, District No. 4 (1898–1953) was typical of rural school playgrounds during the 1940s and 1950s. This photograph was taken April 7, 1950. Pictured from left to right are James Hooten, Cecil ?, Margie Weatherford, Cleata May Dodson, and Joe Dale Moss. (Courtesy of Frances Ainsworth.)

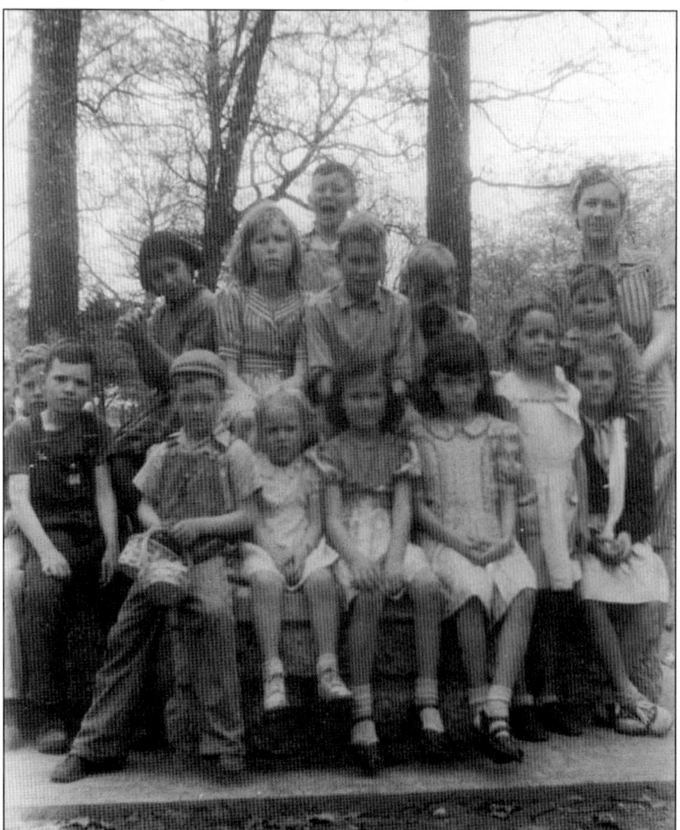

Constance Covey Griffin taught at Waskom School in the Prospect community from 1945 to 1948 as the only teacher for grades one through eight. By this time, Waskom had a lunchroom and the government supplied much of the food and farmers brought in bushels of produce that they did not need. Common meals consisted of pinto beans, fried or boiled potatoes, black-eyed peas, corn, and sweet potatoes, plus a big pan of hot cornbread. Mrs. Griffin took her students on a school picnic in 1946 to Jenkins Park. (Courtesy of Constance Covey Griffin.)

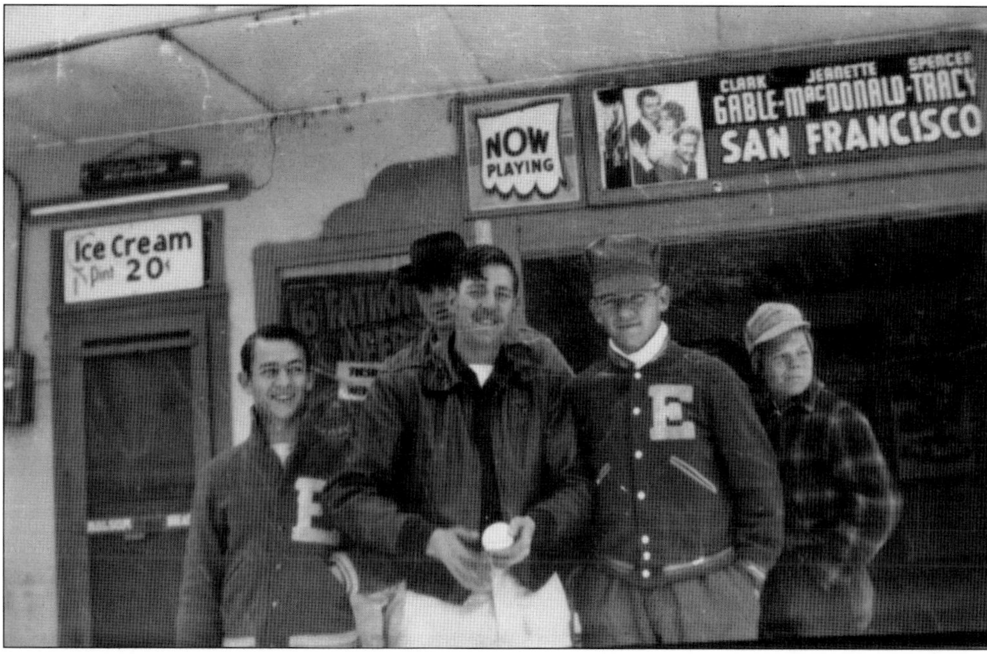


Young people spent many warm days gathered on the town square when friends and families would come to town on the weekends. Standing in front of the Emoryl Theater where they had just enjoyed a Saturday movie are, from left to right, Ernest Cain, Billy Scott, Fred Vaught, Jimmy Cain, and Dick Gaby. The price of a movie on the weekend was 12¢ for anyone under the age of 12 and 25¢ for everyone else. (Courtesy of Ernest Cain.)

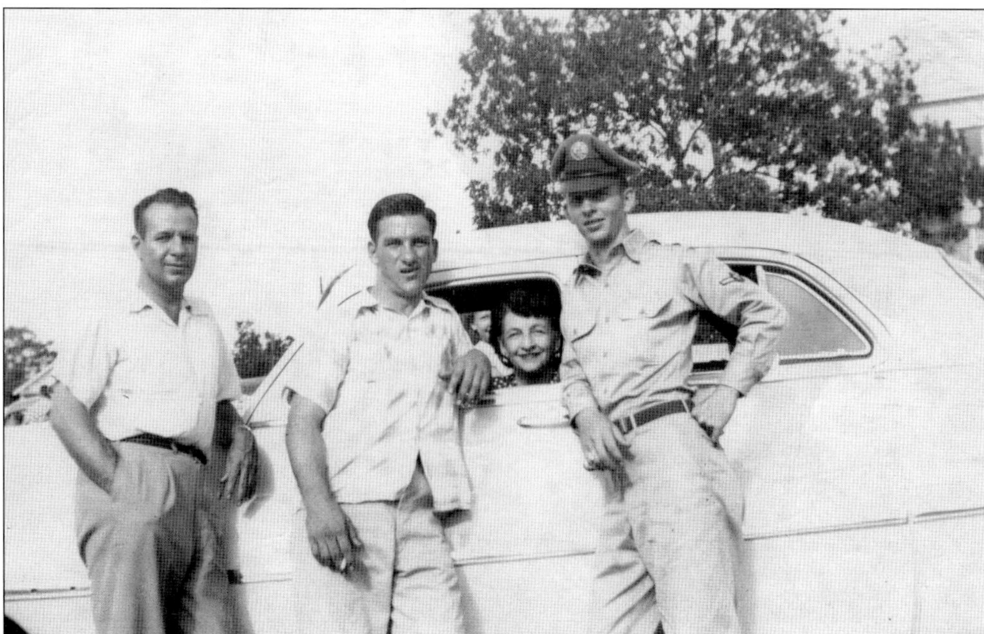

Spending a Saturday afternoon around the courthouse square are, from left to right, Everett Wilson, Don Cain, Ada Kerr Cain, and Ernest Cain, who was home on leave from the military. (Courtesy of Ernest Cain.)

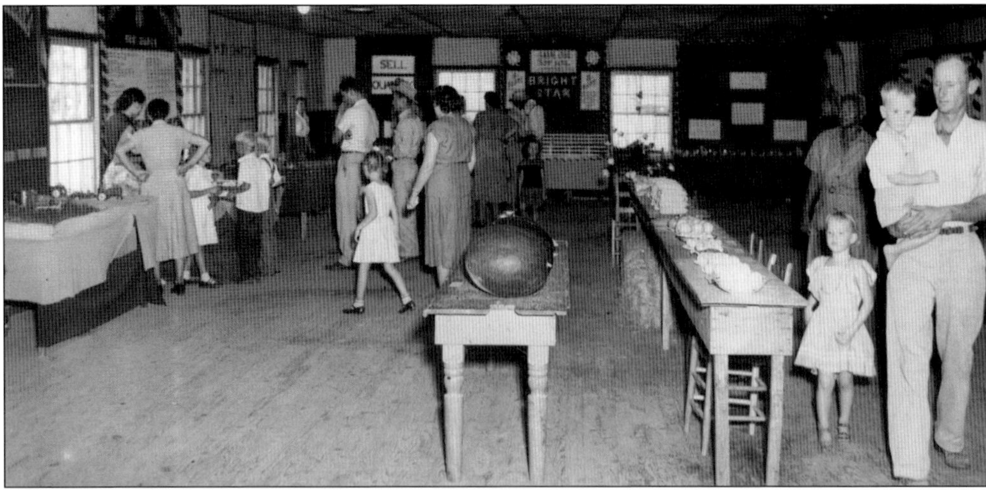


The first annual Rains County Fair and succeeding fairs until the 1950s were held on the courthouse square. Ribbons were awarded for first, second, third, and fourth place exhibits, with cash prizes of $7.50 for first place and $4.00 for second place. Agricultural exhibits included milo, hegari, darso, oats, barley, rye, kaffir, sorghum, and soybeans; sweet clover and Sudan grass; peanuts, apples, peaches, pears, persimmons, figs, Irish and sweet potatoes, turnips, and green snap beans; black-eyed, cream, and field peas, onions, bell peppers, carrots, tomatoes, cabbage, cashaw, pumpkins, watermelon, and ribbon cane stalks and syrup. Textiles included fancy sewing, embroidered pillowcases and towels, dresser scarves, vanity sets, centerpieces, luncheon sets, bedspreads, needlepoint tapestry, infant wear, and quilts. Culinary entries included biscuits, rolls, pone corn bread; pound, angel food, tea, and chocolate layer cakes, doughnuts, half-moon fried apple, potato, custard, and molasses pies; date loaf, peanut brittle, and chocolate fudge. Home Department entries included preserves, jellies, and canned fruits and vegetables. Best School booths, judged on general appearance, originality, quality and quantity, were awarded $5.00 for first place, $2.50 for second, and a ribbon for third.

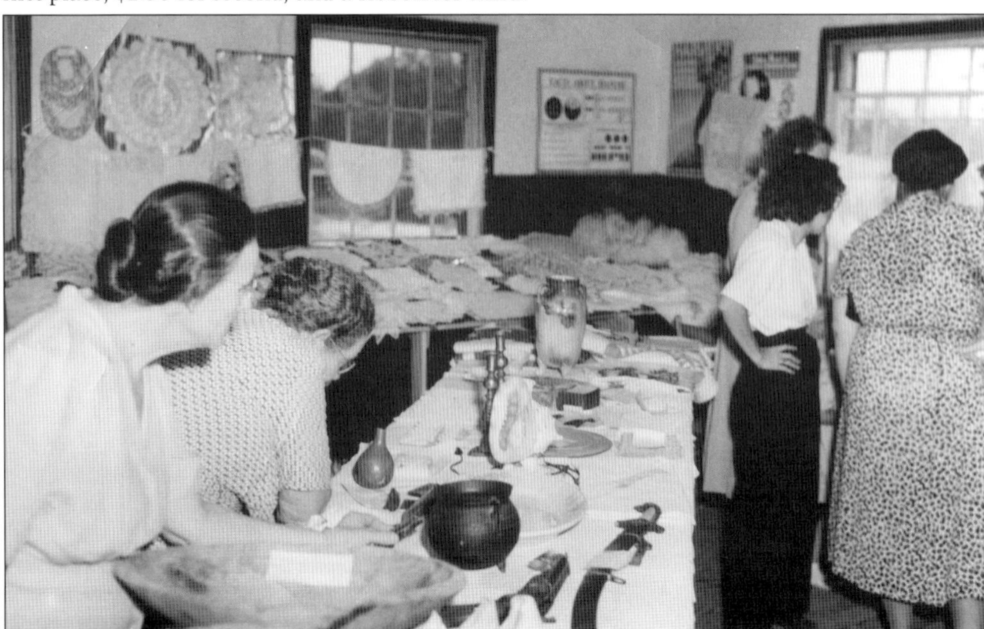

At the Rains County Fair in the early 1960s are, from left to right, Wyndell Stokes, Frank Miears, foreman of the 3J Ranch and livestock superintendant of the Rains County fair, and Floyd Green, a breeder with the prize bull.

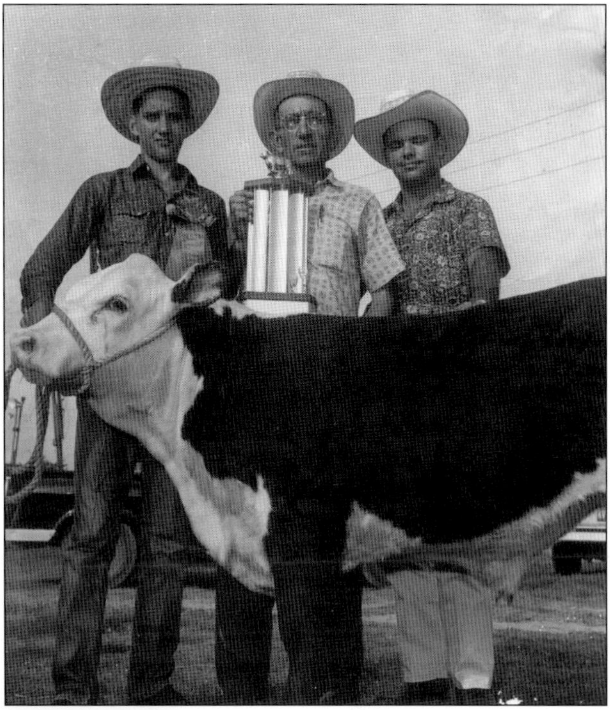

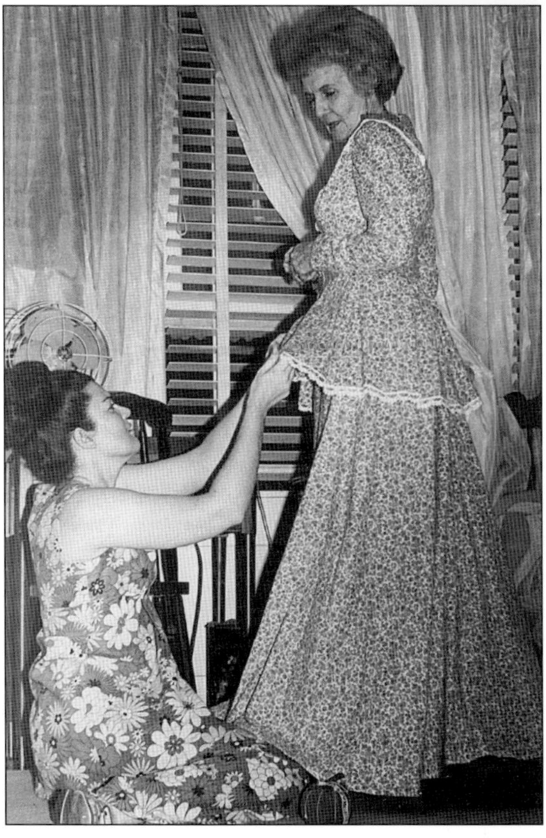

Cay Frances B. House puts the finishing touches on her mother Marguerite Braziel's dress made from cotton sacks for the 1970 centennial celebrations and fair. (Courtesy of Cay Frances B. House.)

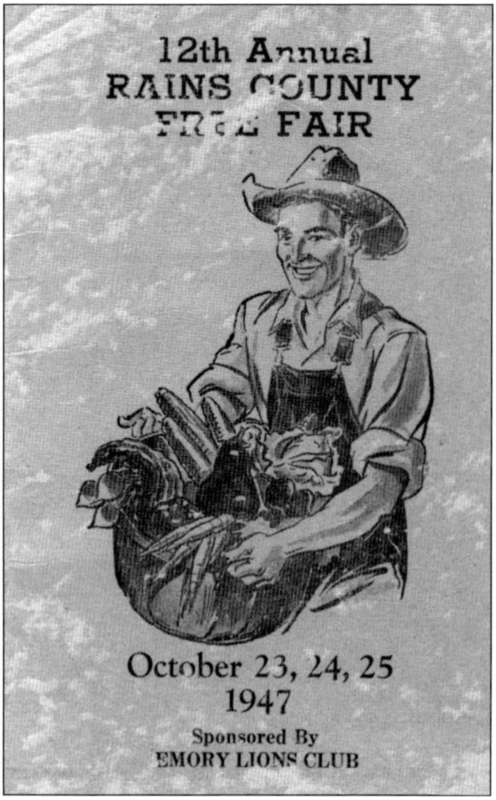


The fair was held on the Emory courthouse square until land for a fairground was purchased. The annual Rains County Fair began in 1930, and no entry fees were charged. Booths were for the various exhibits. Agricultural products included oats, barley, sweet clover, turnips, field peas, and more were judged. Textiles, which displayed fancy sewing, embroidered towels, infant wear, and quilts, plus other items. Culinary entries included breads, cakes, pies, and candies—all homemade. The Home Department is where canned and preserved foods were found. And there were the Best School Booths. Other events were basketball games, sack races, an egg race, a livestock parade, and a carnival. The parade around the square was a real crowd-pleaser. At left is the 1947 Free Fair booklet sponsored by the Emory Lions Club. Below is a list of the 1947 Free Fair Boosters. (Courtesy of Jeri McAree Humphrey.)

## RAINS COUNTY FREE FAIR BOOSTERS

Wilie Carpenter
Post Office Force
Jack Pound
Joel W. Lennon
Odessa Luckett
Eli Allred
Cleo Plunk
R. L. (Jodie) Bentley
Eugie Lynch
L. F. Holley
T. T. Lyles
J. P. Stuart
Jewel McMillon

Miss Victoria Turner
Elton B. Shivers
Ade Childers
Mr. and Mrs. H. O. McCallon
Mr. and Mrs. Ralph Hays
Mr. and Mrs. W. M. Rodes
Mr. and Mrs. F. L. Bullard
Mr. and Mrs. J. H. Houser
Mr. and Mrs. H. D. Garrett
Claud Varnon
J. O. Sisk
Olen Gilley
Mr. and Mrs. Kile Craver

The Rains County Fair is a weeklong event. One of its main activities is country-and-western music and dancing, which includes square dancing. Around the 1950s, the Western attire of skirts and petticoats had become the trademark for female dancers.

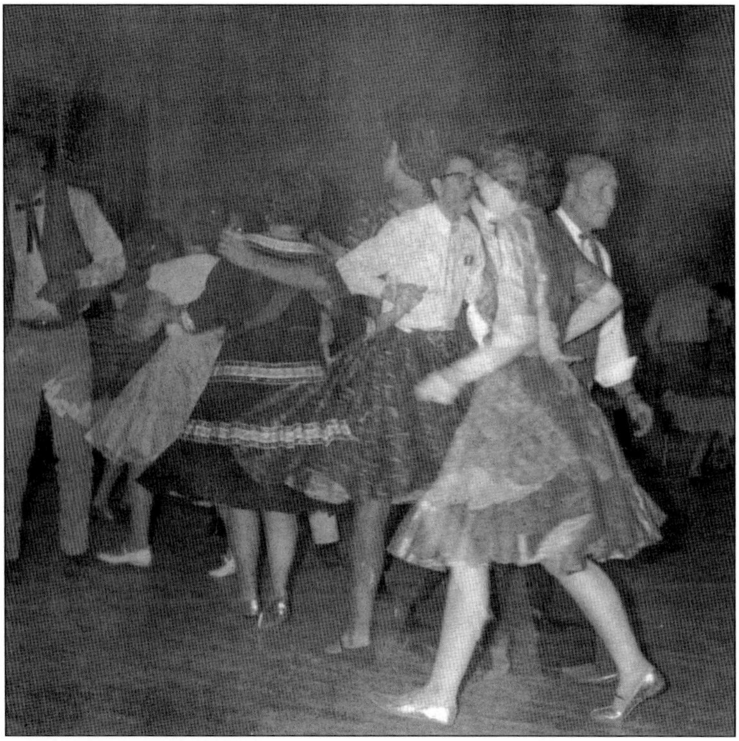

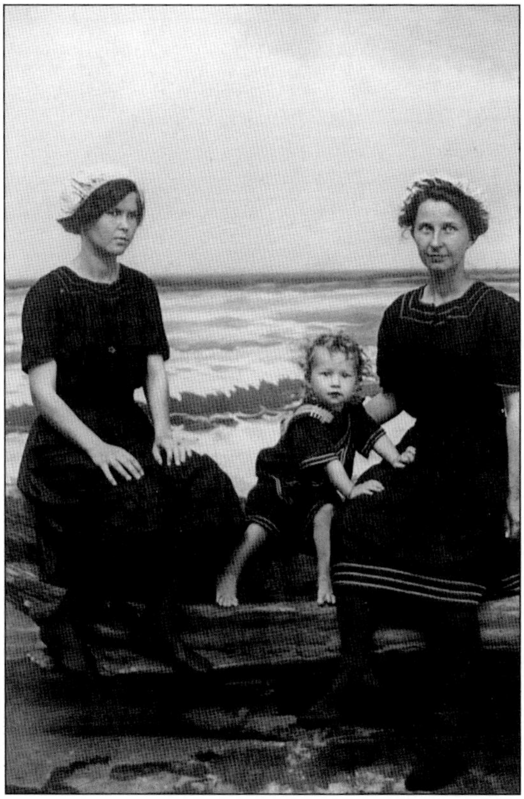

Sisters Mary Tommie Duffey (left) and Ruby Ellen Duffey (right) pose in their swimsuits for a 1910 photograph with one of Ruby's children. Ruby (1888–1934) was Dr. Preston Winford Pearson's (1881–1940) second wife. (Courtesy of Jo Ann Stuart Turman.)

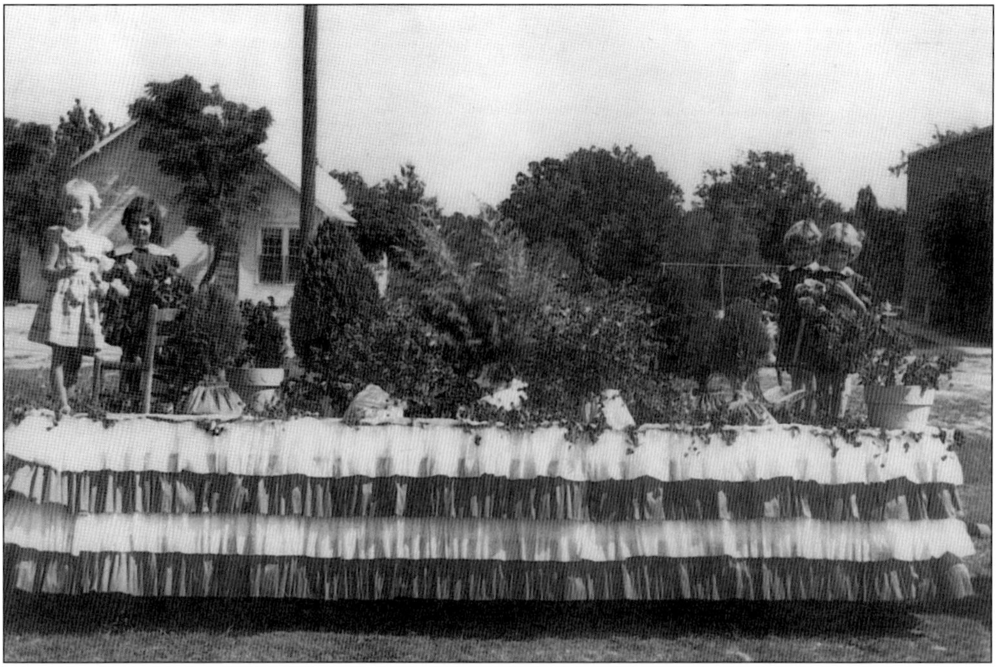

This Emory Ladies Service Club's float is for a Rains County Fair parade in the early to mid-1950s. The Service Club was formed during World War II to help with the war effort. From left to right are Sue Sisk, Jo Orsborn, Pat Peeples, and Pam Peeples. (Courtesy of Maxanne Orsborn Potts.)

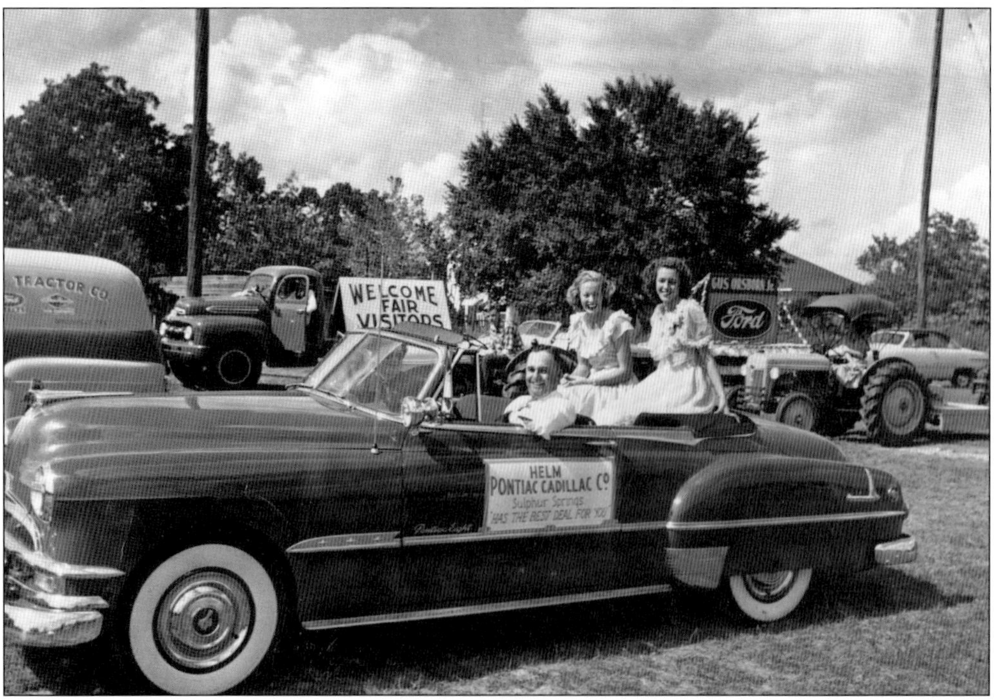


Preparation begins for the 1947 Rains County Fair. Vehicles gathered on an empty lot. The Cadillac was from Helm Pontiac-Cadillac Company in Sulphur Springs, Texas. The car was used as part of the parade to carry the Rains County queens.

*Six*

# Game Plan

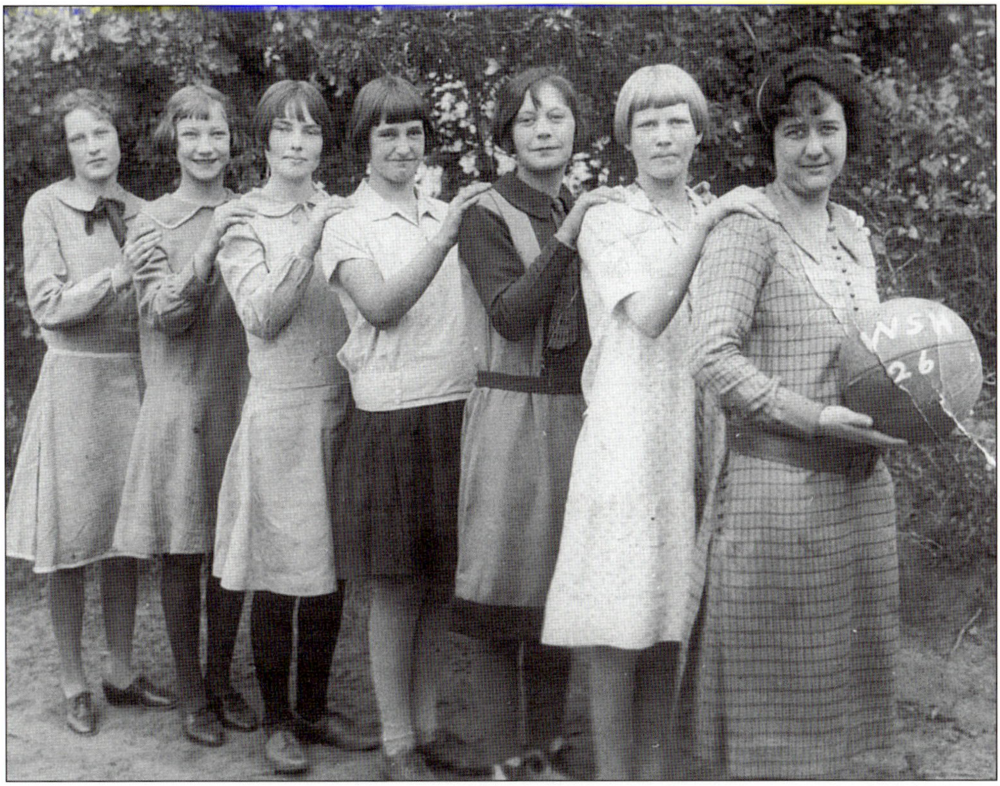


Sports were popular social events at community schools as well as town schools. Football and baseball games had to be played during the afternoons or on the weekends because there were no lighted fields. As the lyrics by Jack Norworth go, "Take me out to the ball game, / Take me out with the crowd; / Buy me some peanuts and Cracker Jack, / I don't care if I never get back. / Let me root, root, root for the home team, / If they don't win it's a shame. / For it's one, two, three strikes, you're out, / At the old ball game." (Courtesy of Constance Covey Griffin.)

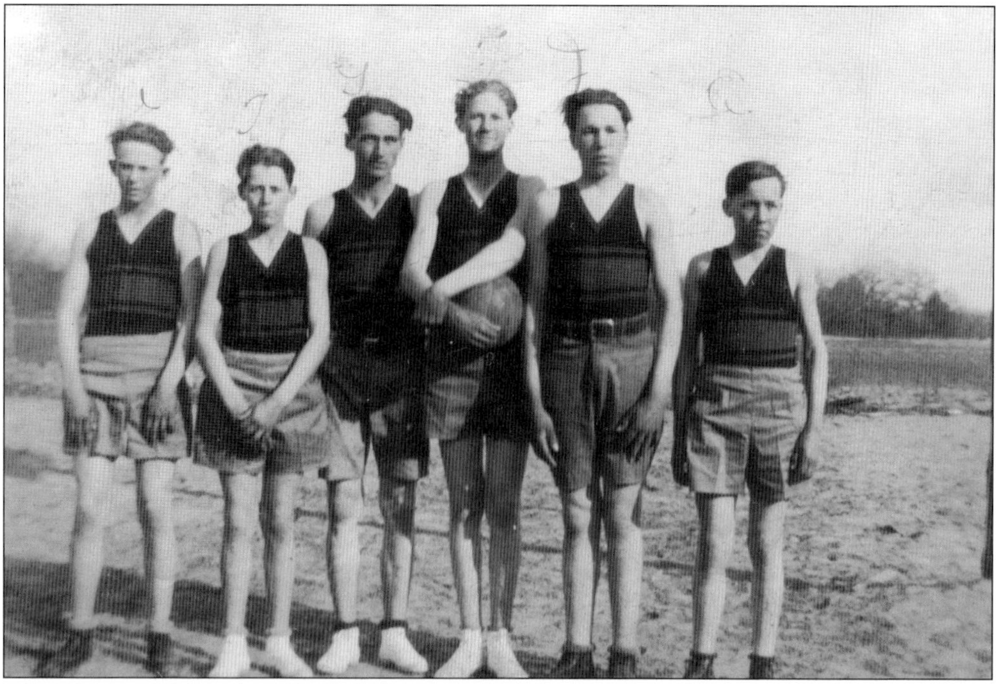

The 1926 New Holmes boys' basketball team included Adolph "Bud" Byram, Tom Fletcher, George Kennemer, Tom Hill, Joe Fletcher, and Edd Fletcher. According to a 1909 *New Holmes Dots* article, the community had a school and a church. (Courtesy of Pat Peeples Adcock.)

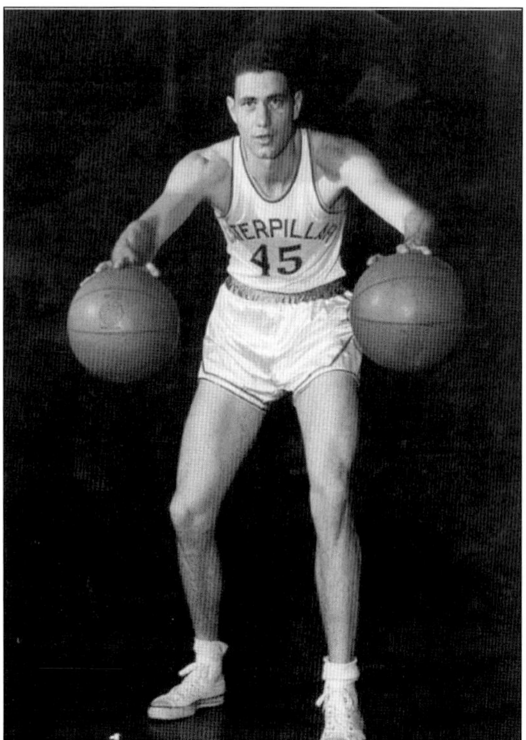


Marcus "Mark" Freiberger was the son of Marcus and Varina Shields Frieberger. At a height of 6 feet, 11 inches, and weighing 215 pounds, Mark began his basketball career at a country school in Rains County. After graduation, he attended the University of Oklahoma, setting all-time scoring records for high school and college. He played for the National AAU Champion Caterpillar Diesels in Denver; Mark was also a member of the U.S. Olympic Champions at Helsinki in 1951–1952. (Courtesy of Gwen Frieberger Holman.)

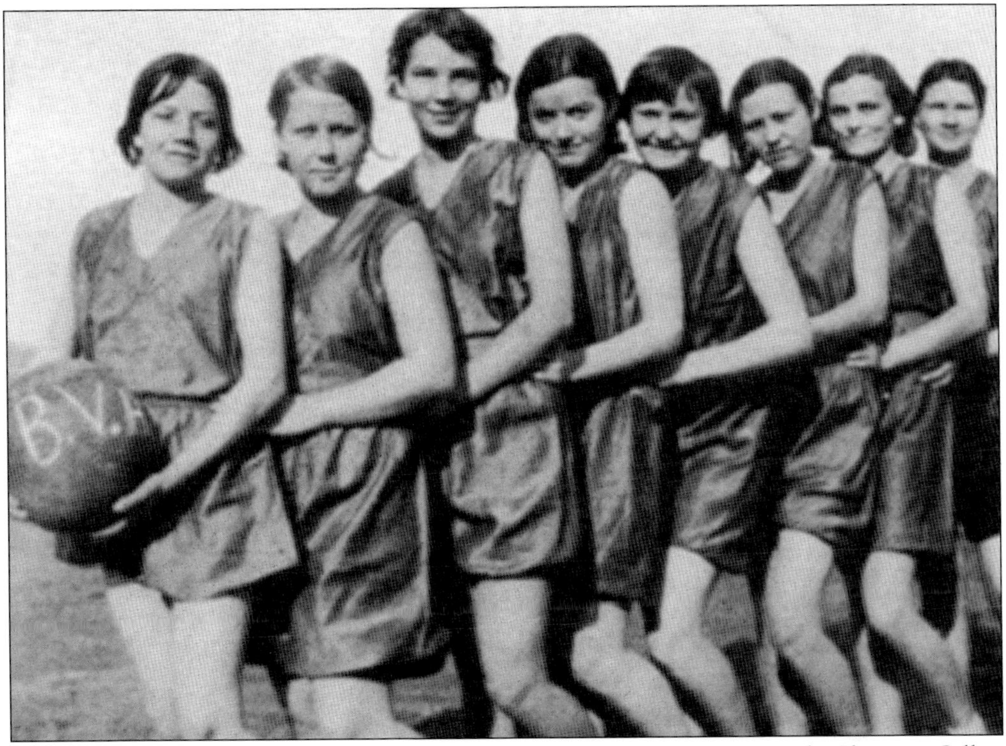

The Bellview girls' basketball team members are Pauline Brown, Marzee Parrish, Christine Gilley, Valla Brown, Reba Alexander, Ozell Alexander, Viola Gilley, and Bonnie Hutchins. (Courtesy of Jeri McAree Humphrey.)

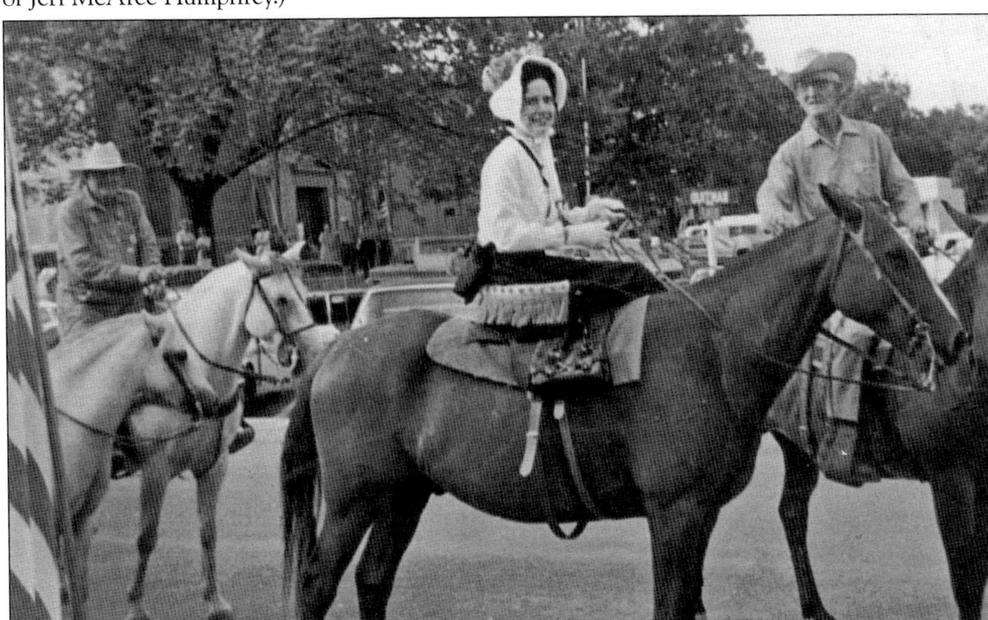

The horses and riders are always an important part of any parade in Rains County. In this picture of riders during the 1970 Centennial celebration are left to right, unknown, Betty Adair, and unidentified. (Courtesy of Linda Terry.)

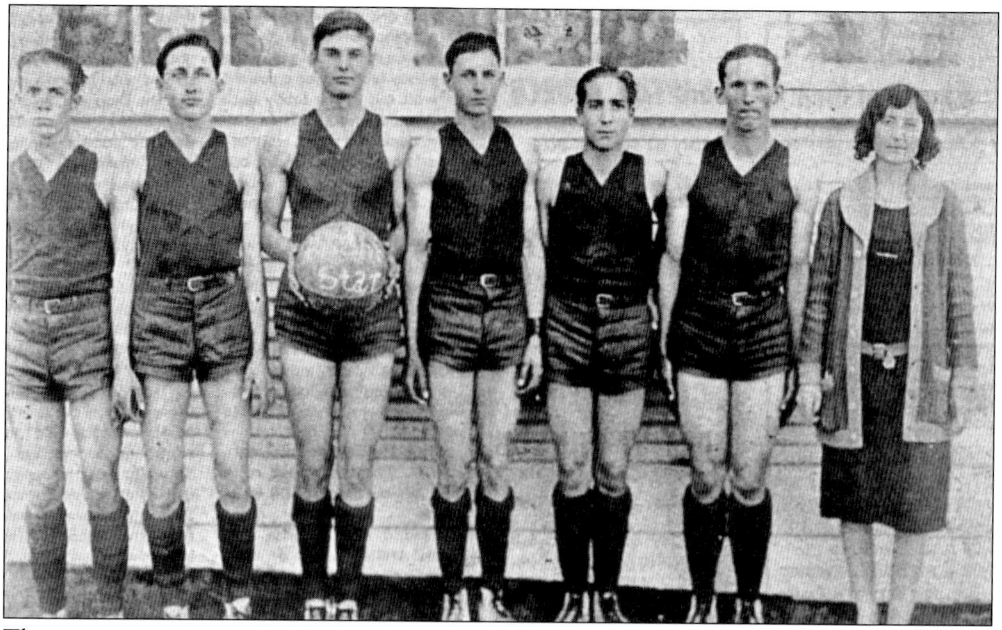

The two main sports at Bright Star were baseball and basketball. Above are the Bright Star boys' basketball team and coach in 1930. This photograph includes, from left to right, Conard Woodson, Henry Walls, Edmund Smith, Lyndell Huddleston, Curtis Woodson, G.B. Bailey, and coach Ardis Goff Alexander.

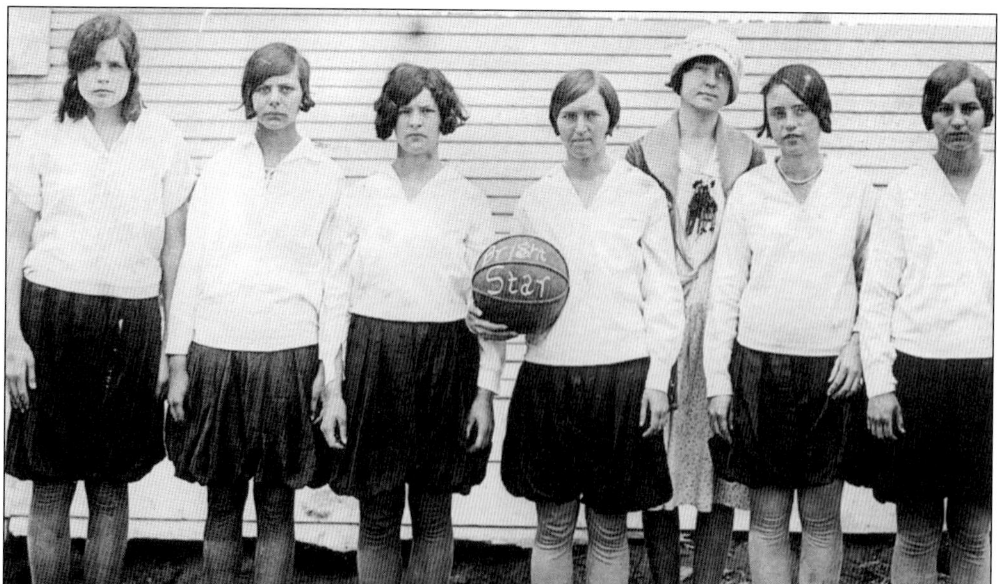

Pictured above are members of the Bright Star girls' basketball team and their coach. From left to right are Rubye Robbins McKeown, Daisy Hass, Ciddie Williams, Lena Felty, coach Ardis Goff Alexander, Arnell Godwin, and Opal Felty. The girls' uniforms were green suits with yellow trim and bloomer-type shorts that reached the knees. Coach Alexander (1903–1989), daughter of W. Lane and Exa Fitzgerald Goff, left her teaching career in 1930 after 10 years in education. She and her husband, F.S. Alexander (1901–1991), the eldest son of George W. and Luana Cook Alexander, operated the Frank S. Alexander Grocery and Feed Store until 1967, when they retired.

Marguerite Montgomery Braziel (1902–1991), the daughter of Caywood and Lottie Norman Montgomery, coached winning teams for years. She took the Emory Kittens to the state championship in 1937. Braziel took Miller Grove's basketball team to the championship game the next year. She returned to Emory School in 1939. (Courtesy of Cay Frances B. House.)

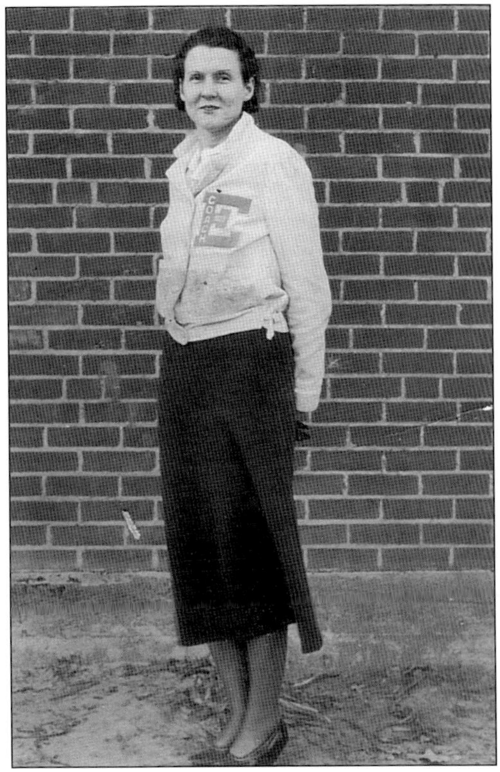

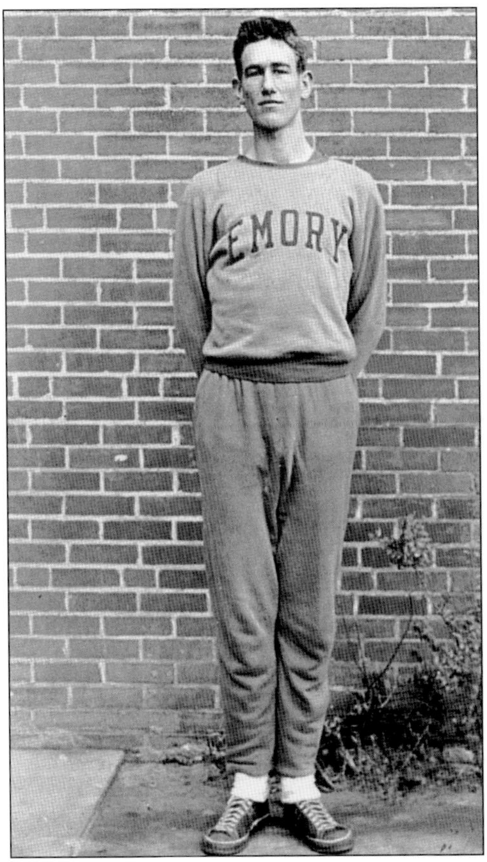


"Tree-Top-Tall" Louis Dale Freiberger, son of Marcus and Varina Shield Freiberger, was in rare form all during the Leesburg tournament for the Emory Lions in 1934 and won the all-tournament center honors, receiving a beautiful gold basketball. (Courtesy of Gwen Freiberger Holman.)

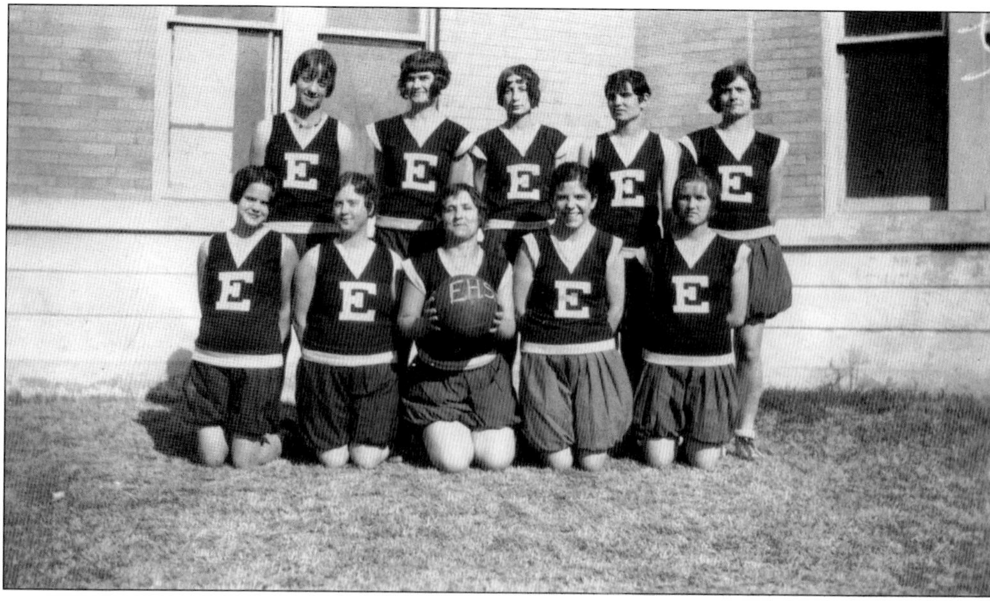


In November 1929, the Emory girls' basketball team received new uniforms in order to give every team worker a red suit. The team elected Nellie Grey Hill as captain and chose the name Blazers. Pictured above are members of the team in practice uniforms. From left to right are (first row) Artie Horsley, Marguerite Wier, Nellie Grey Hill Butcher, Grace Sisk Arrington, and Odeal Morrow; (second row) Beatrice Simmons Hogue, Juanita Smiley, Mozelle Panter, Faye Varnon Melton, and Esta Mae Kennemer Peeples. Below is the same team in game uniforms. The players are in the same order as in the above photograph. (Courtesy of Pat Peeples Adcock.)

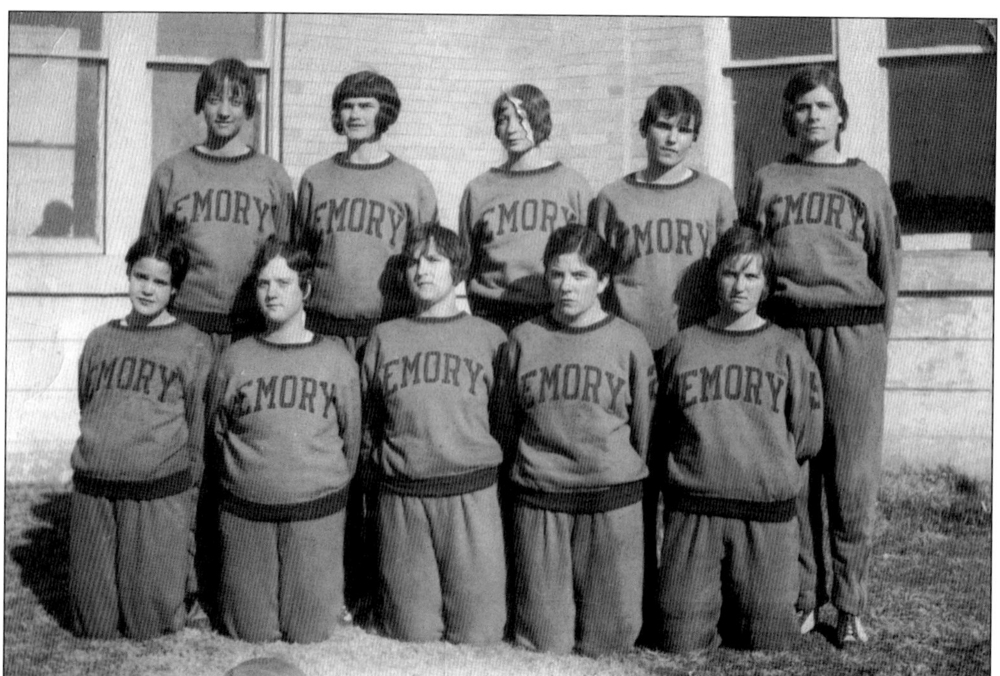

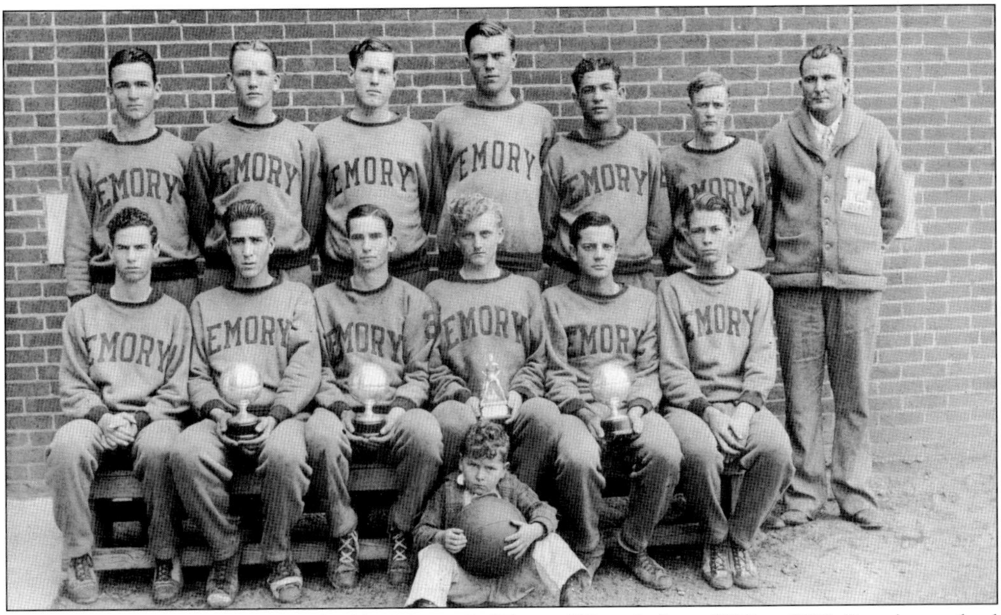

The Emory Wildcats were coached by Morris S. "Fannie" Roach from 1928 to 1935. Roach coached football, basketball, track, and had several championship teams, especially in basketball. The above photograph includes, from left to right, (first row) Phil Nix, Curtis Woodson, Bill Kennemer, Severn Miller, and Homer Bishop; (second row) unidentified, Buster Fleming, Raymond Fitzgerald, Leon Bennett, Robert Killingsworth, Henry W. Gaston, and coach M.S. "Fannie" Roach. The mascot was Coach Roach's son, George Calvin "Hoot" Roach. (Courtesy of Pat Peeples Adcock.)

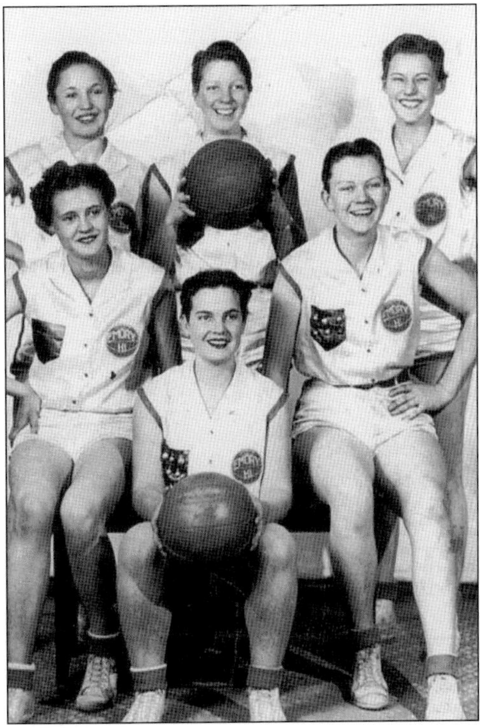

The Emory Kittens played against the Winnsboro Woodchucks on March 20, 1936, in a championship game. This photograph of the Emory lineup includes Mamie M. Davis, all-state forward; ? Scott, all-state forward; ? Gray, forward; Glenna Johnson, captain and all-state guard; Lorraine Hawkins, guard; and Fay Neil Woodson, guard. The team went to Kansas for the national championship game but lost. The tournament winner was the T.J. Courtney girls, who captured the American Tournament title. (Courtesy of Cay Frances B. House.)

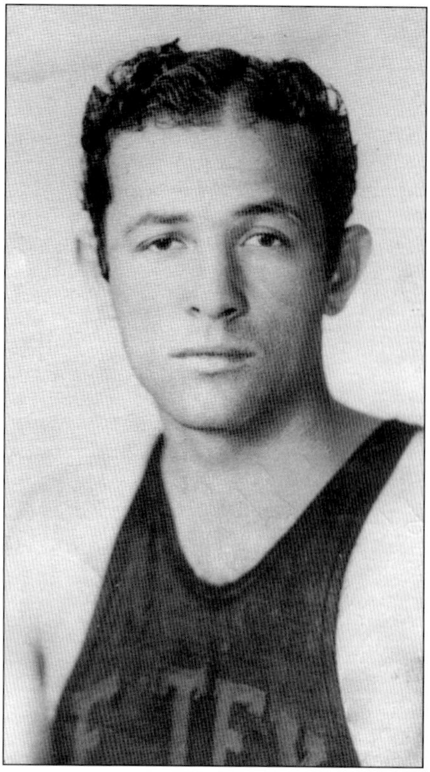

The Emory 1929 senior boys basketball team consisted of Rob Killingsworth (left), Leon Bennett, Raymond Fitzgerald, Buster Fleming, John Stuart, ? Cowan, Woodrow Henslee, ? Powers, Claud Varnon, Roy Clements, ? Henderson, ? Plaxco, Jim Tuttle, and ? Sanders. The boys' season opened on November 22, and tickets were on sale at Nix Drug Store, City Drug Store, and at the schoolhouse. Stuart, Bennett, Fitzgerald, Killingsworth, and Flemings started the game. The Wildcats won over Canton with a score of 29-17.

Below, Craddock Avon Rice (1919–1991) is third from left. He stood six feet tall, weighed 172 pounds, and was one of a 12-member traveling squad. Rice was selected to participate in the 1944 Summer Olympics, but due to World War II, the games were cancelled. Throughout his track career, Rice was never beaten by another Texan. He served as Emory High School principal from 1956 to 1979 and was inducted into the East Texas State Hall of Fame in 1979. Several years later, Rains (ISD) began hosting an annual spring track meet held in his honor, the Avon Rice Relays. (Courtesy of Shirley Hooten and Diane Willis.)

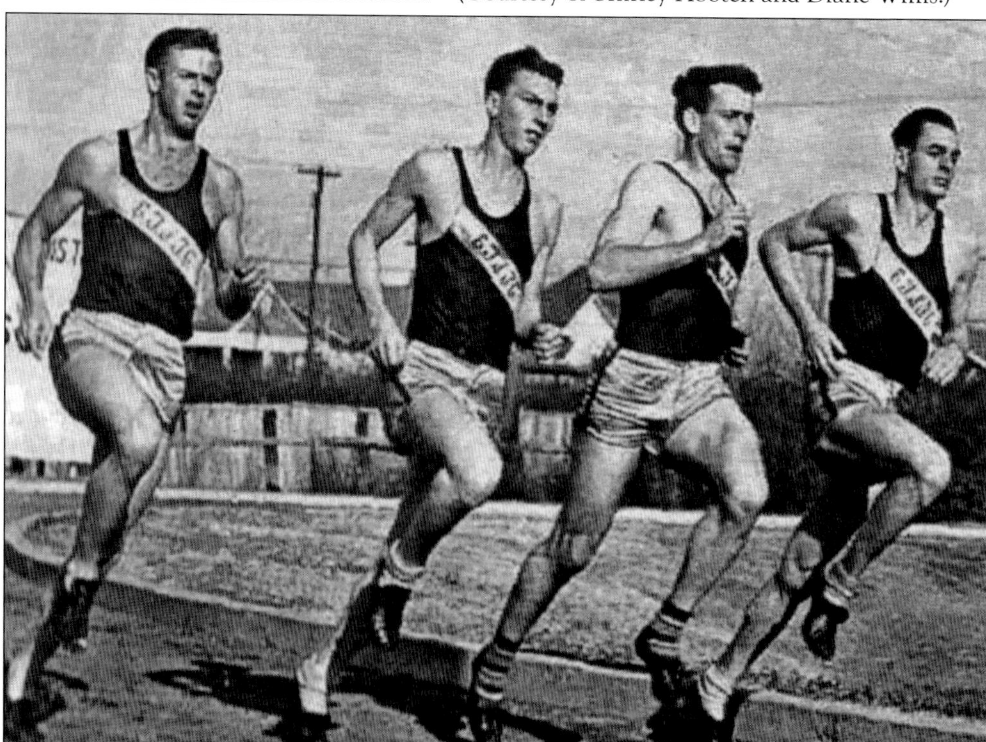

# *Seven*

# The Three Rs

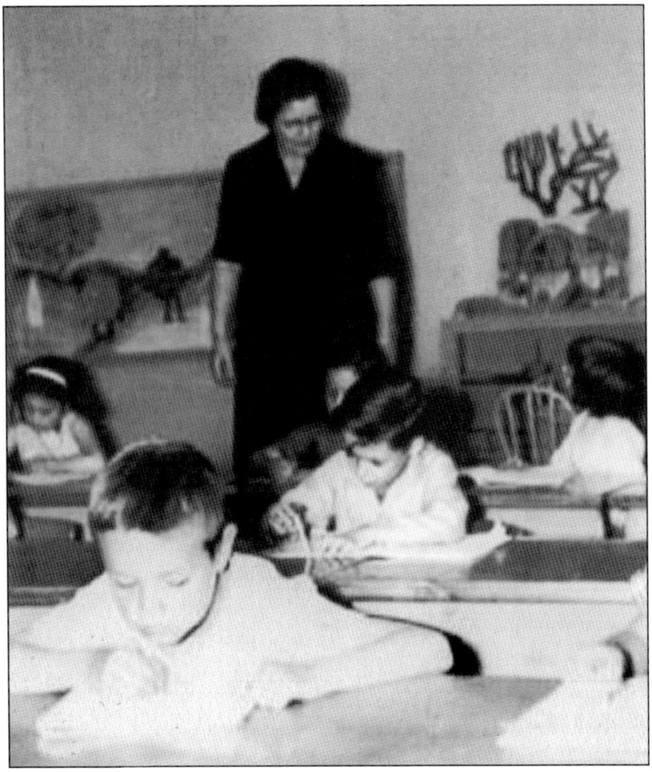

The first documented school in what is now Rains County was a one-room log building known as Union Grove, or Garrett's Hump. Education in the early years was in the hands of the local population. Rural schools operated for many years in Rains County communities, including Emory and Point. The establishment of the first school district, Emory District No. 1, was in 1892; there were over 20 districts by the 1920s. (Courtesy of Phillip Kerr.)

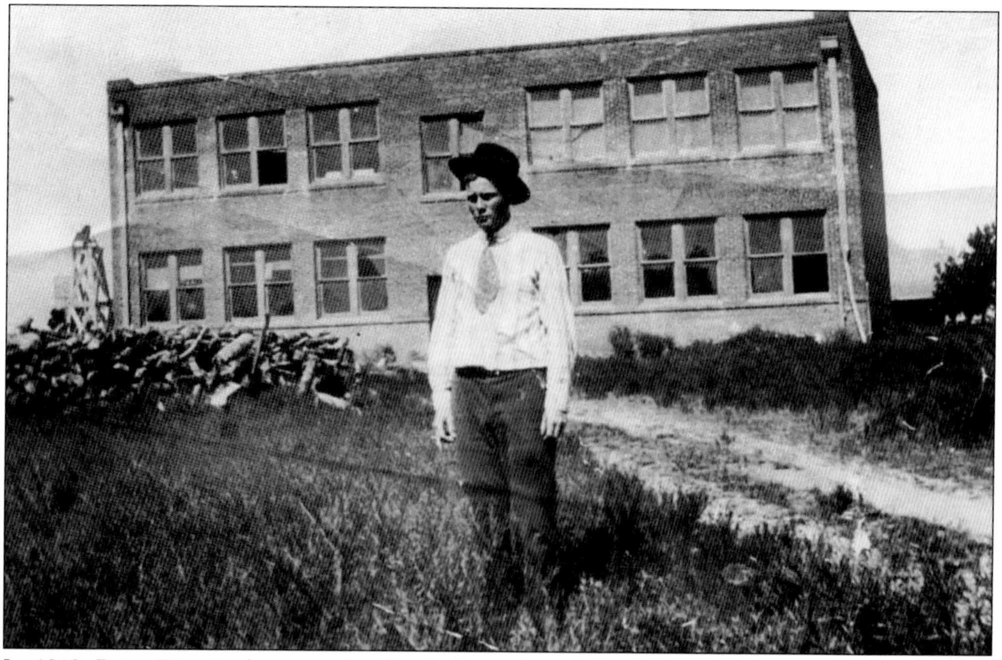

In 1913, Point District became the first Independent School District (ISD) in Rains County. In 1914, its new two-story, red brick building was completed. The photograph above shows Truman J. "Brown" Nelson standing in front of the new 1914 school building. (Courtesy of Edna Nelson Collier.)

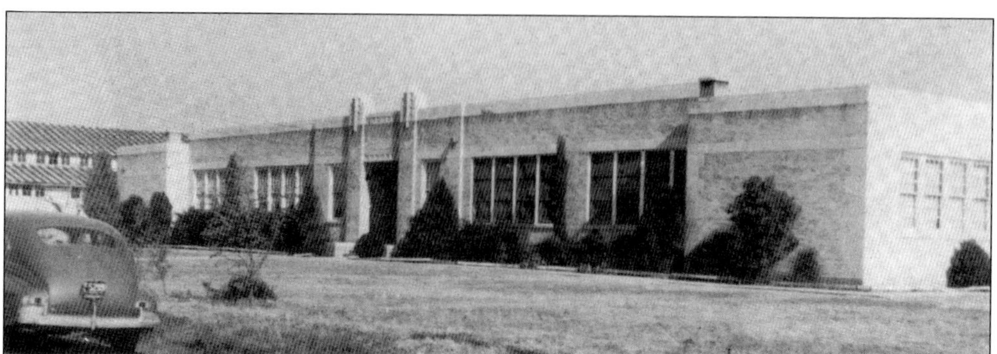

Later, the top floor of the red brick building was removed, but enrollment increased so much by 1939 that the old school building was torn down, and a new brick building was erected by the Work Projects Administration. (Courtesy of Bonita Jo Hooten.)

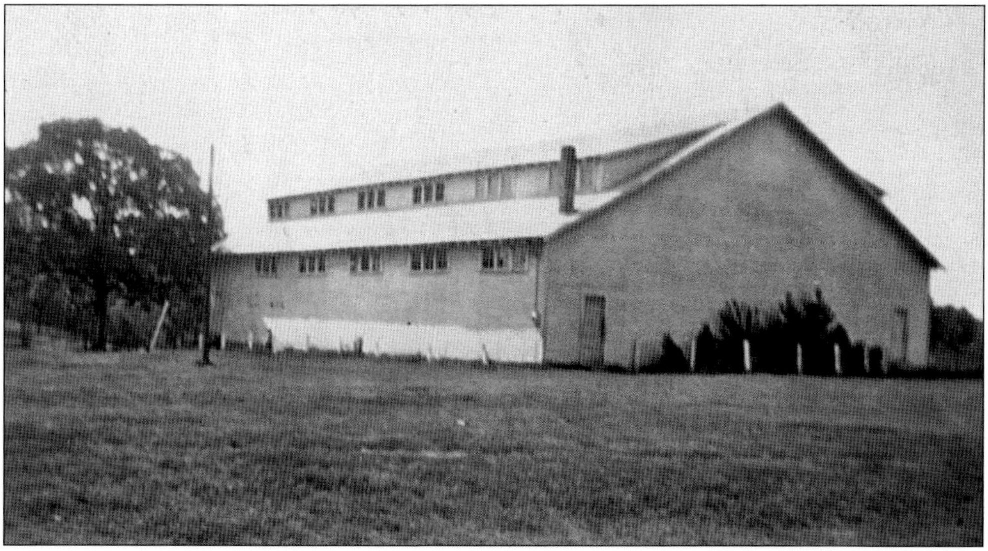

The Emory school board held a special meeting in May 1938 and voted to buy the gymnasium, which was owned by local stock holders for $1,900. The gym was built in 1934 with Public Works Administration labor. Materials were bought by the stockholders, composed of several local citizens. (Courtesy of Pat Peeples Adcock.)

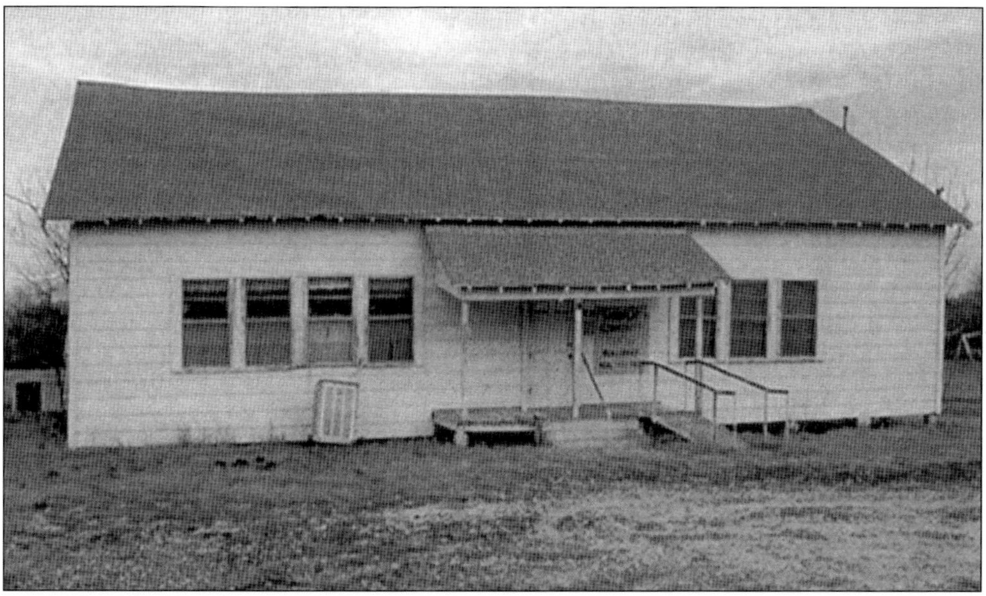

Sand Flat School was one of two African American schools in Rains County. Shown above is the second school building which was a Rosenwald school. Henry and Alice Murray donated land for the school. Attendance averaged about 60 students. Sand Flat School was closed with the advent of desegregation in 1969. The unused building is still standing today. (Courtesy of Elaine Nall Bay.)

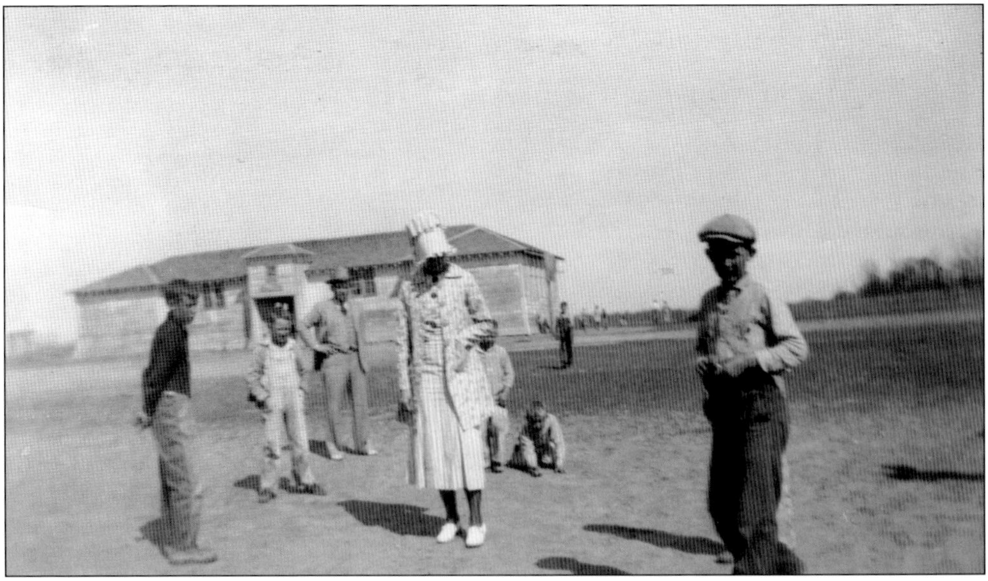

Bellview School District No. 5 was located in the Colony community. During the 1940s, the building had four rooms and a belfry; the bell was used to ring in the school day. At this time, Bellview's lunchroom consisted of long wooden tables and benches as eating space for the students. In 1950, the Bellview Common School was discontinued. According to the Rains County deed records, three acres were bought from John McAree and his wife, Cora, in 1927 to build a new school building at a cost of $100. When the school district ceased to exist in 1950, the buildings were given to the Bellview Community for religious and community purposes. In the 1934 photograph are principal Price Walker (background), teacher Esta Mae Peeples (center), and unidentified students. (Courtesy of Jeri McAree Humphrey and Pat Peeples Adcock.)

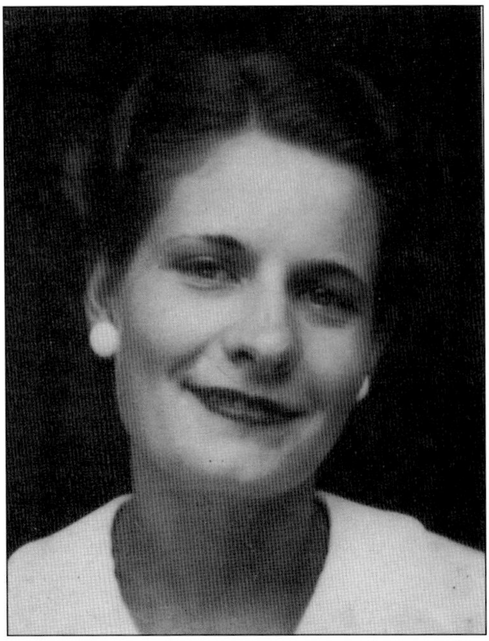

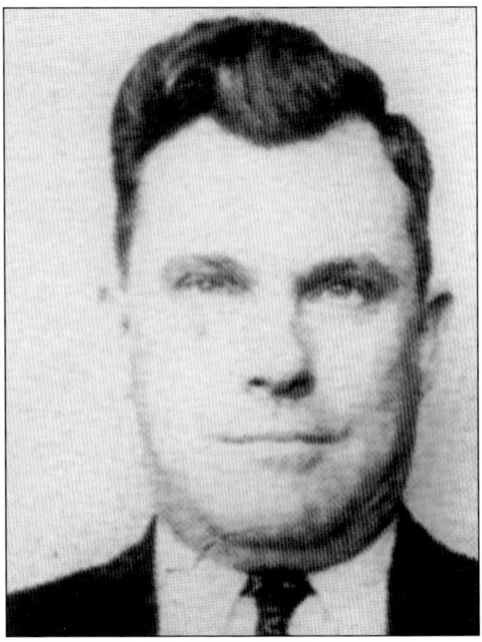

Pictured above are Esta Mae Peeples, teacher; and Price Walker, principal. (Courtesy of Jeri McAree Humphrey and Pat Peeples Adcock.)

The first African American teachers in Rains County were A.C. "Clifton" McMillan (1856–1907) and Dora McMillan (1856–1907), who came from Wood County. They taught at Henry's Chapel School District No. 12 before 1900. The school building was located in the area of Hopewell Cemetery, where A.C. and Dora are buried. (Courtesy of Gwen McMillan Lawe.)

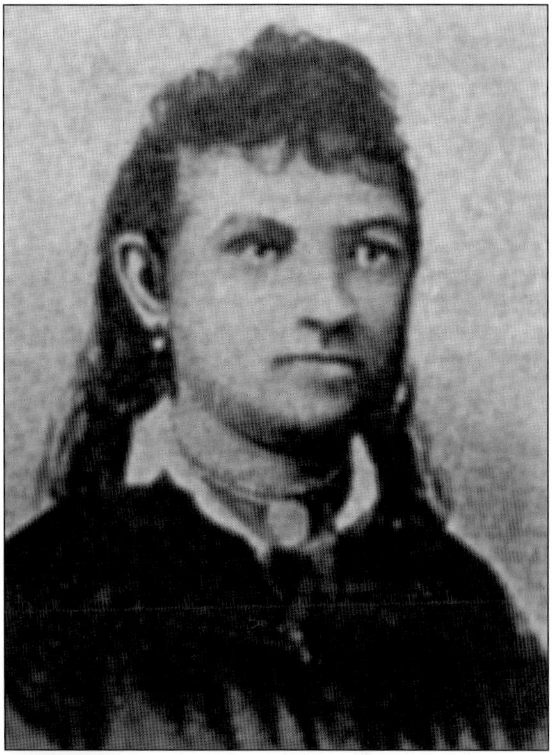

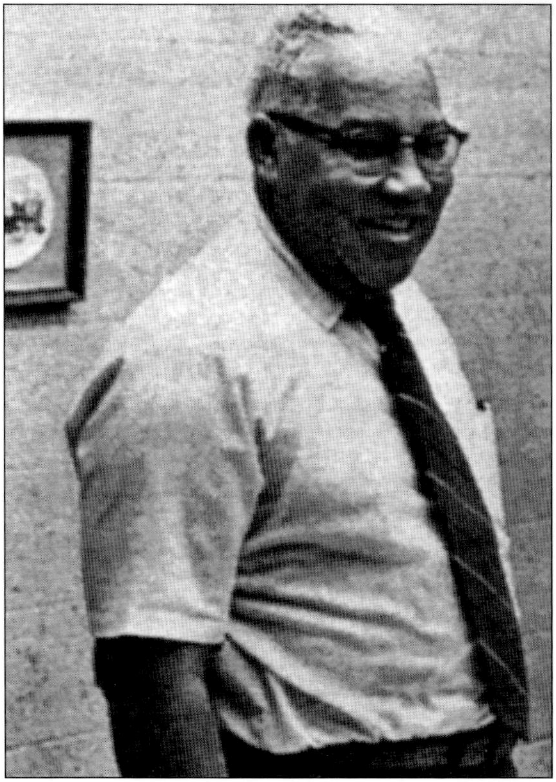

A.C. McMillan (1921–1986), grandson of A.C. "Clifton" and Dora McMillan, followed in their footsteps and had a long career as teacher and administrator in Rains County schools from the early 1950s until 1985. He began teaching at Sand Flat District No. 12, where he had attended school. The A.C. McMillan African American Museum has been established in his honor and is off the square in Emory on Texas Street. (Courtesy of Gwen McMillan Lawe.)

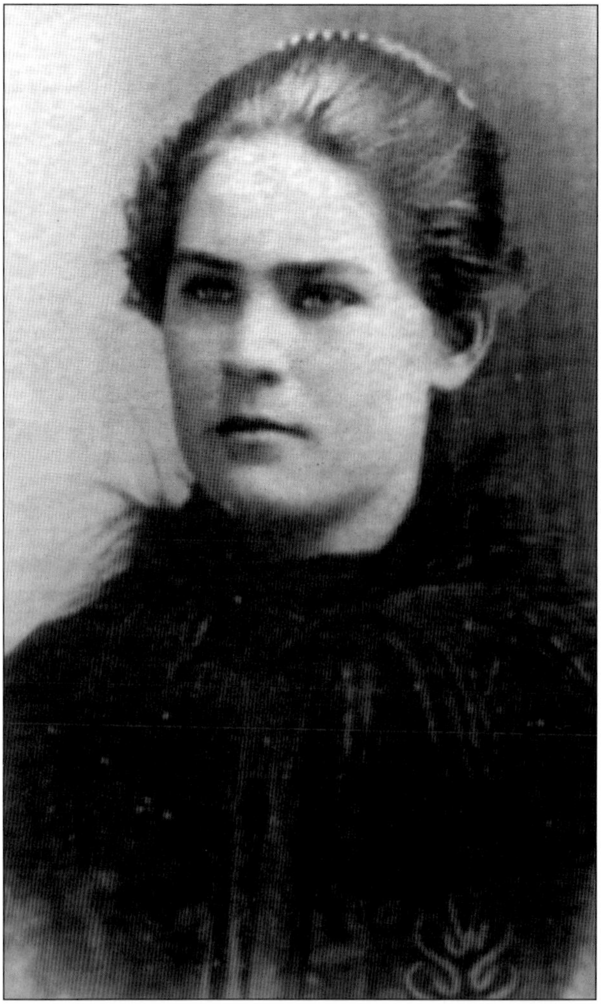

Lucy Carter Bell (1887–1971), daughter of George H. and Mattie A. Carter, and her sister Florence Carter moved to Rains County about 1909. In 1911, Lucy married Floyd Bell of Rains County. That same year, she received a Second Grade Teaching Certificate, which was valid for four years. Her first teaching position was at Boyd School in 1910. Lucy also taught at Cody, Colony, Milsap, Ginger, Woosley, and Emory schools. Her last teaching position was at Bellview School for the 1932–1933 school year.

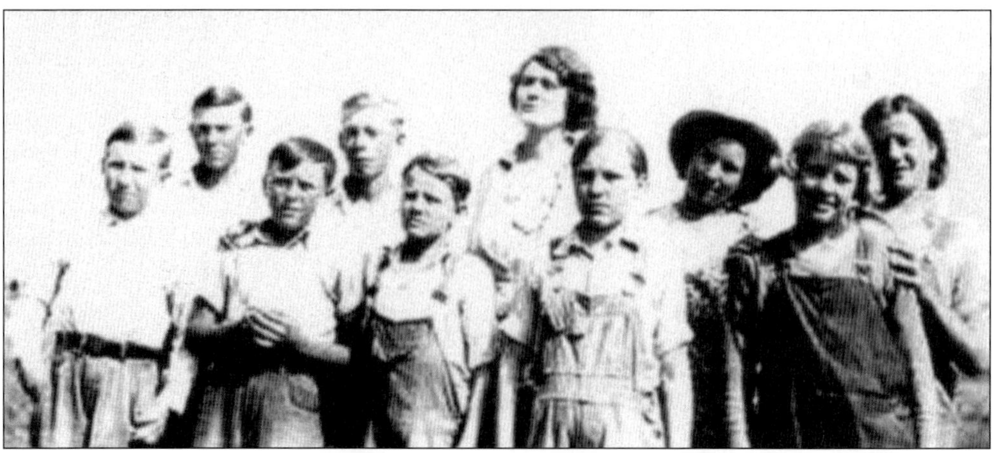

Pictured below are Lucy's sixth-grade and seventh-grade students; on the second row, far right, is Pauline Brown McAree. The Bells lived directly across from the Bellview schoolhouse and adopted a son. (Courtesy of Jeri McAree Humphrey and Jack Bell.)

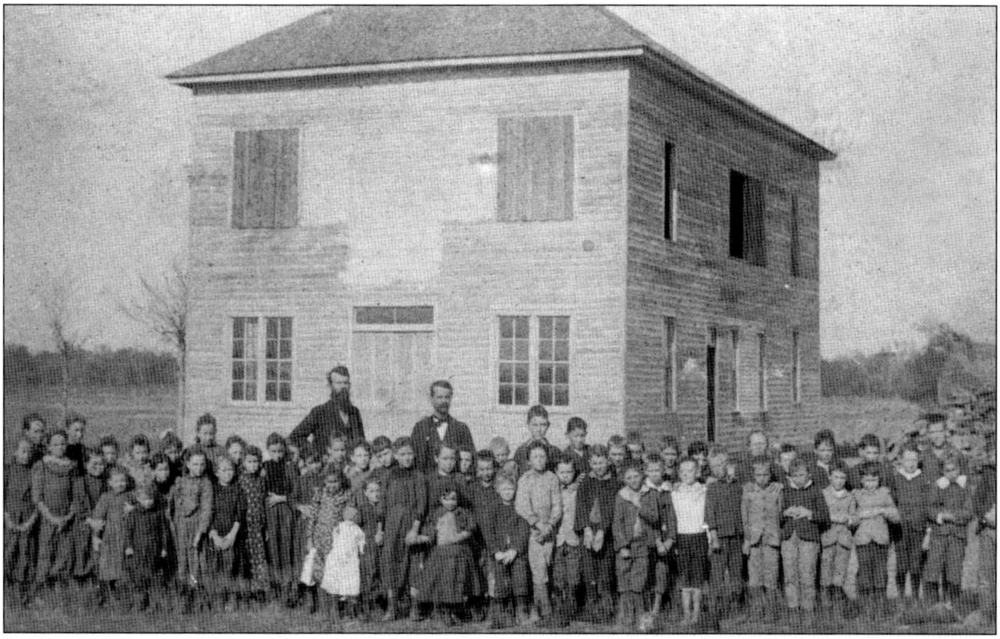

Prior to the Emory public school district, there were 1894 (top) and 1906 (bottom) school buildings. The 1906 building was an old, weather-beaten building constructed without thought of light, ventilation, comfort, or fitness. There was the problem of "tardiness in attendance" during the 1903–1904 school years. An article was published in the *Rains County Leader*, January 15, 1904 asking parents to please help resolve this matter. Excuses offered by students included "I had to help mama," "I had to mail a letter," "I couldn't get off any sooner," "I had some work to do," and "We got up late."

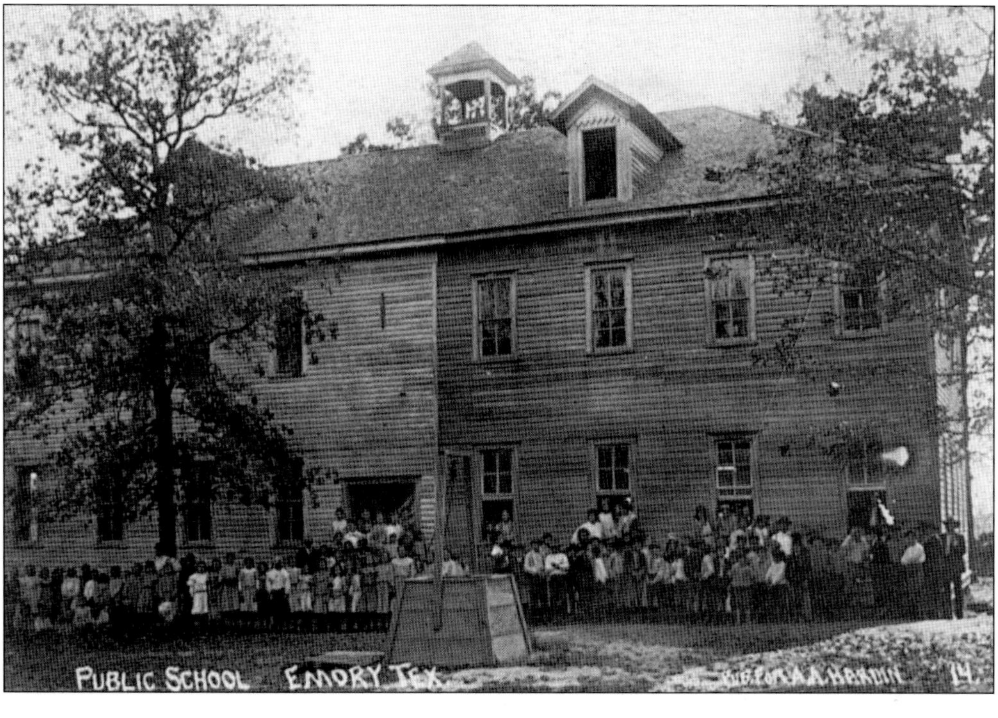

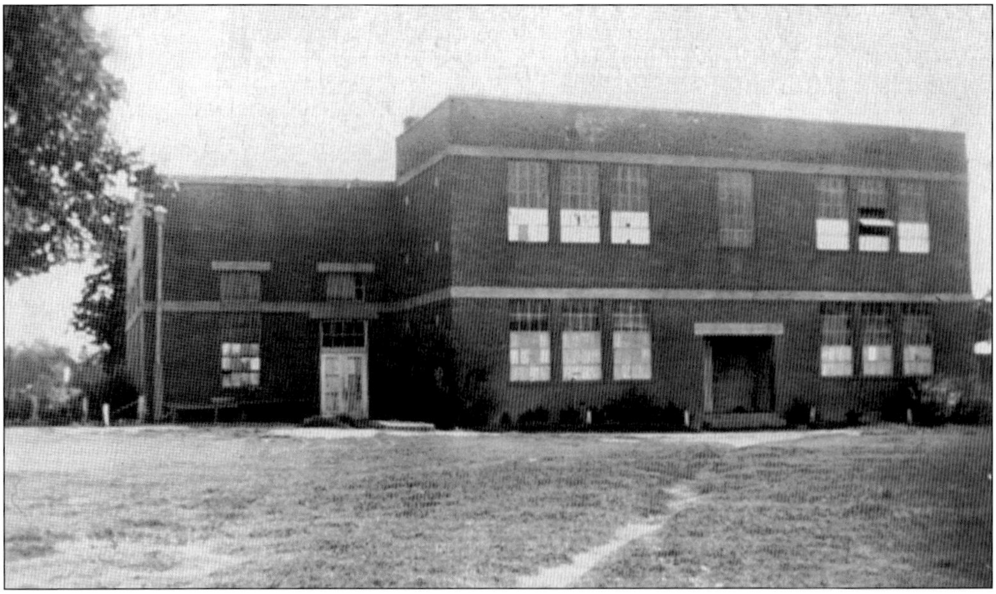

Shepherd Bros. & Company of Greenville was the builder of the Emory school building at a cost of $18,675. A half-day holiday was given so that the school dedication ceremony in October 1922 could be held in the school auditorium. The structure stood on 12 acres with a large, grass-covered athletic field that was free of mud. Below, concrete bleachers served as seating for Emory sports fans. The remains of football victories are still visible behind the school building north of the town square. (Courtesy of Elaine Nall Bay.)

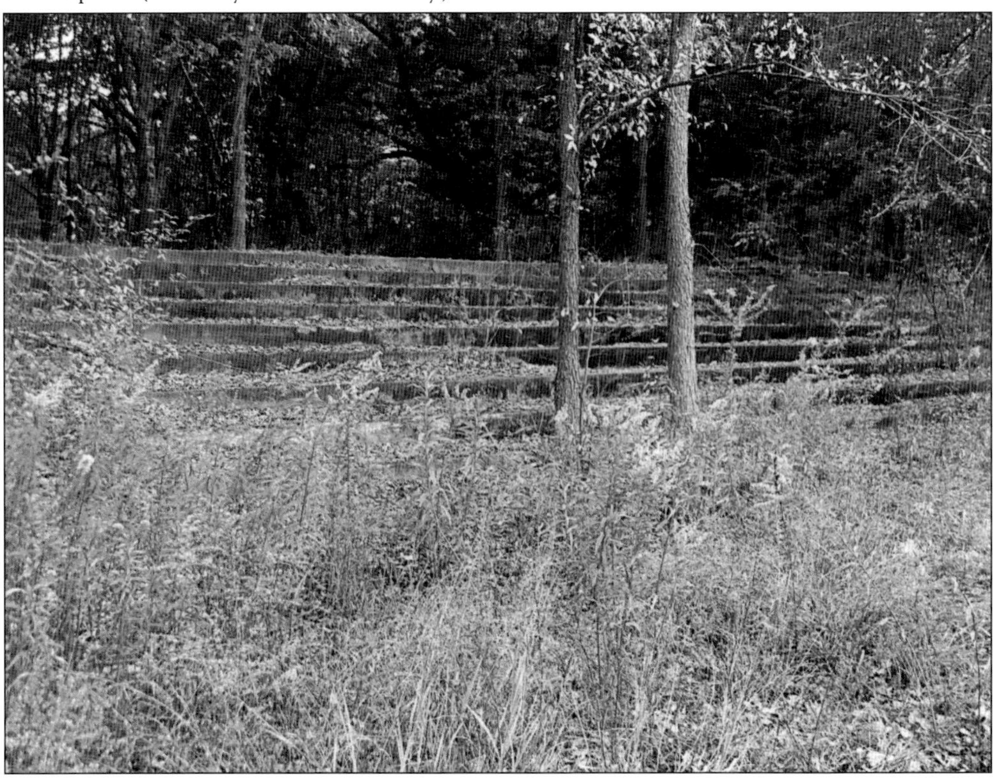

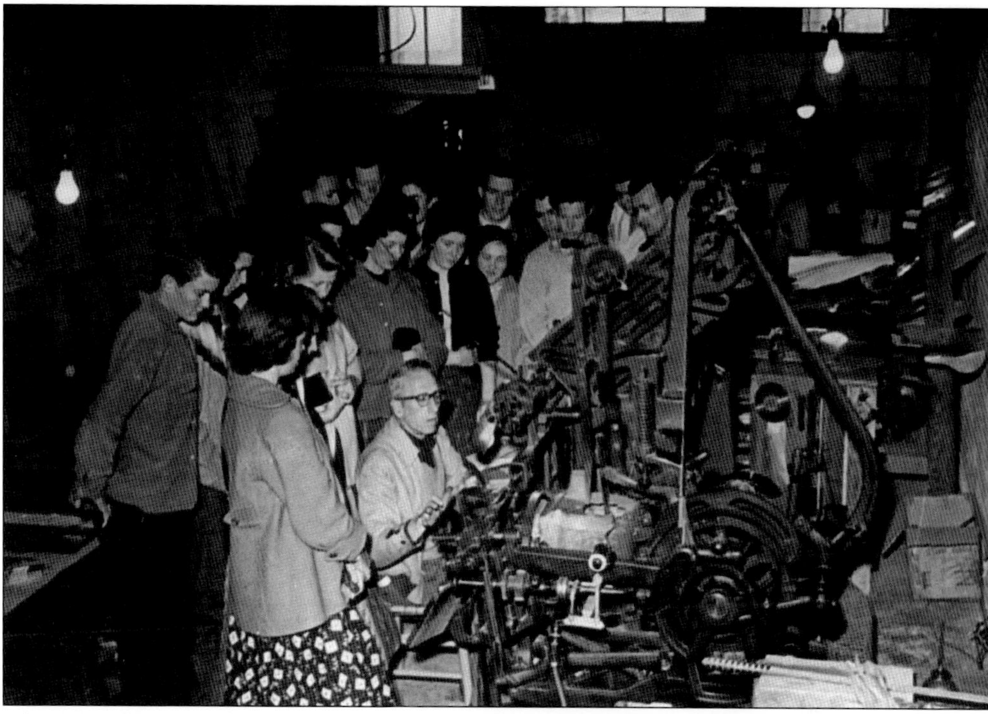

Above, students are shown the old printing equipment of the *Rains County Leader* by linotype operator Earl Hill Sr., editor and publisher of the *Rains County Leader* from 1937 to 1960.

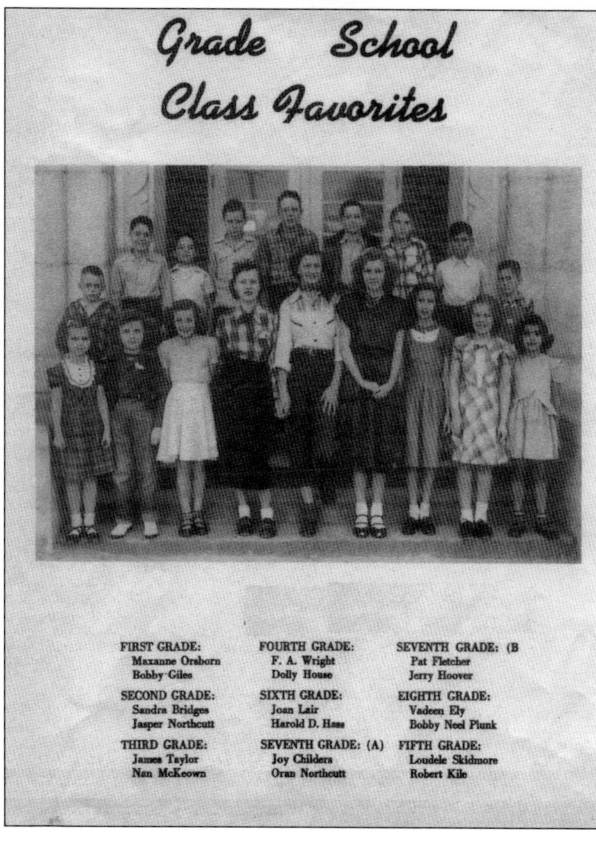


At right are class favorites for the 1950 school year at Emory ISD, including the following: (first grade) Maxanne Orsborn and Bobby Giles; (second grade) Sandra Bridges and Jasper Northcutt; (third grade) James Taylor and Nan McKeown; (fourth grade) F.A. Wright and Dolly House; (fifth grade) Loudele Skidmore and Robert Kile; (sixth grade) Joan Lair and Harold D. Hass; (seventh grade A) Joy Childers and Oran Northcutt; (seventh grade B) Pat Fletcher and Jerry Hoover; (eighth grade) "Vadeen" [Vadean] Ely and Bobby Neel Plunk.

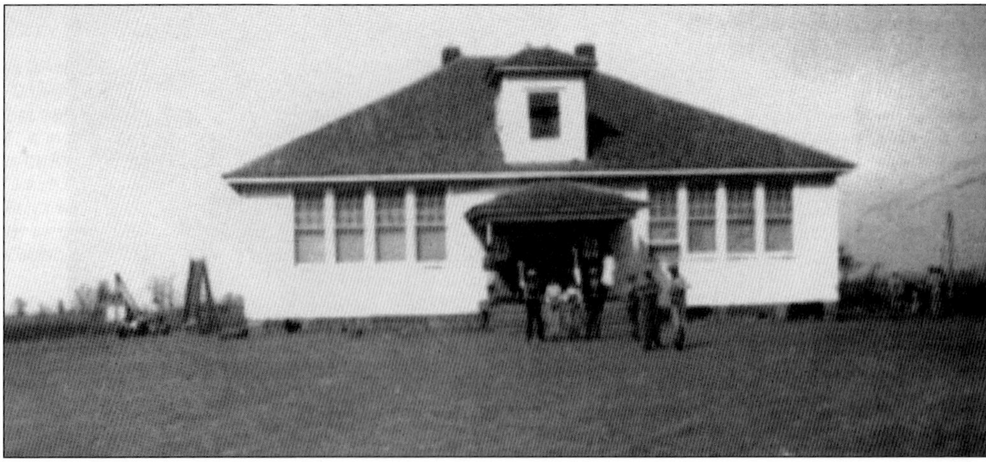

Living in the Pilgrims Rest community with his bride Hallie Mae Horsley, in the 1926–1927 school year, "Mr. Earl Sybert taught 6th–8th grade at Ginger school along with Marie Amis and Rosa Reeves," noted the *Rains County Leader* on October 29, 1926. During the 1930s, Sybert served as the clerk of Rains County and worked in an abstract office before moving his family to West Texas. (Courtesy of J. ARN Womble.)

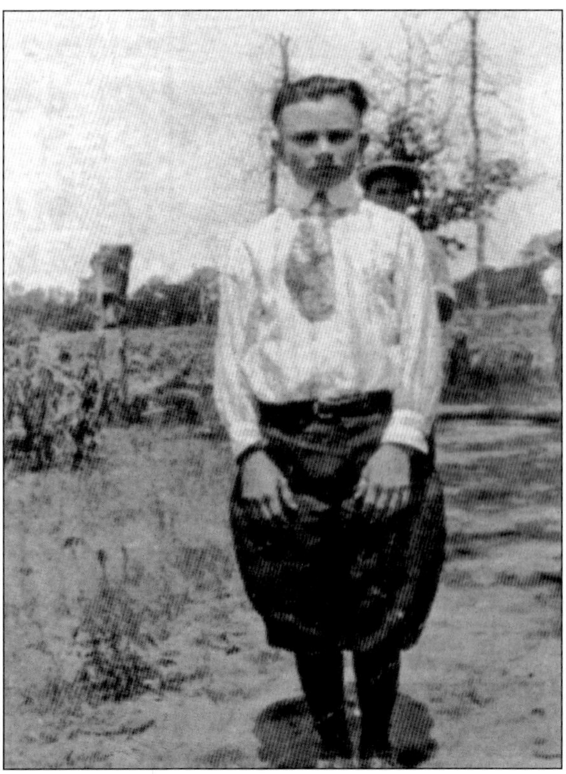

James Earl Sybert, son of Jesse Thomas Sybert and Lucy Ann Moore, began school at Hogansville about 1910. As was customary, students brought their lunch to school in metal buckets. One of the common lunch items was hard-boiled eggs. Boys would often hold the eggs in the palms of their hands and crush the shell against their foreheads. On one occasion, Earl ran out of the house for school and grabbed his lunch. At school, he followed the usual routine of cracking the egg against his forehead. Only this time he had a big surprise: he had picked up a raw egg. Earl became a teacher and taught at the Ginger School, pictured above. (Courtesy of J. ARN Womble.)

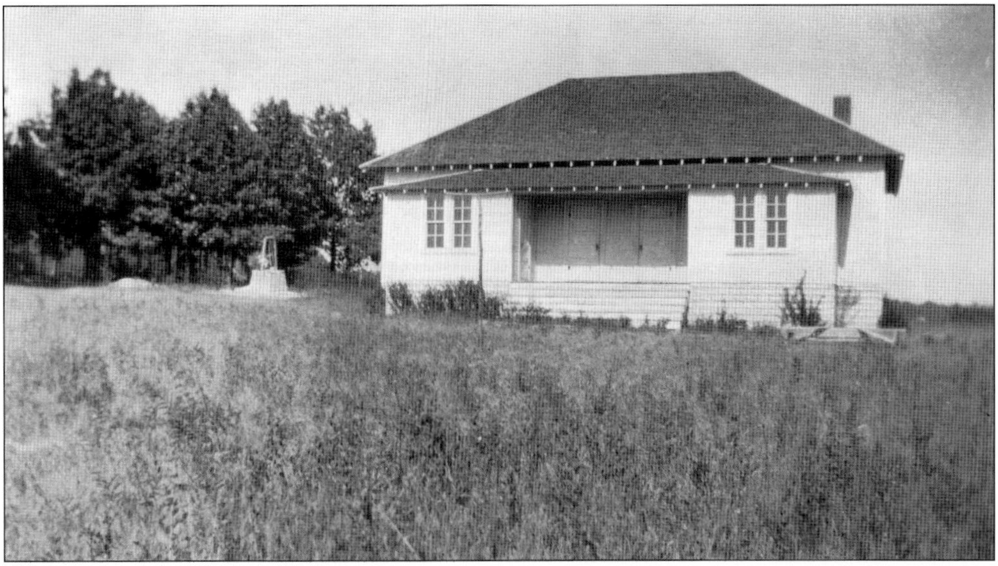

The Rocky Point School had a long porch across the front, lights that hung on a wall with a fuel tank above, and two entrances. Grades one, two, and three had class in the front room, while grades four, five, and six used the middle room, and the last room was for grades seven and up. The 1930 graduation exercises were held in the Emory School auditorium. Graduates from Rocky Point Grammar School in April 1930 were Frank Davis, Walter Harbin, Leonard Lynch, C.B. Meyer, Edward Moreland, Edith Moreland, Vestell Russell, Milton Sanders, and Lois Waren. The teachers for the 1929–1930 school year were Mrs. Yandell and Faye Calloway. (Courtesy of Pauline Hultman.)

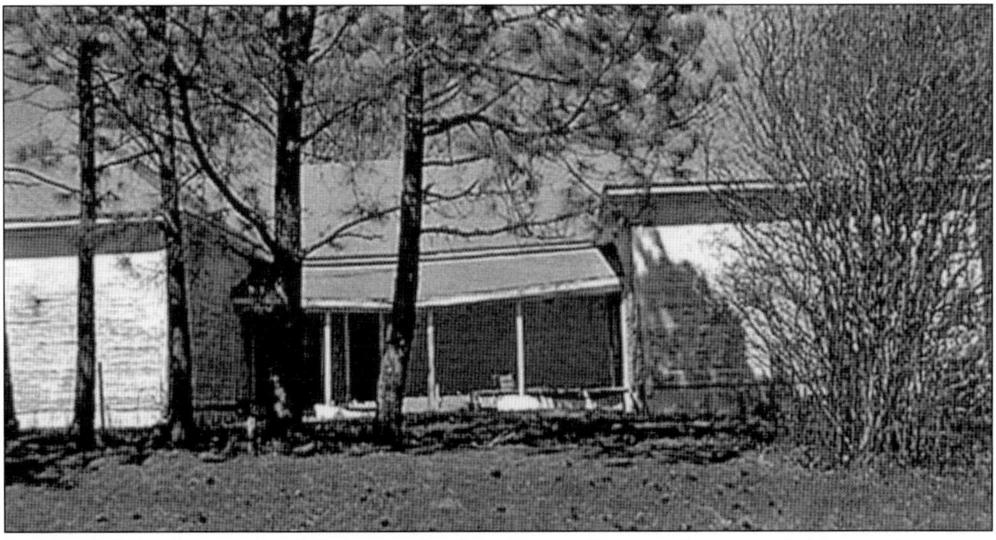

Richland School was one of the two schools in Rains County that served African American children. In December 1921, Mattie and Maudie Daniels sold one acre for $100 to the trustees for Richland School District no. 19. In 1925, a building with a large front porch between the two wings was nestled in Richland Community among two churches, two stores, and a Dairy Queen. Inside were six rooms that served grades 1 through 10. The new school building was fully equipped for domestic science and vocational agriculture departments. The historic building burned in 2002. (Courtesy of Elaine Nall Bay.)

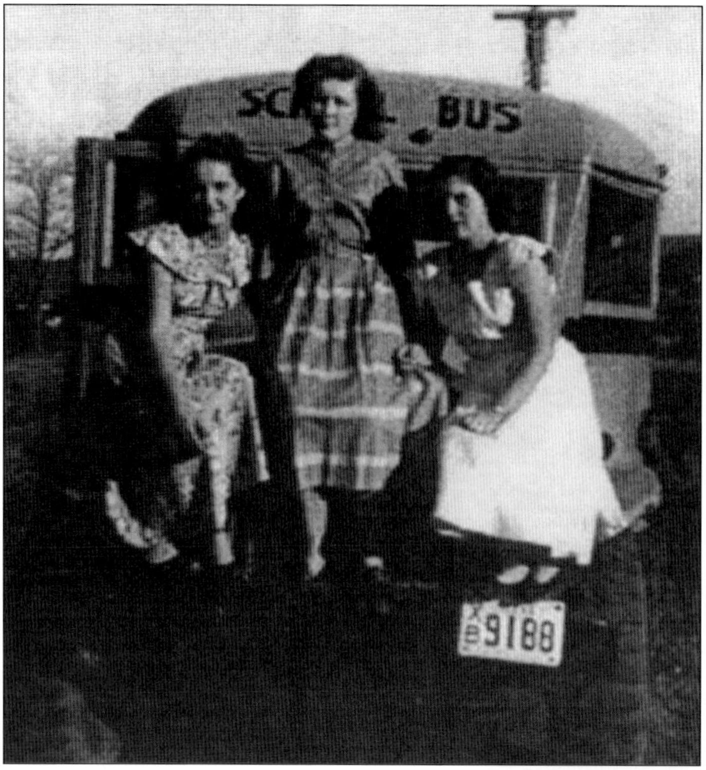


The first bus operation for the Point school began in 1935. The bus service for Point served the communities of Woosley, Flats, Lynch, Cody, Wattsville, and Waskom in later years. From left to right, Betty Cunningham, Freddie Prince, and Genell Watts sit on the back of the school bus in 1950. (Courtesy of Genell Watts Lankford.)

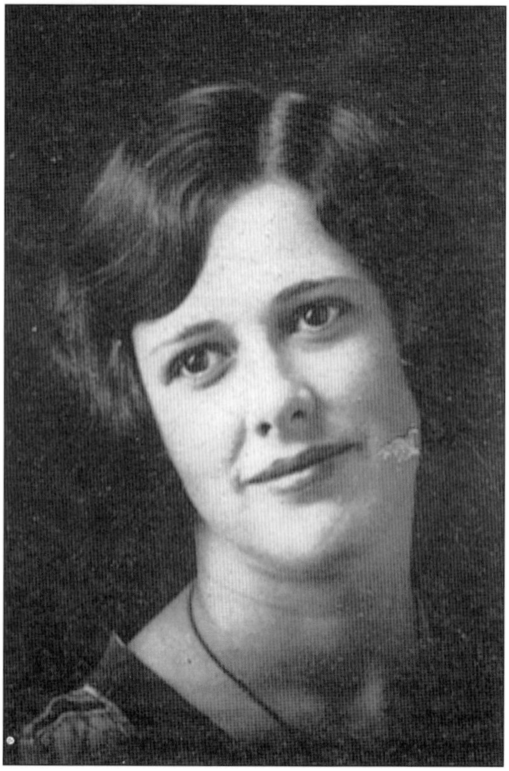

Vera Clewis (1910–1986) married Gus Orsborn Jr. in 1927. She received a bachelor's degree with a major in English and a minor in math and then a master's degree in commerce from East Texas State University; Velma taught for 38 years in many of the county's schools, including Gritt, Alba, Point, Antioch, New Holmes, Henry's Chapel, and Emory. The Orsborns had two daughters, Maxanne and Jo Nell.

*Eight*

# Never Forgotten

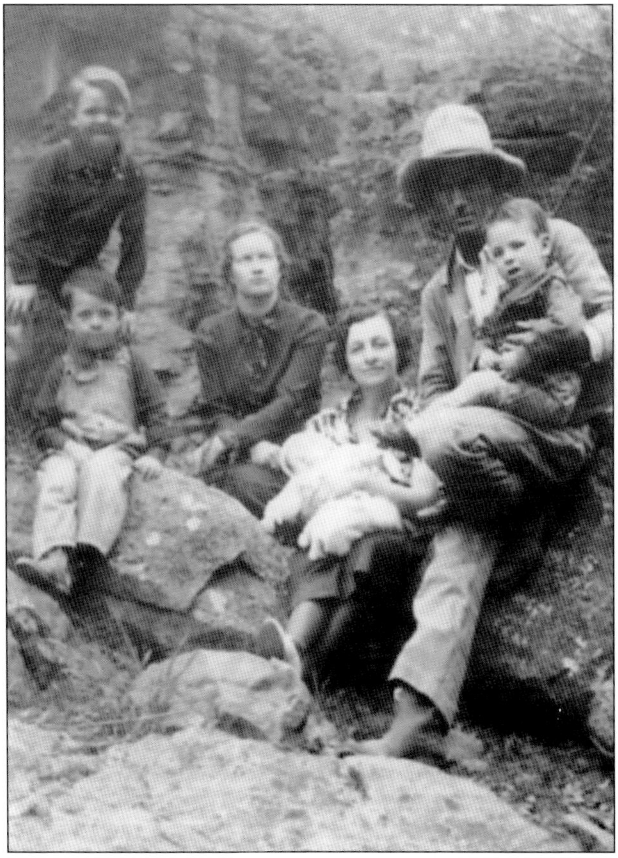

Following are glimpses into the lives of numerous people and families who came to Rains County over the years. Their lives, efforts, and struggles influenced the evolution of the small communities of Emory and Point into what Rains County is today. Rains County may not have become the small, rural area that attracts many visitors annually without the history book of their lives.

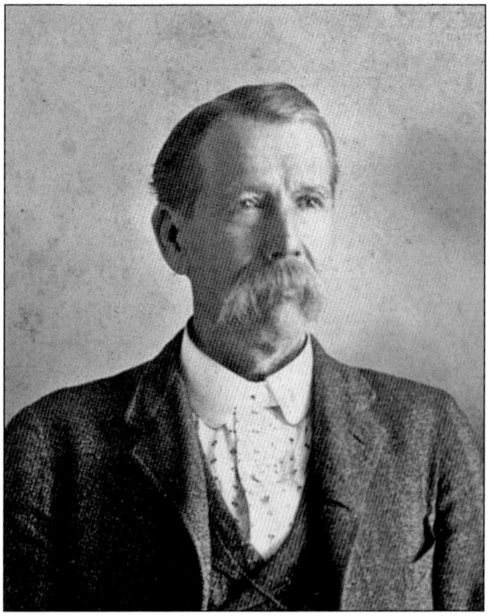

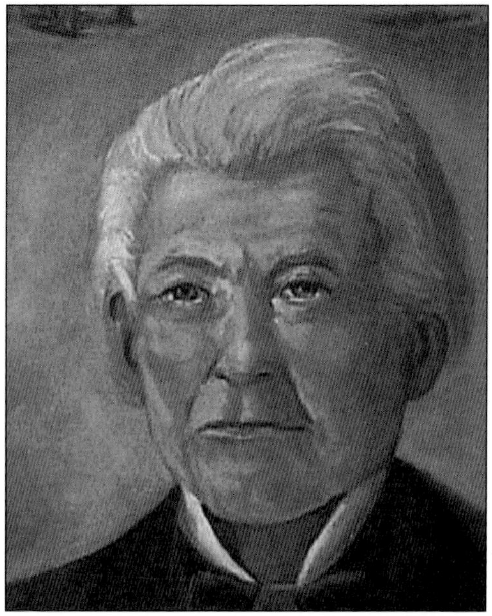

Emory Rains (1800–1878) is remembered as the "Founding Father of Rains County, Texas." Physically, Rains was a tall, stately man of elegant bearing. He never grew a beard, and his jet-black hair turned to silver. He always wore a wool shirt with an open collar. He married Marana Anderson (1802–1885) in 1822. "Mrs. Marana Rains always kept the coffee pot on the fire and a cup of coffee was the treat to visitors who called in those days," wrote the *Rains County Leader*, Pioneer Edition, in August 1939. To their union, 13 children were born—12 of them living to maturity. Eleven of their children were Pilmira, Mary Ann, Sally, Liz, Marana, Ellen, Minerva, John D., Presley, Miria, and Mahalia Kathleen. At age 29, Emory, not being able to read or write, was taught by Jonas Harrison by practicing writing in damp sand around Patroon Creek, Shelbyville, Shelby County, Texas, where their land deed is recorded in Spanish. Rains went on to become a self-taught lawyer and held many public offices. At age 66, he rode a mule to Austin to assist in the passage of the bill establishing Rains County. Rains bought 640 acres two miles northeast of Point where he spent the remainder of his life. Emory Rains, E.P. Kearby and Capt. Tom M. Cain surveyed Rains County. Emory Rains died Monday, March 3, apparently from a stroke. Postmaster Elijah Bibb, a dear friend, built Emory Rains's coffin as he had requested. (Courtesy of Jeri McAree Humphrey.)

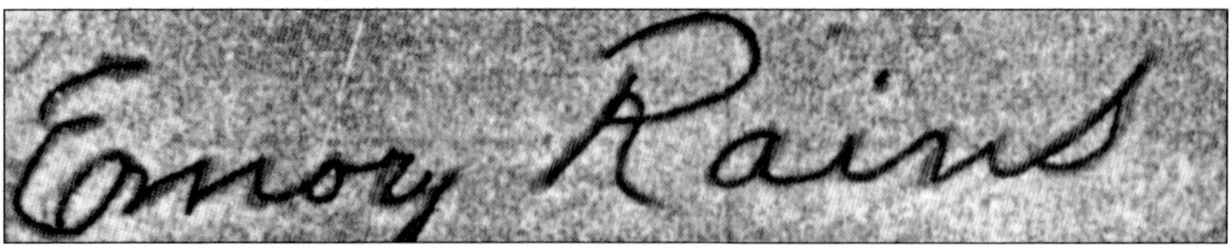

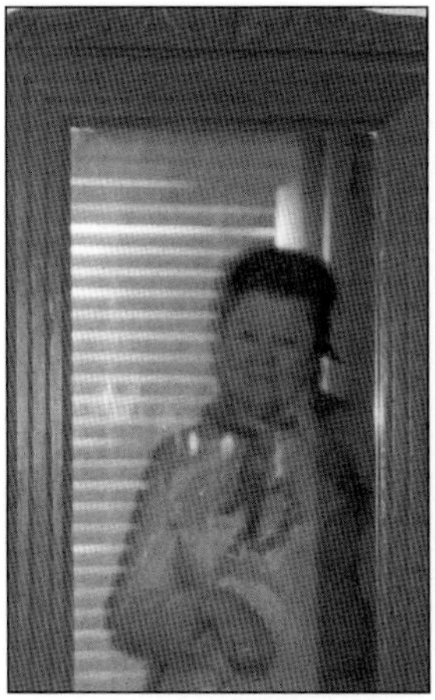 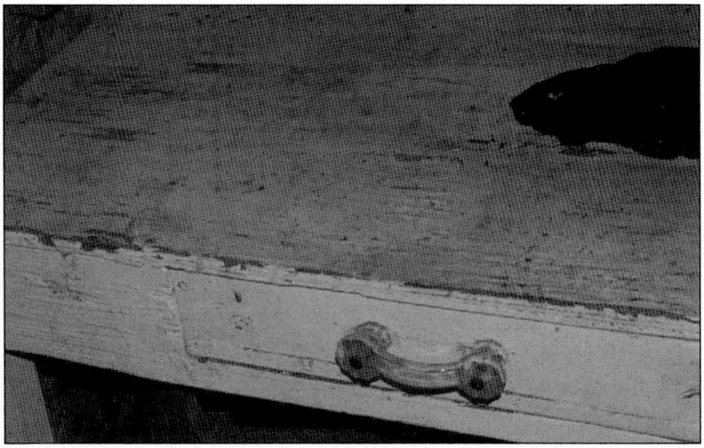

The precious Rains family organ fell off the wagon while they were moving and broke into many pieces as transporters were trying to evade troublemakers. Emory Rains salvaged parts of the organ and made a framed mirror. Cay Frances B. House is a direct descendant of Emory Rains, and her reflection is seen in the mirror pictured on the left. The dough table pictured on the right also belonged to the Emory Rains family and now sits in home of his great-great-granddaughter, Cay Frances. (Courtesy of Jeri McAree Humphrey.)

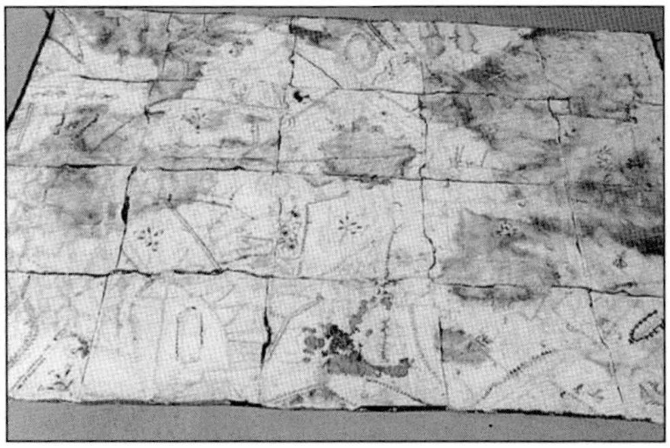 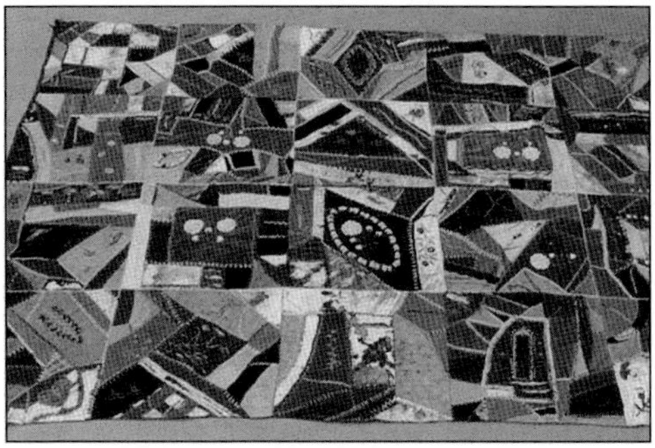

Recently, an original quilt that Marana Rains, wife of Emory Rains, quilted has surfaced. The over 100-year-old quilt is 65 inches by 82 inches and consists of 16-inch blocks. The old quilt was in the possession of Presley Rains Montgomery, who received it from his mother. His grandchildren gave the quilt to Cay Frances B. House for safekeeping. The quilt was taken to Melanie Sanford, a textile conservationist in Red Oak, Texas, to be preserved. The appraiser dated the quilt as having been made between 1880 and 1895. Eventually, the 125-year-old quilt will be encased and hung in the Rains County Historical Society's building for the pleasure of all Rains County residents and visitors. (Courtesy of Melanie Sanford, textile preservationist.)

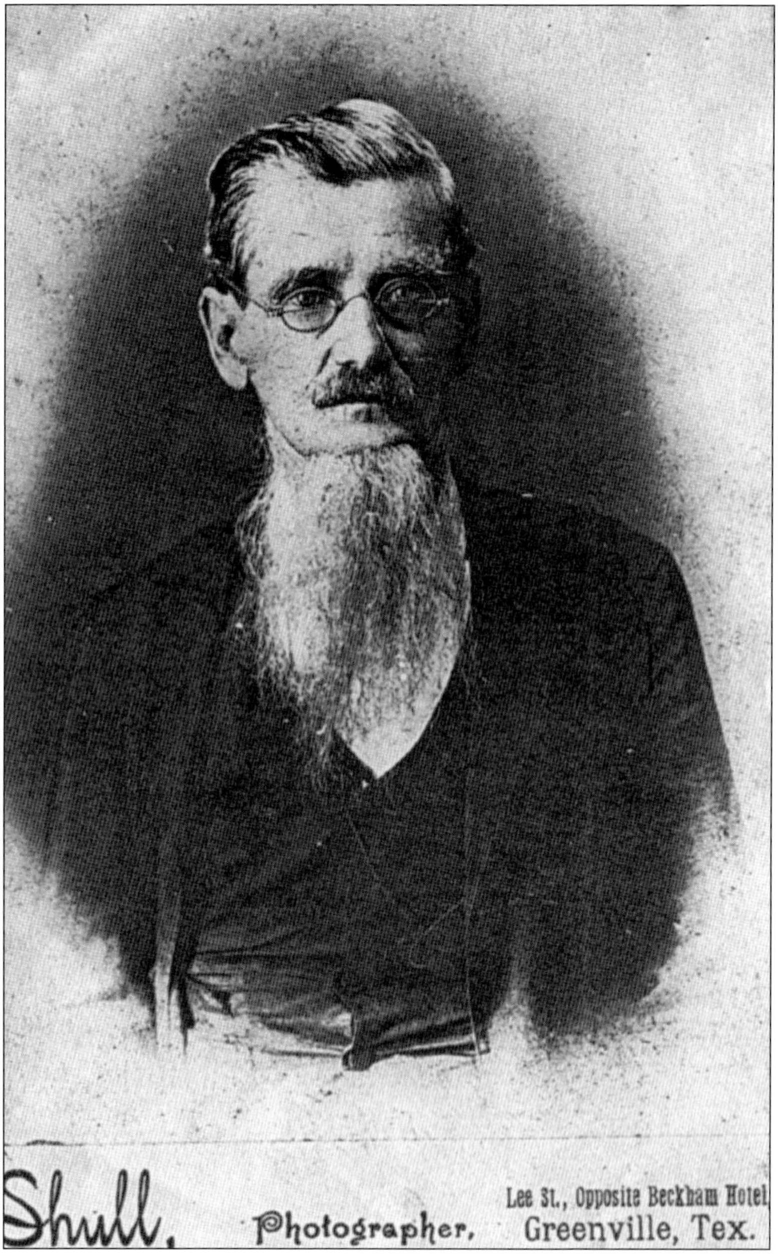


A Missouri native, Ambrose Fitzgerald (1827–1893) traveled by a wagon drawn by a yoke of oxen for his adventure to the exciting "promised land" of Texas and reached Nacogdoches County in 1846. Here, he received a grant of 640 acres from Mercer's Colony. Fitzgerald was on his original 640 acres as four new counties were formed: Henderson, Van Zandt, Wood and Rains. He was the first clerk of Van Zandt and Wood Counties. After the Civil War, Fitzgerald returned home and became tax assessor, district clerk, and county clerk for Rains County. In the early 1870s, he was a teacher at the school held in the Emory Masonic Lodge. In 1857, he was ordained and became a Baptist circuit-riding minister. It is said that he baptized over 2,500 people and served as a Baptist minister for over 50 years. He baptized James Stephen Hogg, the first native governor of Texas. (Courtesy of Mary Ann Fowler Fitzgerald.)

Carrie Etta Roan (1875–1959) moved from Tennessee to Hunt County, Texas. She married James A. Amis (1872–1939) in 1894. They moved to Alba in 1902, Ginger in 1906, and Emory in 1909. A versatile businessman, Amis operated a sawmill, lumberyard, truck farm, cattle and hog farm, pickle factory, and undertaking business. He sponsored the successful flight of a hot air balloon over Emory in 1914 and led efforts to build Highway 19 through Emory. (Courtesy of Carolyn Warren.)

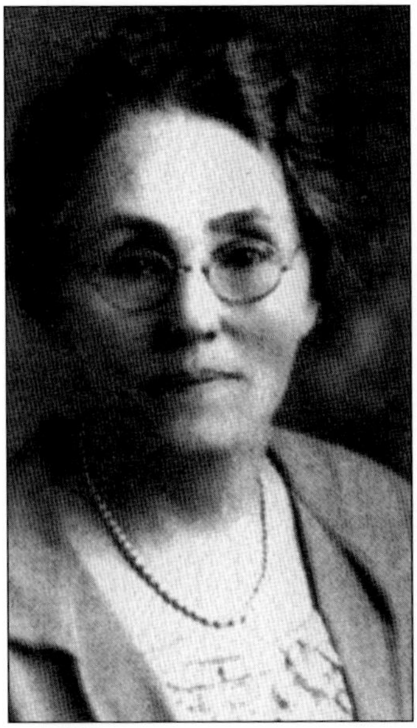

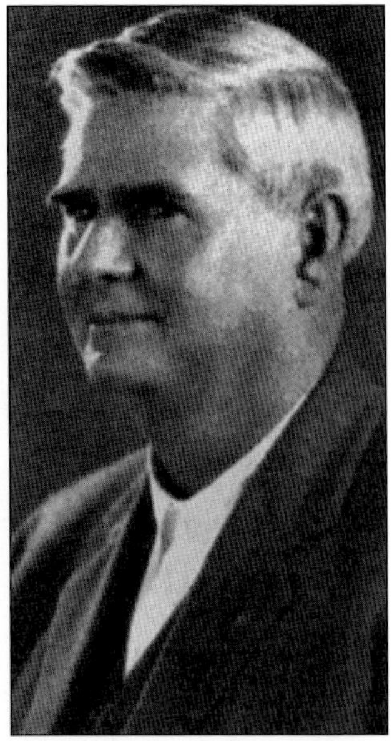

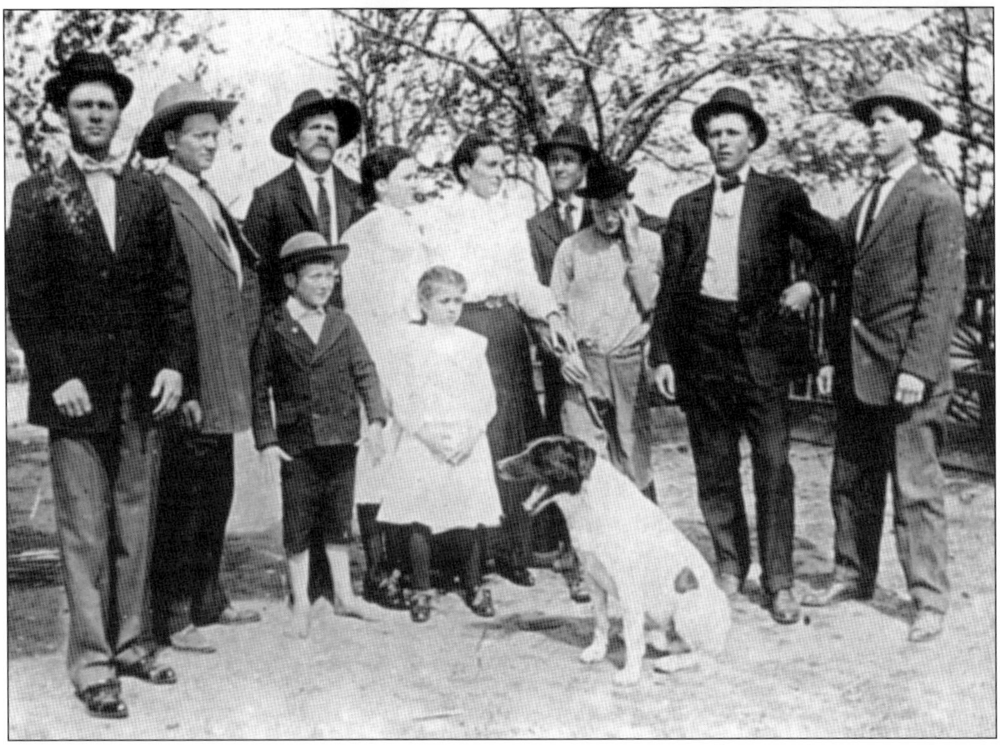

The William Drake Fenter family came to Rains County from Arkansas about 1900. Family members always expressed a hankering to go back to Arkansas. In this photograph are, from left to right, (first row) Roy D., Dovie Jane, and Hattie C.; (second row) Joseph Andrew, William Marion, William Drake, Malinda Hughes Fenter, Sam Montgomery, Charlie H., James Franklin, and Holly Artemas. Joseph Andrew operated a barbershop in Point for 64 years without ever putting out a business sign or a barber pole. Those who needed his services knew where to find him. According to Ronnie Fenter, "He gave me my first haircut." (Courtesy of Ronnie M. Fenter.)

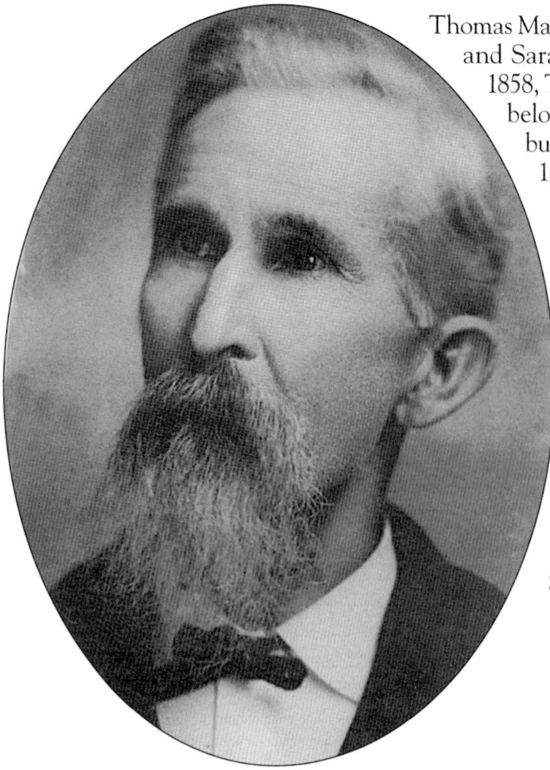

Thomas Mabry Cain (1832–1915), son of George Douglas and Sarah Cain, moved to Texas around 1850. In 1858, Thomas married Elizabeth B. Hooker, shown below. Tom began his merchandising business, but when the Civil War began, he joined the 11th Texas Calvary. He carried the title of captain all his life, although he was only a private. In 1875, Tom and Elizabeth moved to Emory. Tom owned the Cain & Ballew General Store with son-in-law J.W. Ballew. Cain was Rains County postmaster from 1896 to 1898, served as Rains County representative in the 14th and 16th state legislatures, and served in the 28th Texas Legislature for two terms. His business ventures were cotton ginning, a gristmill, and cattle trading. The cotton gin and gristmill were damaged during the 1894 tornado. (Courtesy of Jo Ann Stuart Turman.)

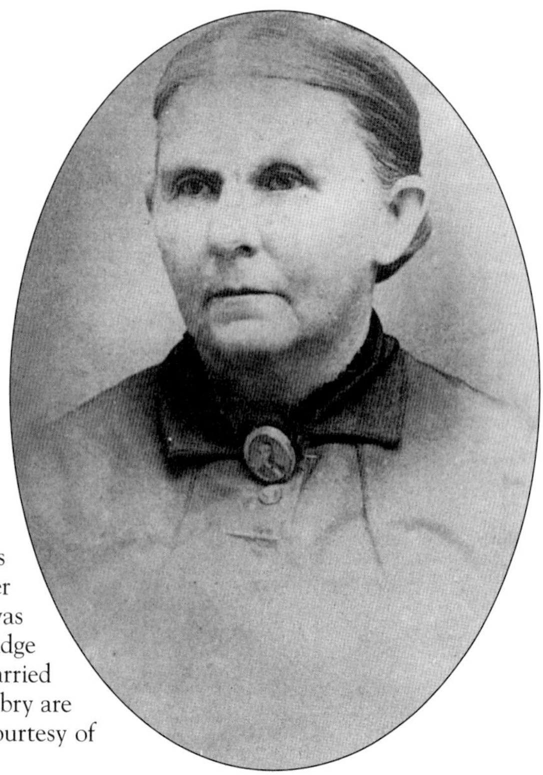

Elizabeth Bass Hooker Cain (1840–1893) was the daughter of James Walker Thomas Hooker and Mary Elizabeth Kitching. Her family was among the earliest settlers in the Hooker Ridge Community. In 1858, Elizabeth B. Hooker married Thomas Mabry Cain. She and Thomas Mabry are buried in the Hooker Ridge Cemetery. (Courtesy of Jo Ann Stuart Turman.)

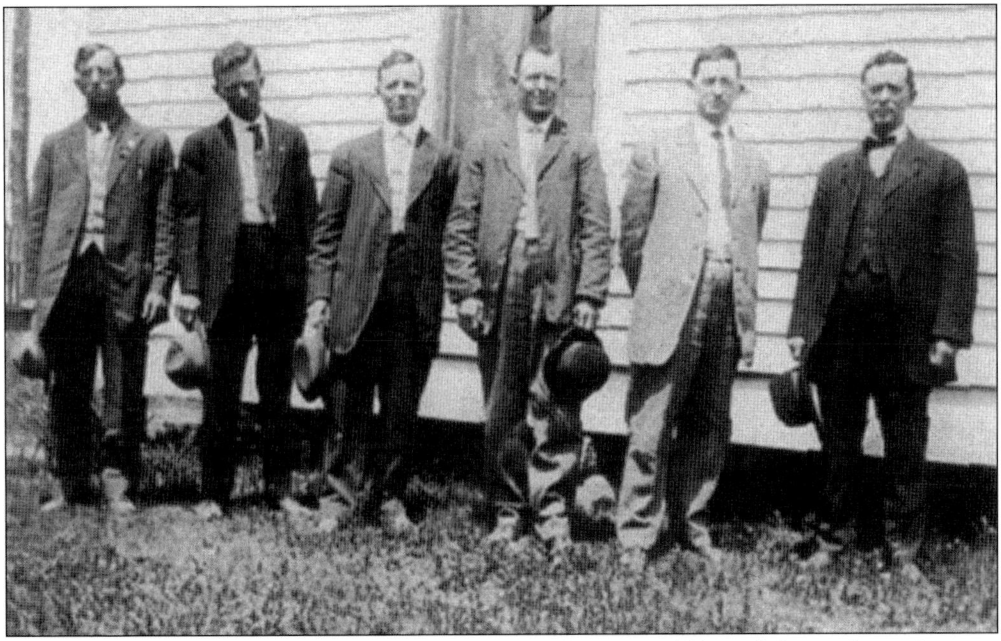

On April 26, 1912, the *Rains County Leader* wrote, "The Fitzgerald boys, left to right are Lonnie, Buckner, Ambrose, Sam, and Bruce, and cousin Joe Fitzgerald, dined at the home of Ambrose Fitzgerald Wednesday. This is first time all these brothers have been together in approximately three years. They are the sons of the late Rev. Ambrose Fitzgerald." (Courtesy of Bob and Mary Ann Fowler Fitzgerald.)

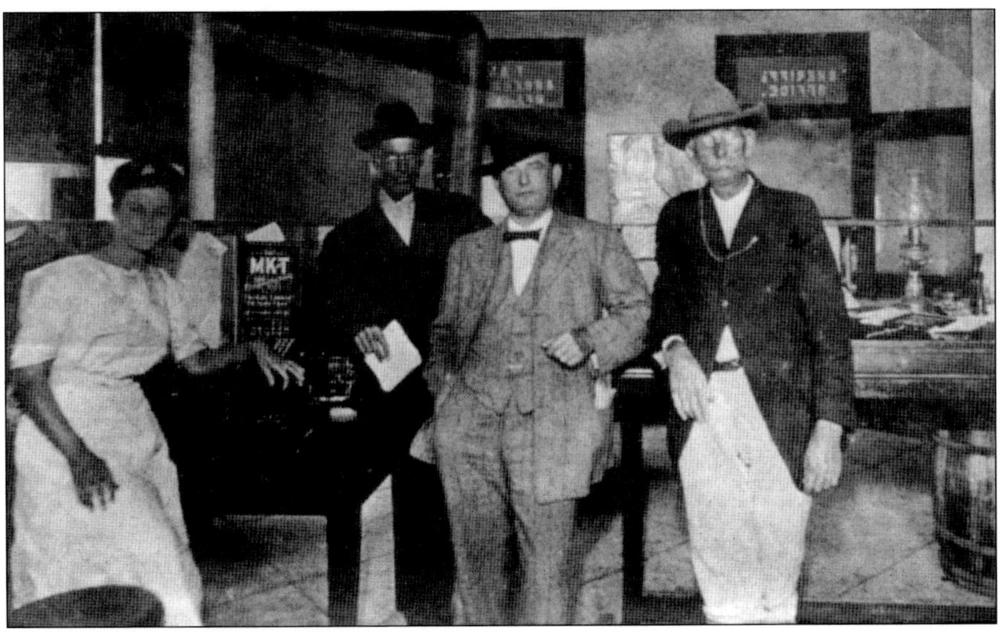


Seen in the sheriff's office in 1915 are, from left to right, Eula Morgan, Rev. C.M. Martin, W.W. Berzette, and George Morgan, sheriff. Rev. Martin served as county treasurer and had the record of marrying more couples and baptizing more born-again people than any other resident preacher in Rains County. (Courtesy of Mary A. Cain White.)

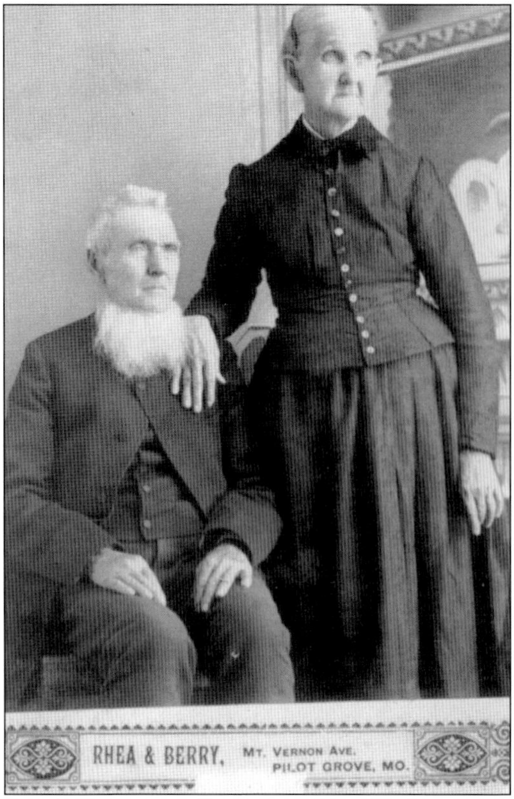


Alston Phillips and Jane McAlister migrated from Missouri and are enumerated in the 1880 Rains County census with their sons—N.E., Gideon, and Henry. All three sons are listed as 1880 Rains County road volunteers. (Courtesy of Jo Ann Stuart Turman.)

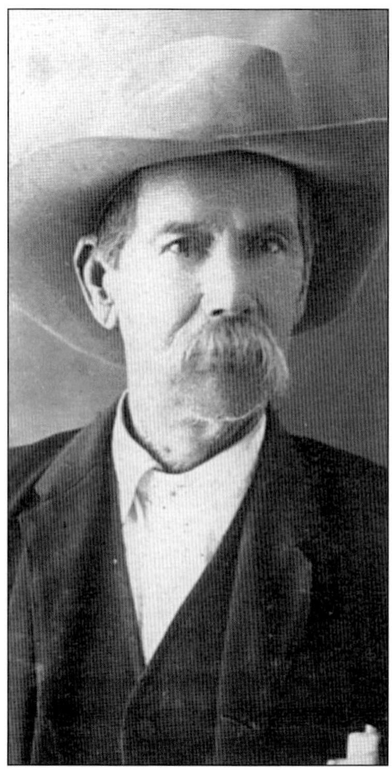

The *Rains County Leader* wrote on October 30, 1908, "Uncle Press Rains of Point, a lifelong resident of Rains County, died at a hospital in Dallas last Sunday morning from injuries received in falling from a trestle Thursday before. He had been visiting the Fair for several days and had been robbed of all the money he had just a day or two before he was hurt. It is not known how the accident occurred, but we learn the police are making an investigation. His remains were shipped . . . to Point Tuesday morning and interred in the Coats' graveyard near Center Point Tuesday evening, in the presence of a large crowd of relatives and friends. He was a son of Emory Rains, an alcalde under the Mexican rule, and father of the homestead law of Texas, and for whom Rains County and the town of Emory were named. Uncle Press Rains was the first Sheriff of Rains County by appointment when the county was organized, and was afterwards elected to the office. He was an ex-Confederate soldier and in pioneer days fought the Indians back from the borders of civilization. The deceased leaves two sisters, Mrs. T.A. Williams and Mrs. Maraney Williams of Point, one in Oklahoma and one in this county . . . With him one of the oldest landmarks of the State has passed away from our view." (Courtesy of Jeri McAree Humphrey and Cay Frances B. House.)

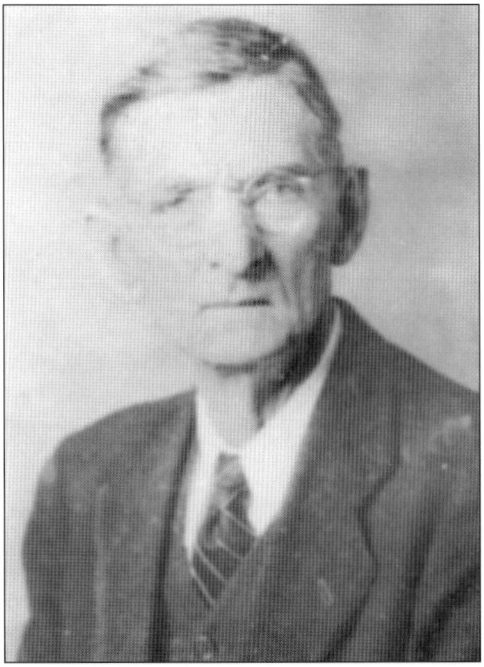 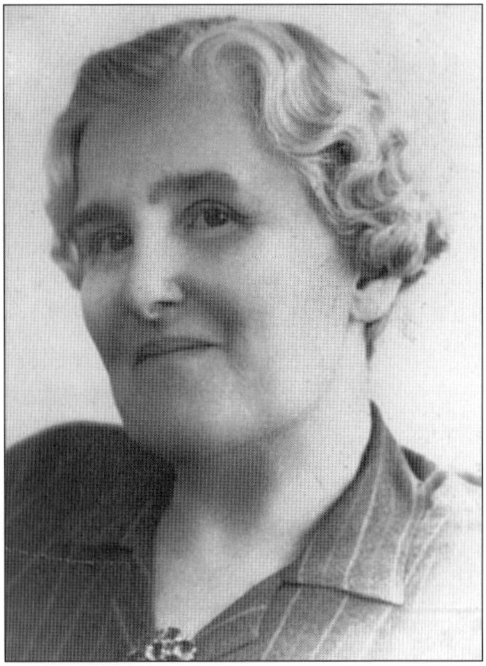

Tom W. Hill Sr. (1873–1937) was the son of Rev. and Mrs. W.P. Hill. His family migrated to Rains County in 1894. In 1905, Tom purchased the Rains County newspaper, which has remained in the Hill family since that date. Katherine "Kate" Nelson Turner Hill (1875-1961) was the daughter of Lewis Conner Turner and Harriett Wrenn. The Wrenn family moved to Texas when Kate was an infant. Her father was an M-K-T bookkeeper, which caused the family to move a lot. In 1898, Kate came to Emory after teaching kindergarten in Mineola, Wood County. After a year's courtship, she married Tom W. Hill Sr. in 1899. Tom and Kate are buried in the Emory City Cemetery. Pictured below is an 1887 *Rains County Leader* office replica located in the Rains County Historical Park. It contains original printing equipment dating from 1890 to 1920 that was donated by the Hill family. (Above images, courtesy of Earl Clyde Hill Jr.; below image, courtesy of Elaine Nall Bay.)

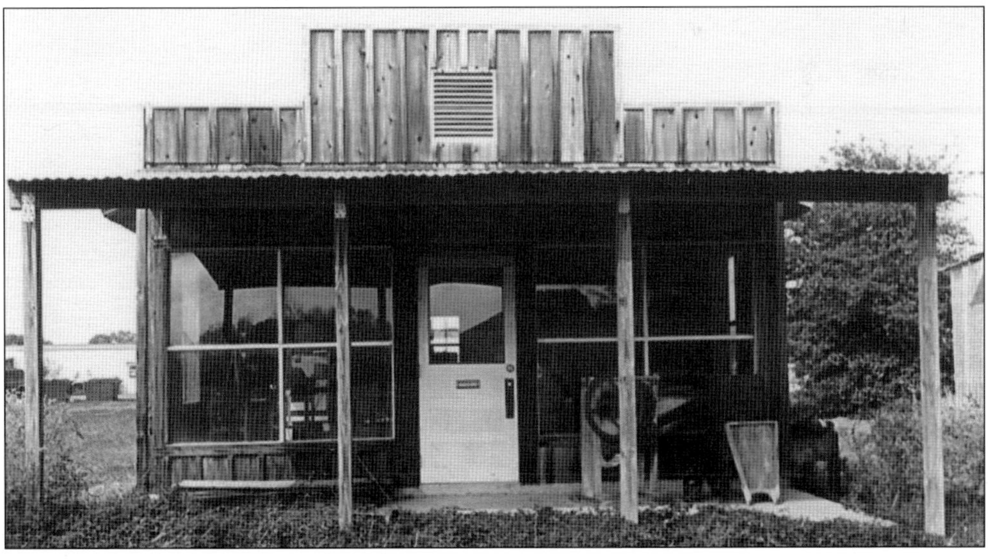

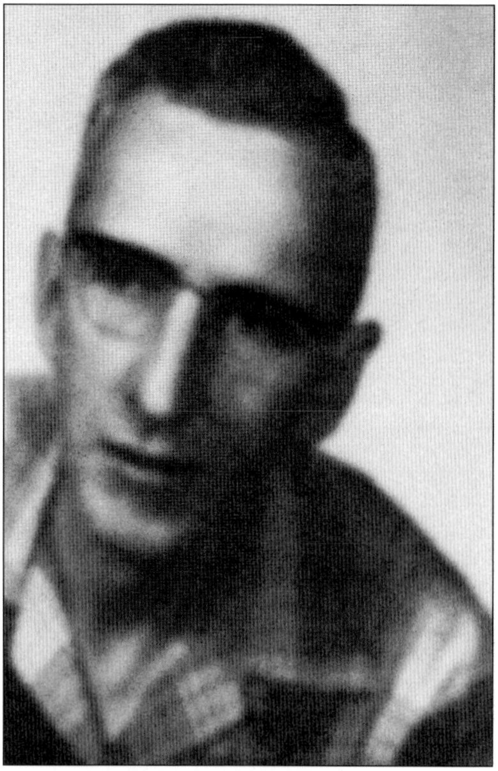

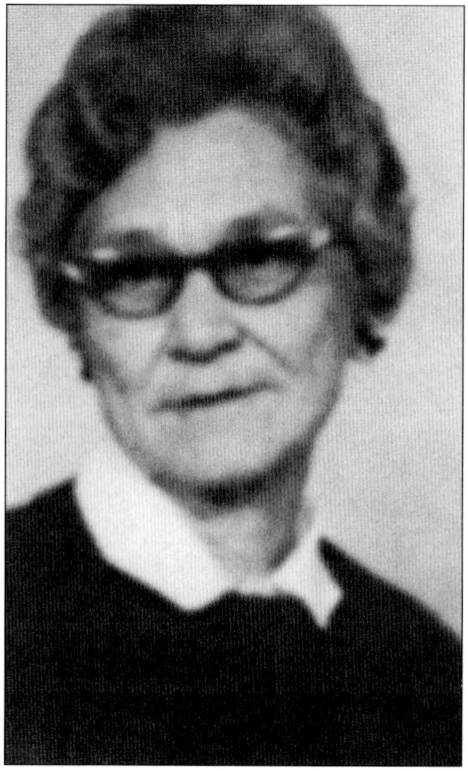

**RAINS COUNTY LEADER**

**TOM W. HILL, Publisher.**

Entered in the postoffice at Emory, Texas, as second-class mail matter.

SUBSCRIPTION PRICE
(In Rains County)

| | |
|---|---|
| 1 year | $1.50 |
| 6 months | 75c |
| 3 months | 40c |

(Payable in advance)

**Out of County Subscriptions**

| | |
|---|---|
| 1 month | 25c |
| 3 months | 60c |
| 6 months | $1.10 |
| 12 months | $2.00 |

(Payable in advance)

All subscriptions discontinued at the expiration of time paid for

Upon the death of Tom W. Hill Sr. in 1937, his fourth son, Earl Clyde Hill Sr. (1905–1960), continued as editor and publisher of the family business, the *Rains County Leader*, until his death in 1960. Since his father was the newspaperman, Earl had to help at the shop and learned to set type at the early age of 10. He married Loree Owens (b. 1904), who had come to Rains County in 1930 to teach mathematics and science at Emory High School. Earl was very talented, being a church organist, an avid fisherman, and an artist. Both are buried in the Hill family plot at Emory City Cemetery. He also took time out for community affairs. The subscription advertisement at left is dated 1921. (Courtesy of Earl Clyde Hill Jr.)

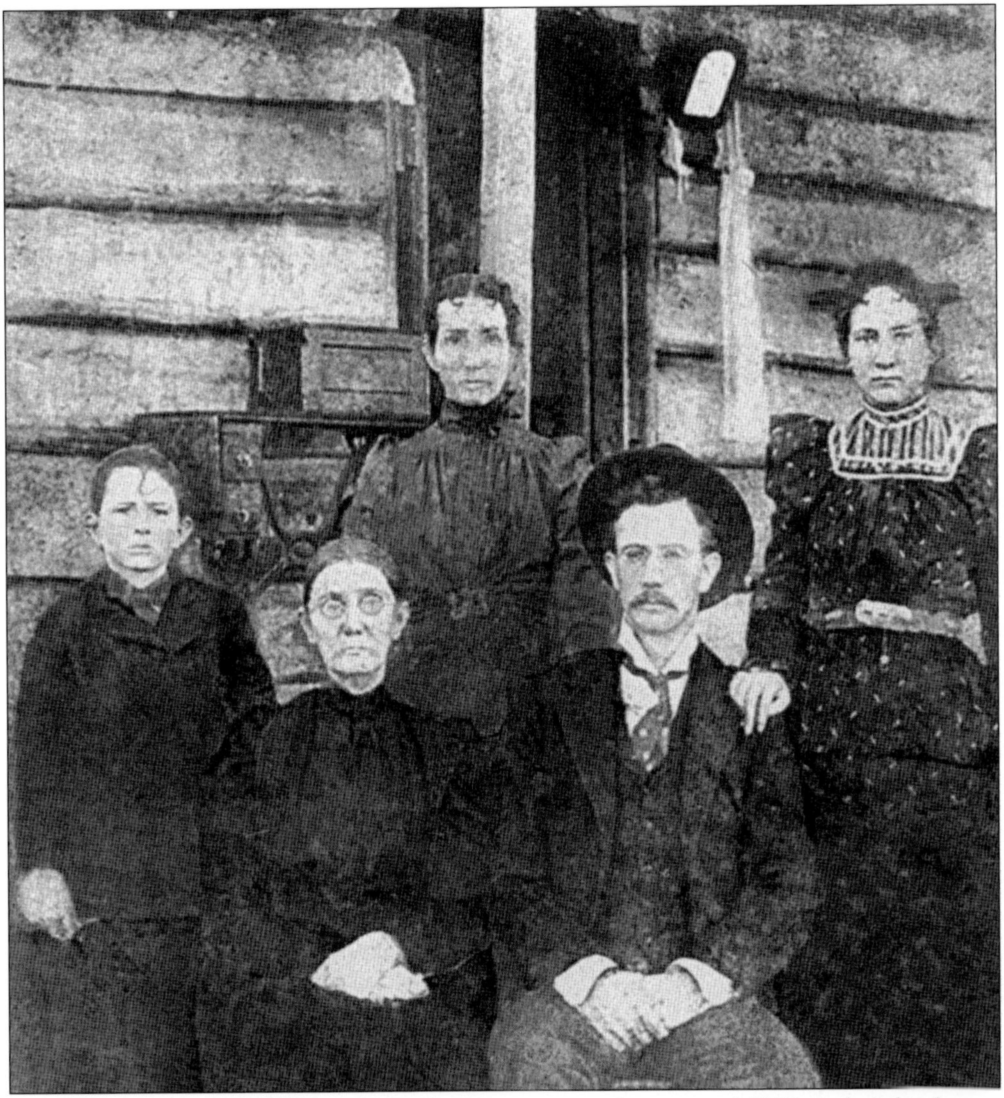

The T.W. Donaldson (1849–1919) family portrait was taken around 1900 at their log home, 3.5 miles northeast of Point. From left to right are (seated) Mary Foster (born 1832, the mother of America Donaldson) and Jim Foster (born 1852, brother of America Donaldson); (standing) Jim Levi Donaldson (1891–1907), America Foster Donaldson (1849–1927, Jim's mother), and Fannie Donaldson Pelky (born 1886, America's second daughter). The family is buried in the Coats Cemetery northeast of Point. Two of T.W. and America's children had died before 1900 at the time of this photograph.

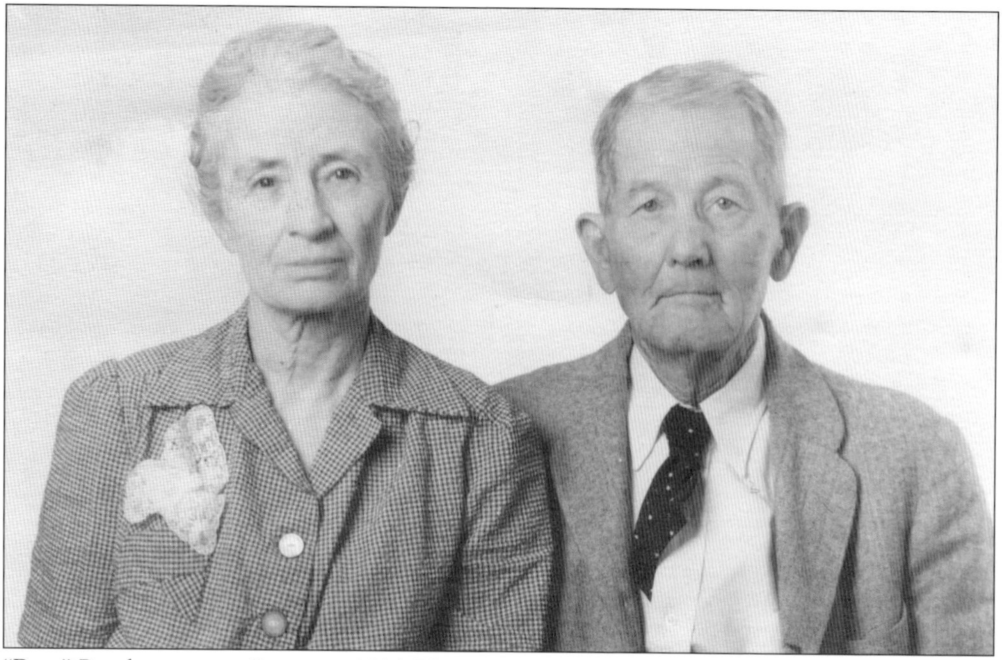

"Doss" Peeples came to Emory in 1886. He was a successful cotton farmer and businessman. A *Rains County Leader* advertisement dated July 1904 lists "Doss" as a partner in the Robertson & Peeples Ice Company as well as being the first occupant of the Henry building with a large stock of merchandise. In 1939, Doss was the oldest member of the Methodist church. According to the *Leader*, in 1939 Peeples was 80 years old and had the very first birthday party of his life. A large cake was served with lemonade. Above are William D. "Doss" Peeples (1859–1947) and Derinda A. Peeples (1873–1964). Below are Esta Mae Kennemer Peeples and Paz Peeples, son of William D. and Derinda A. (Courtesy of Pat Peeples Adcock.)

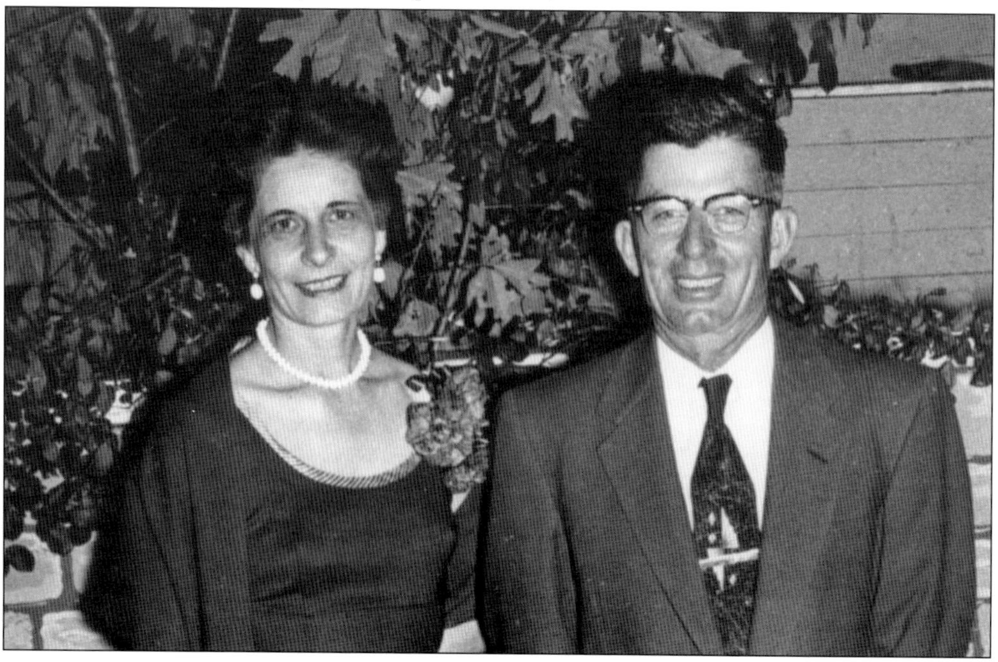

Emeline Cook, born about 1860, and Frank McAree married at the ages of 15 and 25, respectively. Frank died at age 39 and is buried in the Colony Cemetery along with their three sons. In 1887, Emeline married Thomas P. Pope, a cattleman, who also raised top-quality horses. After the deaths of her children and her mother, Emeline was admitted to North Texas Hospital for the first time in 1904. Thomas died in 1913, at age 53, from tubercular enteritis. Emeline died at the Terrell State Hospital and is in an unmarked grave on the hospital grounds. (Courtesy of Ronnie M. Fenter.)

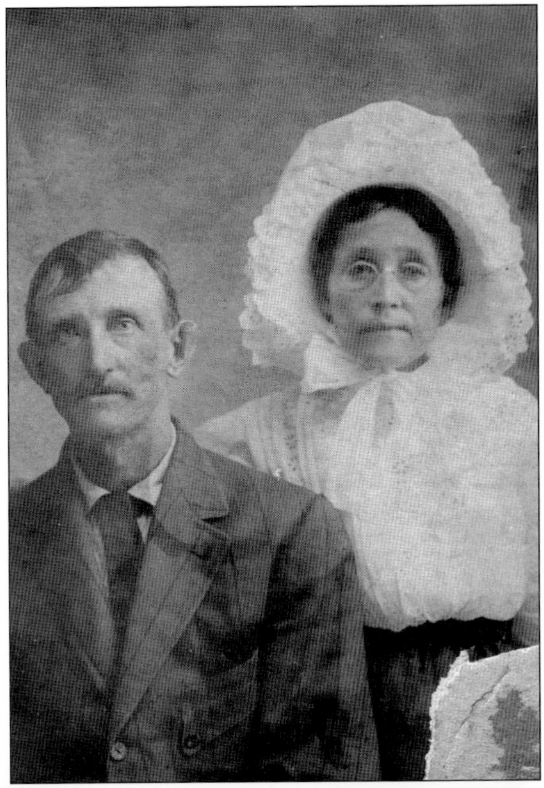

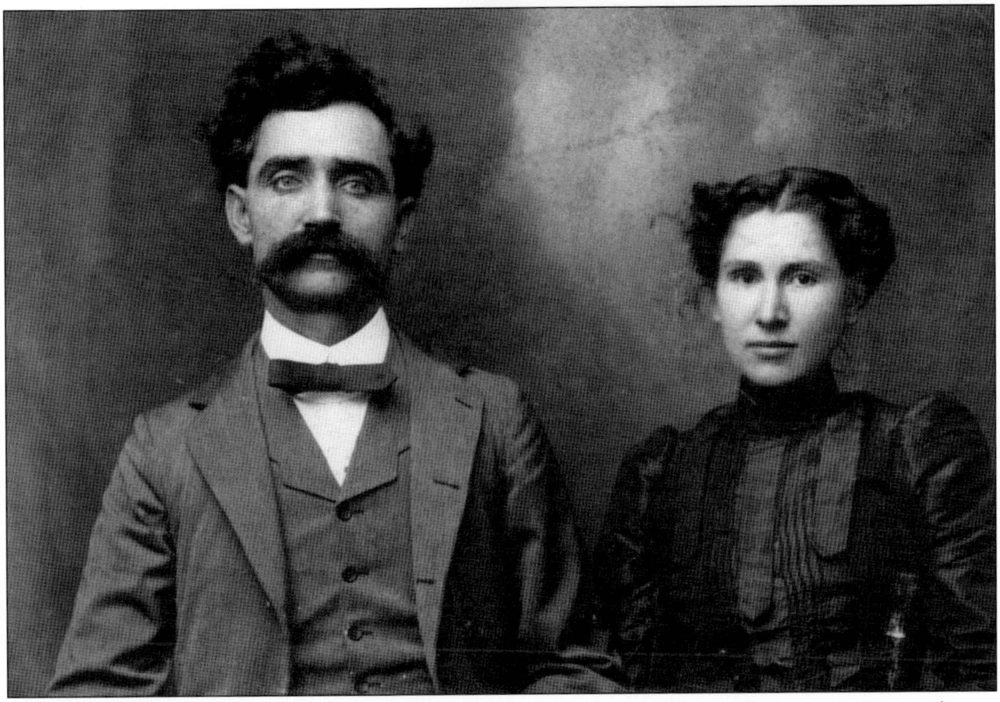

Gus Orsborn Sr., age 35, and Nellie Williams, granddaughter of Emory Rains, age 20, are shown in their wedding picture about 1901. (Courtesy of Maxanne Orsborn Potts.)

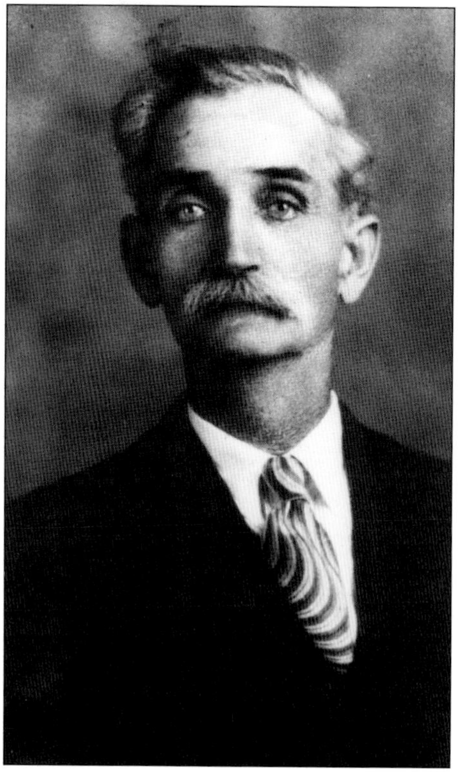

Law enforcement ran in the Orsborn family. Gus Orsborn Sr. (1866–1953) lost his parents at a young age and went to live with his older sister, Mattie Virginia, and her husband, A.C. Sparks. At the age of 35, Gus Sr. married the granddaughter of Emory Rains, Nellie Williams, age 20. Nellie died while her children were young and is buried in the Emory City Cemetery. In 1896, Gus Sr. ran against Oscar Dick for election as Rains County sheriff and was defeated by four votes in the race. When Dick died before taking office, Gus Sr. was appointed sheriff. He was elected to the office in 1898, 1890, and 1902. And 18 years later, he was asked by citizens to run for sheriff again and served his fifth and sixth terms in 1922 and 1924. (Courtesy of Maxanne Orsborn Potts.)

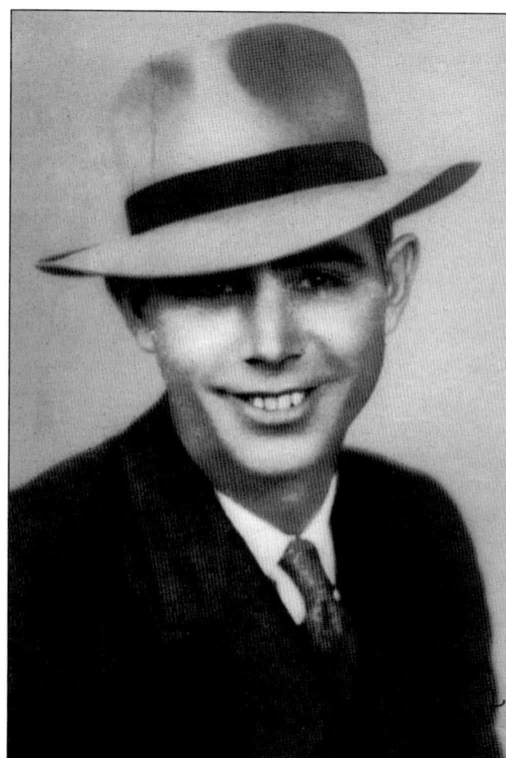

In 1934, Gus Orsborn Jr. (1901–1983) was elected sheriff of Rains County. He was reelected in 1936, 1938, and 1940. His brother Max Orsborn (1906–1968) served as deputy at times during Gus Jr.'s terms in office. After serving in the Navy during World War II, Max returned to Rains County and was elected sheriff in 1946 and 1948. All three Orsborn sheriffs are buried in the Emory City Cemetery in the Orsborn plot. (Courtesy of Maxanne Orsborn Potts.)

Guy Mortimer Stuart (left), son of S.J. and Sarah Jane Forbis Stuart, and his cousin Raymond Stuart Hill, son of Maude Stuart and Thomas P. Hill, are in their dress uniforms during World War I. Hill owned a service station in Wills Point, Van Zandt County, but he and his wife, Sadie, lived in Rains County's Ginger community a large portion of their lives. (Courtesy of Jo Ann Stuart Turman.)

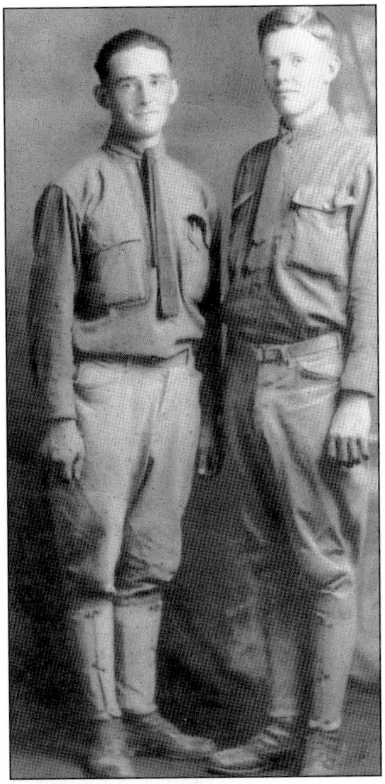

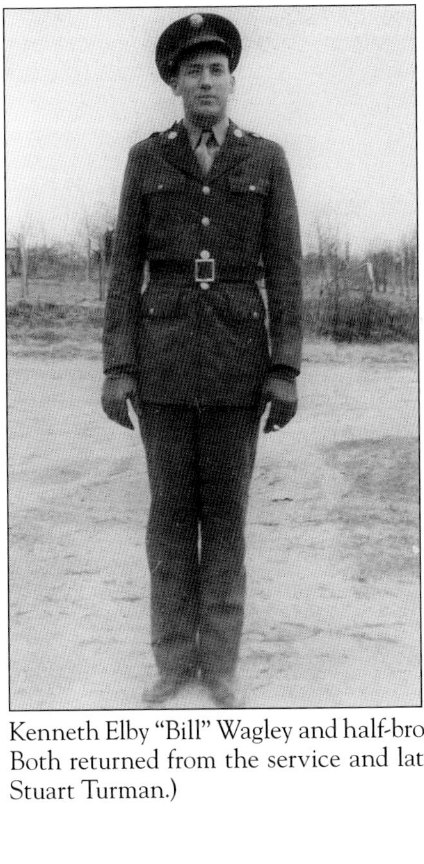

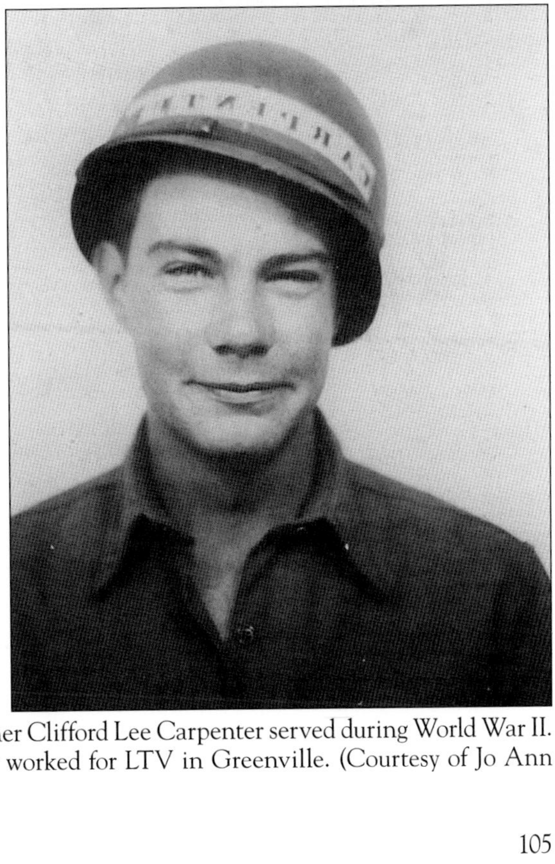

Kenneth Elby "Bill" Wagley and half-brother Clifford Lee Carpenter served during World War II. Both returned from the service and later worked for LTV in Greenville. (Courtesy of Jo Ann Stuart Turman.)

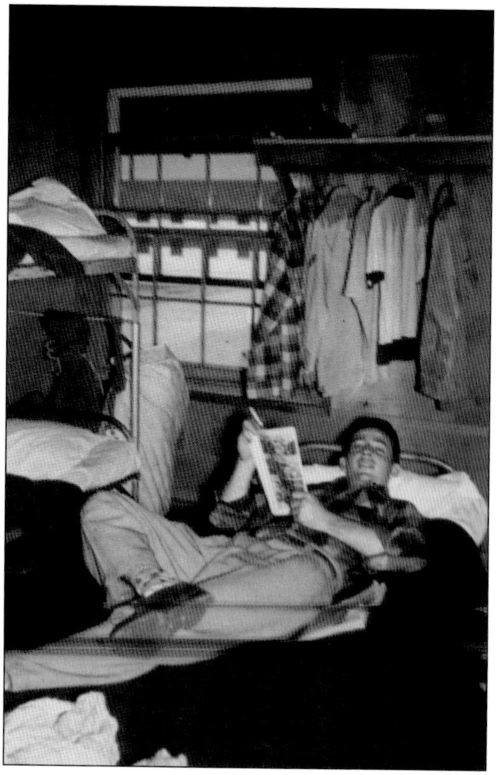

Ernest Cain lies in the barracks at Keesler Air Force Base in Biloxi, Mississippi. He was a young man attending electronics school in 1951. After basic and electronics training, Ernest was assigned to the Air Defense Command during the Korean War in order to help protect the United States from invasion. (Courtesy of Ernest Cain.)

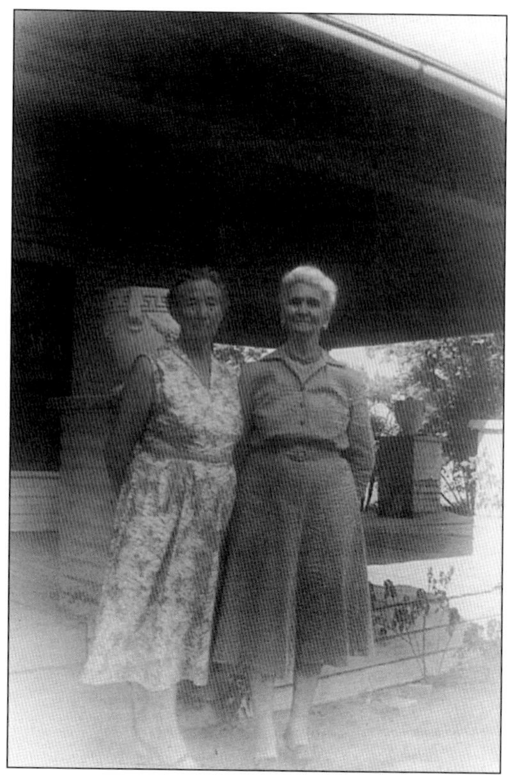

Almeta Brooks (1889–1974, left) and her sister Lula Jane Brooks (1885–1965, right) were daughters of Oscar Barryman "O.B." Brooks. They lived in the Dougherty community until they married. Lula Jane Brooks married John Braziel; they donated land for the first church in the Dougherty community. Almeta Brooks first married George Henry Wagley who died in 1923; she then married Van Carpenter. (Courtesy of Jo Ann Stuart Turman.)

# *Nine*

# Looking Back

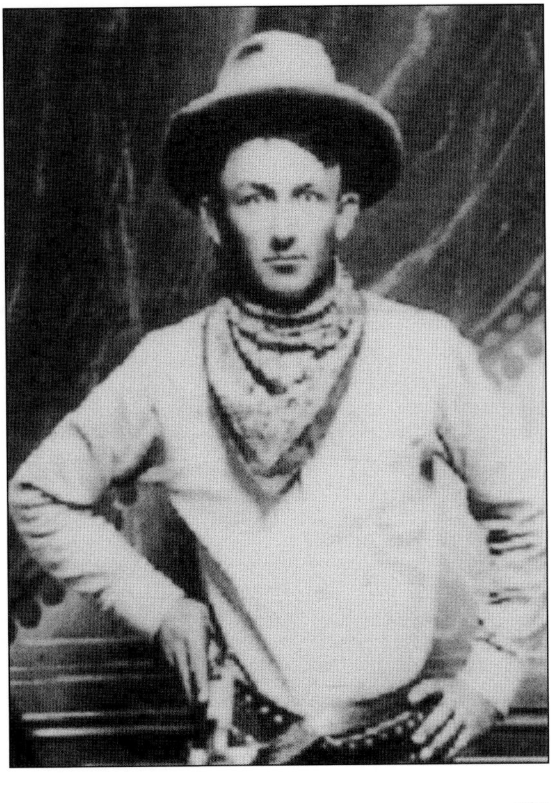

A moment may only last a second, but it may become a memory that brings joy, tears, and laughter. Helen Keller once said, "What we have once enjoyed, we can never lose. All that we love deeply becomes a part of us." This photograph of an unidentified man was in the files of the *Rains County Leader*.

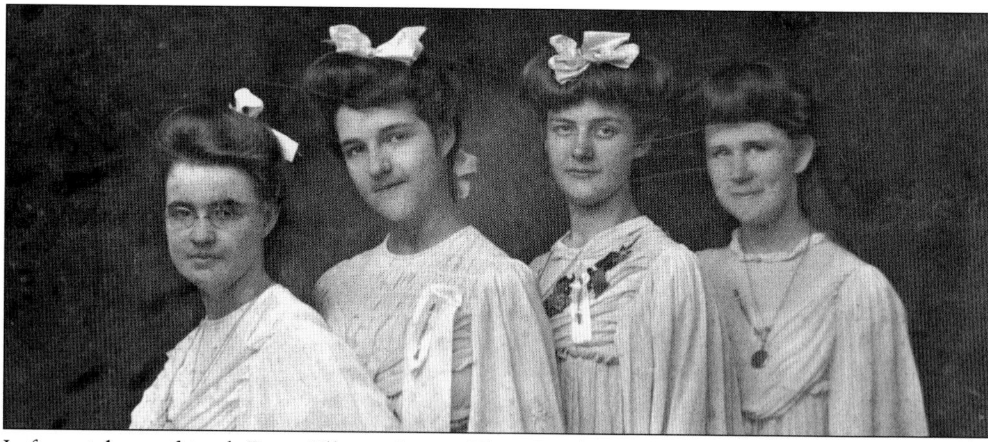

Left to right are friends Betty Elliott, Annie Glass, Bertha Crabb, and Mitt Stewart. The young ladies are dressed in the typical attire of the early 1900s, when women's clothing became lighter in construction and materials. A popular style was the lingerie dress, made of feather-light white cotton inset with strips of open-worked lace and net.

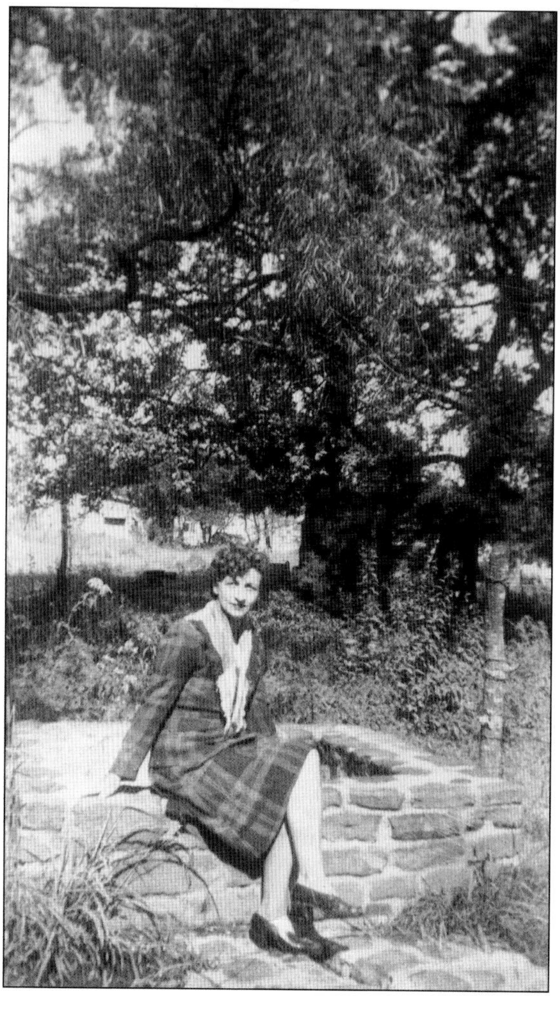

In 1943, Ada Cain, daughter of Wm. J. "Dick" Kerr and Alice Isobell McCloskey, was sitting at the old spring in the Emory city park. This was the original location of Springville, which was named for the many springs in the area. Springville was the name for Emory before the county was formed in December 1870. The springs still run through the park, which is now named in honor of Ruby McKeown. (Courtesy of Mary A. Cain White.)

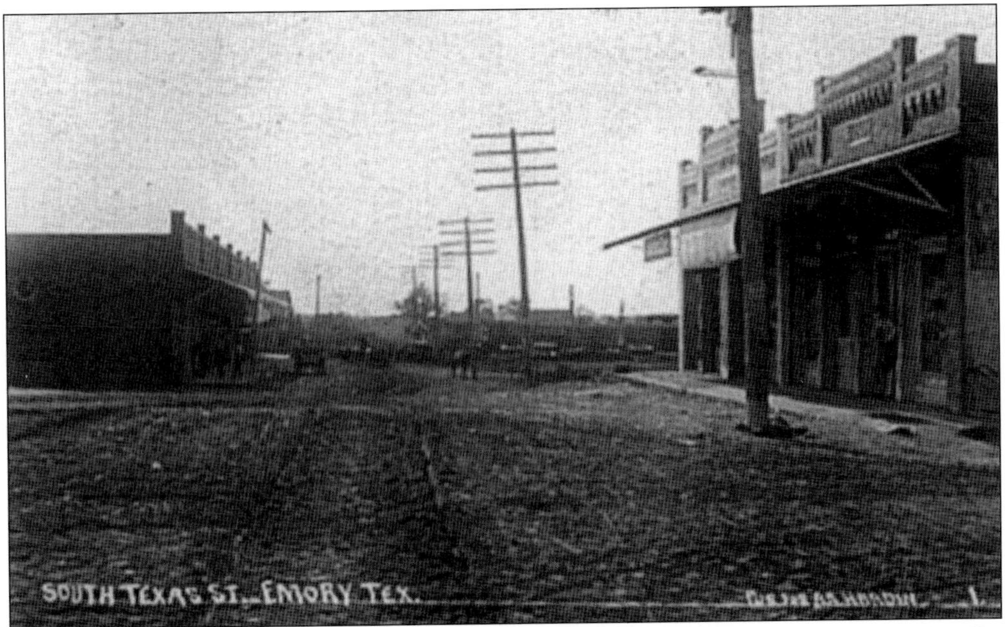


Above is a view of the dirt street, Texas Street, that still runs north to south through Emory. The block of buildings on the left are the Alexander Buildings, erected by brothers Ed and George Alexander; the business at the forefront of the block of buildings on the right is the Henry Building, owned by Emma Henry.

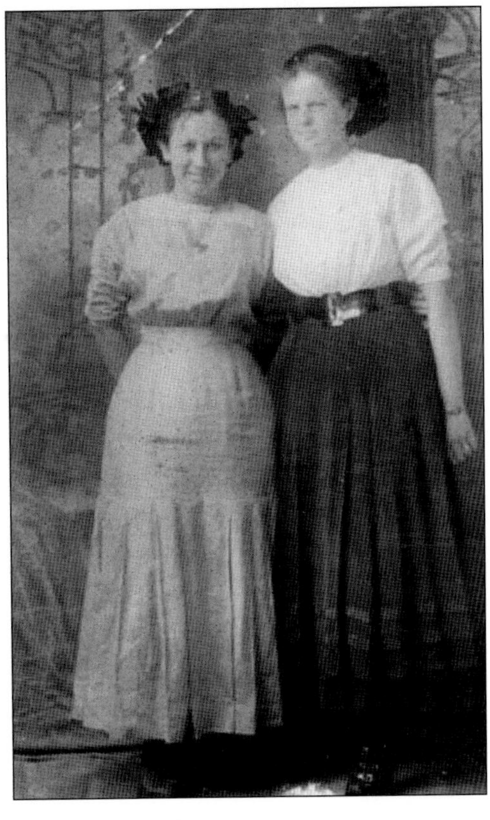

Friends Charlsie Johnson Matthews (left) and Arrie Ruth Holmes (right), attended Pilgrim Rest school. Ruth was the daughter of William Frederick Holmes; she married Robert Green "Bob" Horsley in November 1911. The Horsleys moved to west Texas and are buried at Snyder, Texas. Ruth and Bob Horsley (1888–1967) are the grandparents of actor Lee Horsley. (Courtesy of Terrie Keck.)

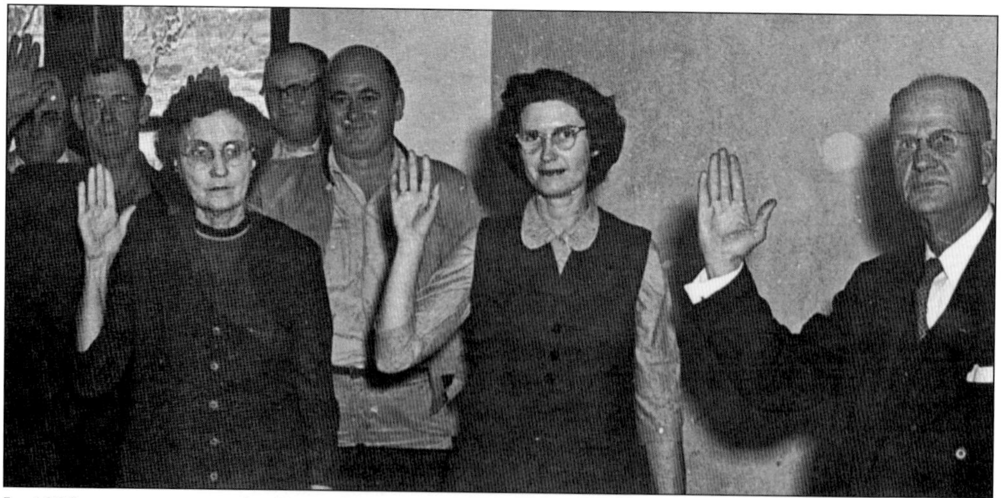

In 1920, women across the United States won the right to vote, but they were not allowed to serve as jurors in Texas. In 1950, a Texas Constitution amendment gave women living in Texas the right to serve on jury panels. This picture shows the swearing-in of the first two women jurors in Rains County by Judge Berry. No one has been able to identify the women at this time.

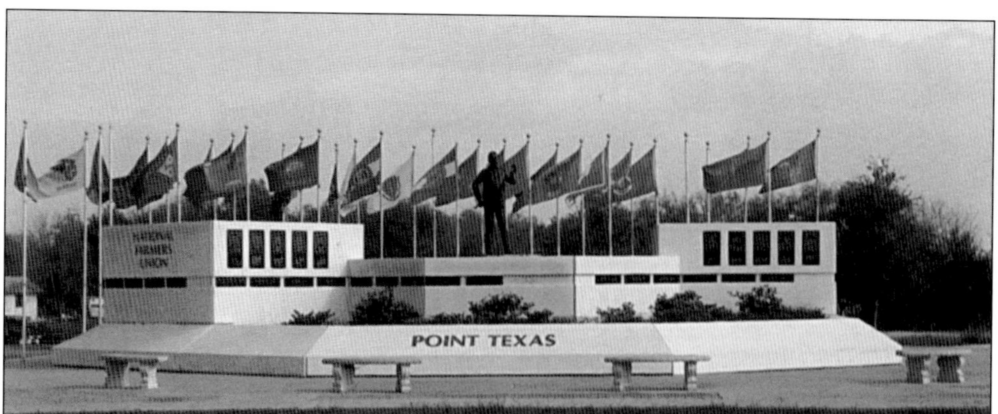


The monument in remembrance of the organization of the National Farmers Union, which was organized in Point, is located in Point on Highway 69. People Organizing Ideal Neighborhoods Today, Inc. (POINT) helped raise money for the memorial. The monument displays all the retired National Farmers Union state flags. A new United States flag was presented by Congressman Ralph Hall. The 2006 Labor Day ceremony included posting six new flags for six states: Maine, Massachusetts, New Hampshire, Vermont, Connecticut, and Rhode Island. (Courtesy of Elaine Nall Bay.)

This outhouse served the Weldon and Lynn Bridges family and remained in use as late as 1973. The date it was built is unknown. It was donated and moved to the Rains County Historical Park by Joe and David Bridges, sons of Weldon and Lynn, in April 2000. (Courtesy of Elaine Nall Bay.)

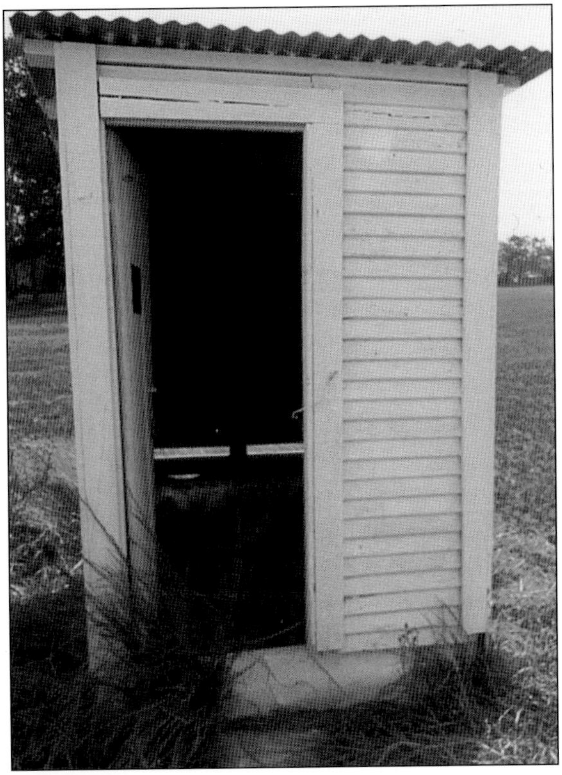

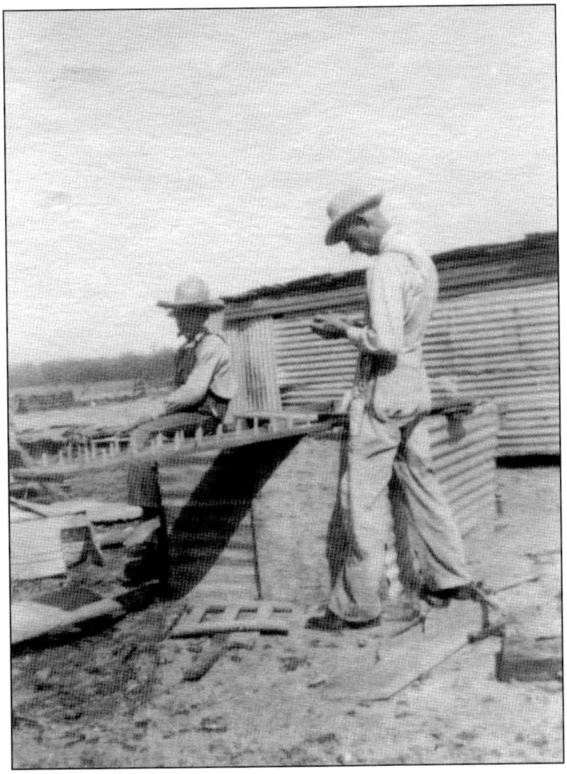

The Kennemer family lived in the Smyrna community. "Little Jim" attended New Holmes School, which burned in 1902. Preaching and school were held in the Kennemer home until new buildings could be constructed. James Edward "Little Jim" Kennemer Sr. married Bettie Caddell (1888–1978); they first lived in a log cabin, but James built a new house in 1917. Pictured are James Edward Kennemer Sr. (1886–1979) and his son, Kenneth Wayne, building a frame for their tomatoes. (Courtesy of Pat Peeples Adcock.)

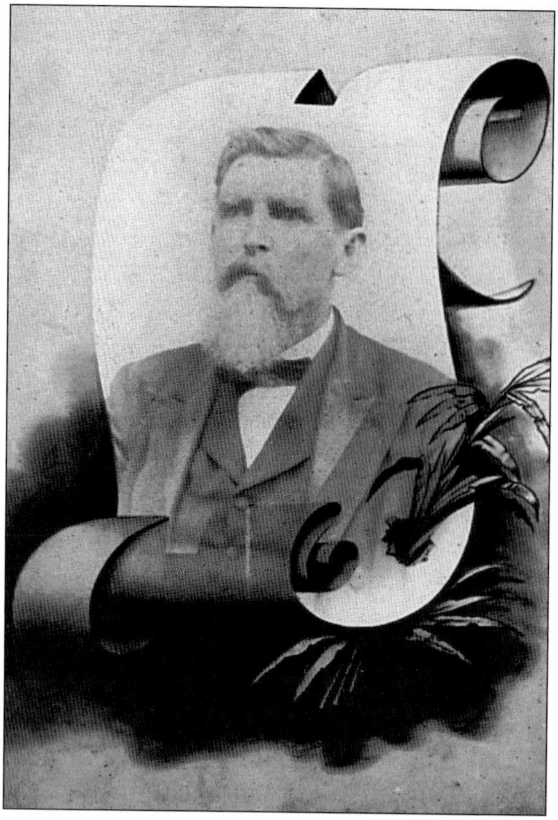

Stephen James Stuart, son of James R. Stuart and Clarissa Mitchener, was born February 25, 1846 in Sumner County, Tennessee. Three of the Stuart brothers joined the Confederacy. S.J. Stuart and his brother William Marcus Stuart were paroled n 1865 after being captured in Louisiana. At age 24, S.J. set out for Texas on his favorite horse, Dexter, and settled in Rains County along with the Phillips and Corbin families, who married into the Stuart family. S.J. Stuart married Sarah Janie Forbis on July 8, 1877, in Rains County, Texas. He was a schoolteacher and was elected as one of the first surveyors of Rains County. S.J. (1846–1919) and Janie (1859–1935) are buried in Forbis Cemetery, which was begun by Janie's father. At left is a portrait of S.J. Stuart. Below is the survey crew. Pictured from left to right are unidentified, Lon Stuart, S.J. Stuart, and unidentified. (Courtesy of Jo Ann Stuart Turman.)

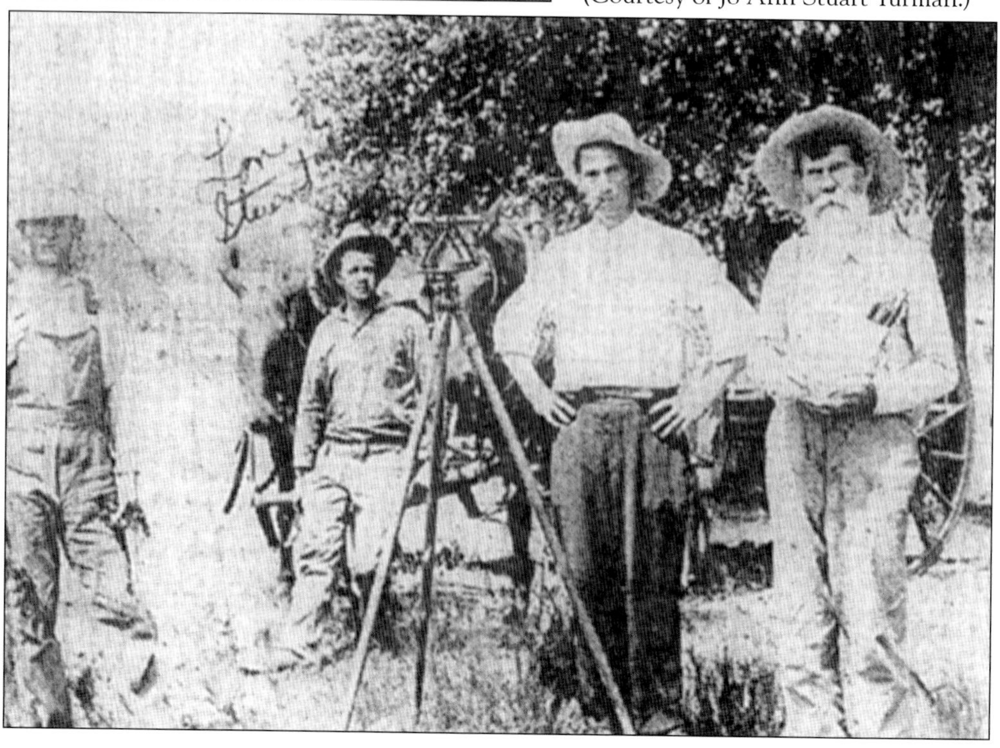

Before having a post office in Point, the people had to go six miles to Springville for their mail. The Post Office Department named the town "Point" and established the post office December 1879. Hattie Ballew was the first postmistress, working as such for a couple of months. Dr. E.A. Sweptson, her successor, erected a small building, which he used for both the post office and his medical office.

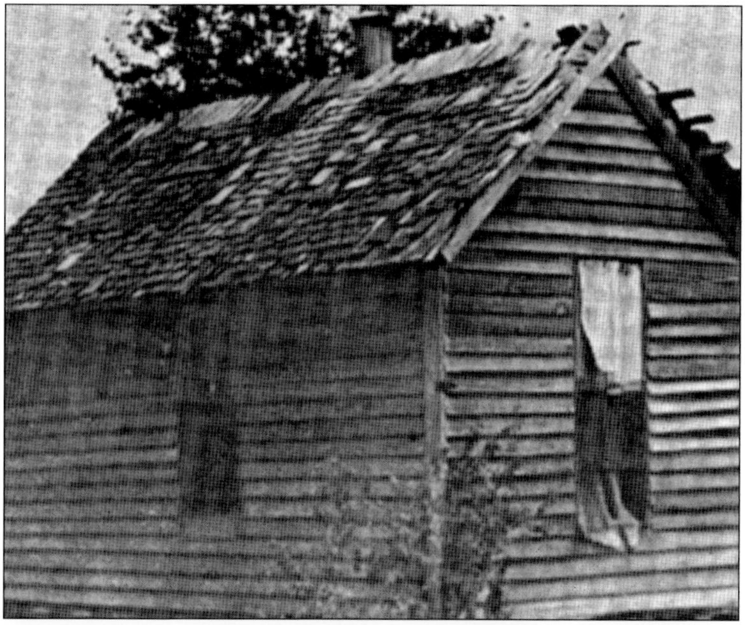

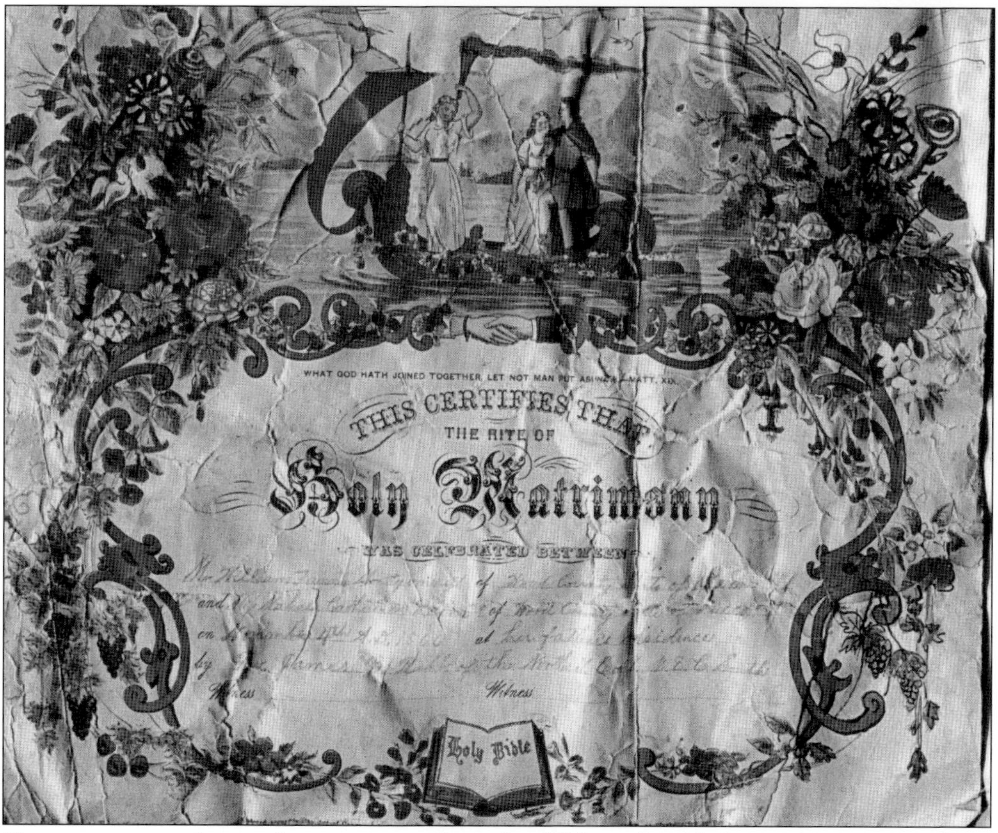

WHAT GOD HATH JOINED TOGETHER, LET NOT MAN PUT

THIS CERTIFIES THAT

THE RITE OF

Holy Matrimony

WAS CELEBRATED BETWEEN

Witness

Witness

Holy Bible

Shown is an original copy of a marriage certificate dated "November 4th A.D. 1866," uniting William Fannin Montgomery and Mahalia Kathleen Rains in Holy Matrimony. The ceremony was performed at the home of the father of the bride, Emory Rains. (Courtesy of Cay Frances B. House.)

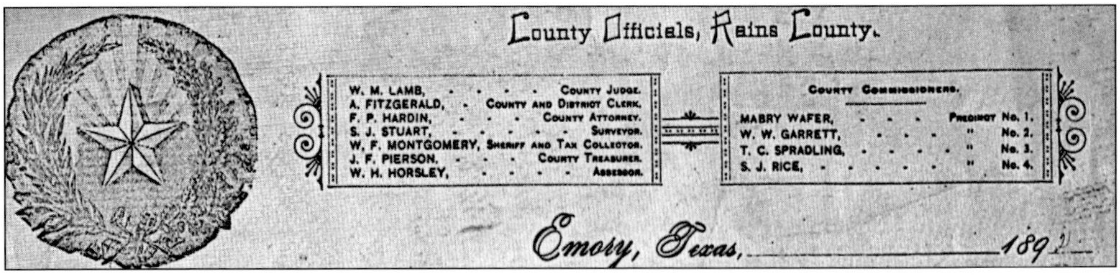

County Officials, Rains County.

W. M. LAMB, County Judge.
A. FITZGERALD, County and District Clerk.
F. P. HARDIN, County Attorney.
S. J. STUART, Surveyor.
W. F. MONTGOMERY, Sheriff and Tax Collector.
J. F. PIERSON, County Treasurer.
W. H. HORSLEY, Assessor.

County Commissioners.
MABRY WAFER, Precinct No. 1.
W. W. GARRETT, " No. 2.
T. C. SPRADLING, " No. 3.
S. J. RICE, " No. 4.

Emory, Texas, 189

Above is the official letterhead stationery listing the Rains County officials and dated 1892. Listed are W.M. Lamb, county judge; Ambrose Fitzgerald, county and district clerk; F.P. Hardin, county attorney; S.J. Stuart, surveyor; W.F. Mongomery, sheriff and tax collector; J.F. Pierson, county treasurer; W.H. Horsley, assessor; Mabry Wafer, Precinct No. 1 county commissioner; W.W. Garrett, Precinct No. 2 county commissioner; T.C. Spradling, Precinct No. 3 county commissioner; and S.J. Rice, Precinct No. 4 county commissioner.

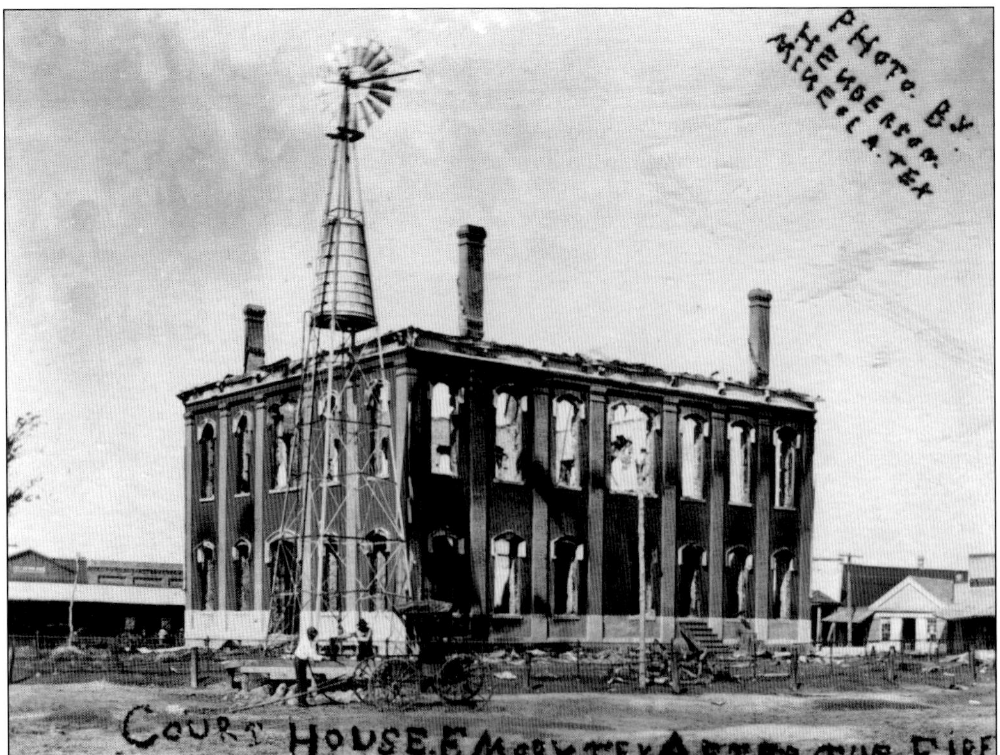


The second Rains County courthouse burned in May 1907. Records were salvaged due to a steel vault having been put in the building.

For expansion purposes, the windows to the steel courthouse vault were closed, and an addition was added to the north side. This jail cell was on the top floor along with a large room that served as the jail. When the courthouse was remodeled back to its original floor plan, the north addition was removed. The cell was donated to the Rains County Historical Park. (Courtesy of Elaine Nall Bay.)

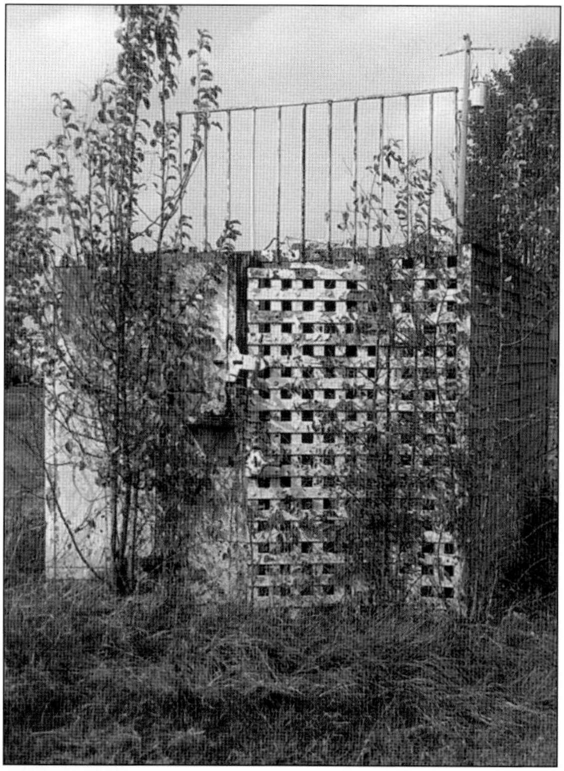

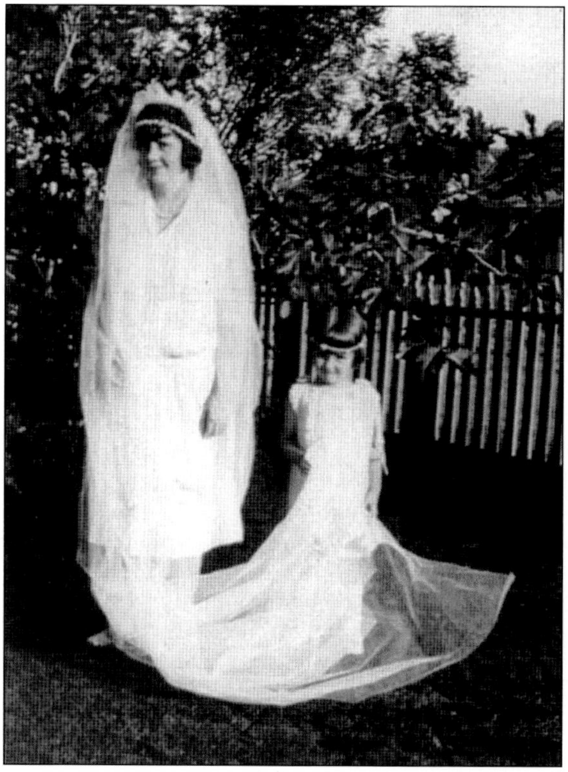

Aletha Amis (1898–1986) was the daughter of Rains County businessman James Alexander and Carrie Etta Roan Amis. Aletha graduated from Emory School in 1915 and earned her six-months teaching certificate to teach at Rocky Point school for the school term in 1916. On Wednesday afternoon of June 17, 1925, Aletha had a pretty home wedding on the lawn of the Amis residence. Pictured are Aletha and her niece Carolyn Glass, who served as ringbearer. (Courtesy of Alton W. Ashworth, Jr.)

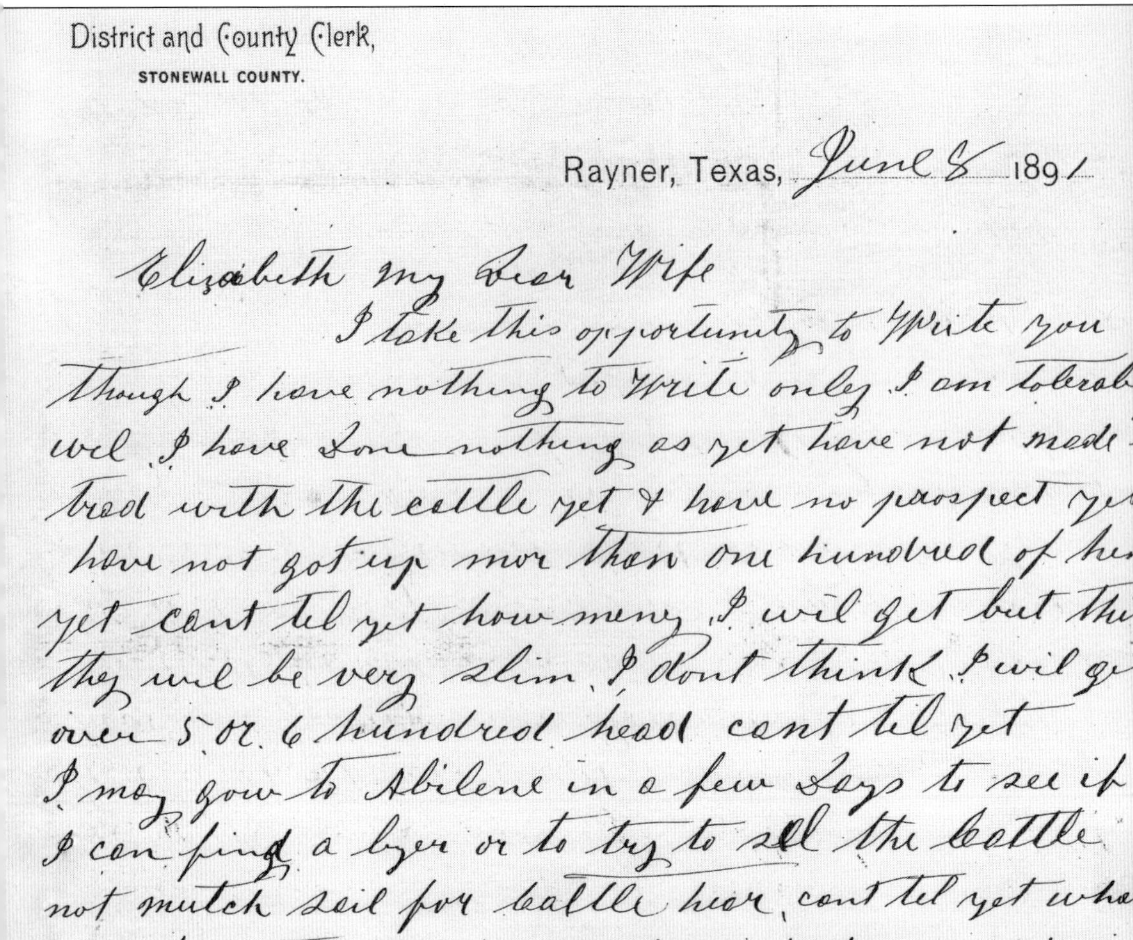

District and County Clerk,
STONEWALL COUNTY.

Rayner, Texas, June 8 1891

Elizabeth my Dear Wife
I take this opportunity to Write you
though I have nothing to Write onley I am tolerab
wel I have Done nothing as yet have not made
trad with the cattle yet & have no paospect yet
have not got up mor than one hundred of hen
yet cant tel yet how meny I wil get but thi
they wil be very slim I dont think I wil ge
over 5 or 6 hundred head cant tel yet
I may gow to Abilene in a few Days to see if
I can find a byer or to try to sell the cattle
not mutch Deil for cattle hear cant tel yet wha
wil Do yet gras is good Know had a good rain
hear thers Day Knight cattle wil get fat I
think cant tel when I wil get Back home
But as soon as I can
Rite to me Your Afect Husban T M Cai

This original handwritten letter was sent by Tom Cain to his wife, Elizabeth Hooker Cain, while he had gone to West Texas to buy and sell cattle in 1891. (Courtesy of Jo Ann Stuart Turman.)

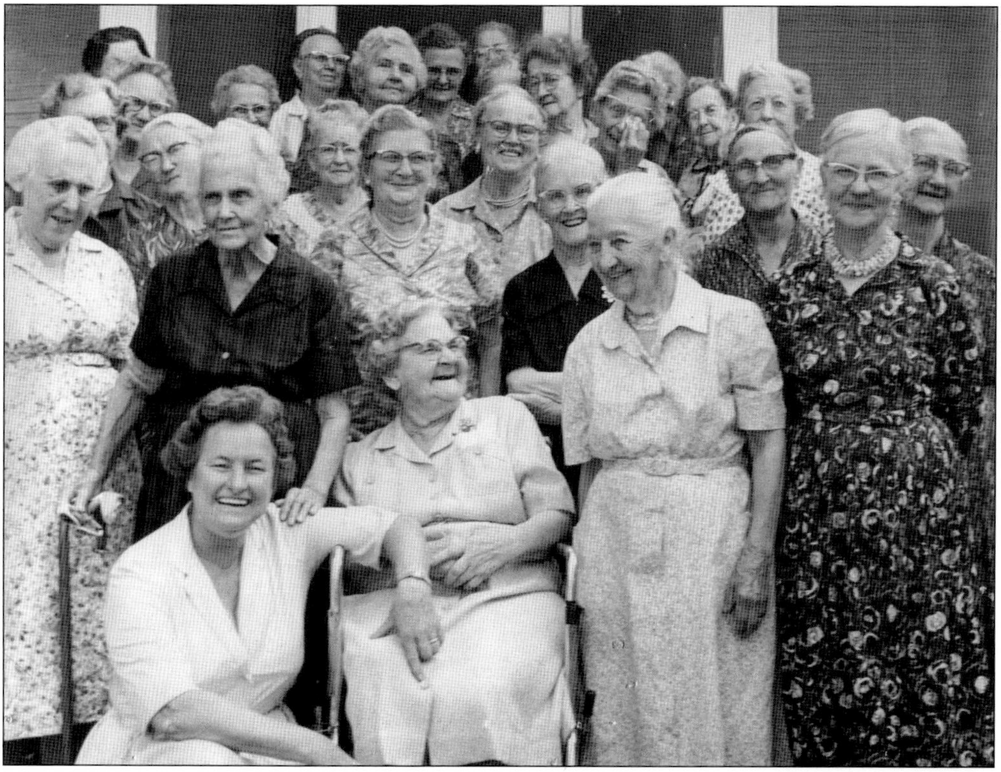

The "Gay Seventies" met together at Helen Johnston's home in Emory. They are, from left to right, (first row) Helen Johnston, hostess, Odessa Bishop, Pearl Allred, and Bessie Prather; (second row) Mary (Austin) Traylor, Mrs. H.A. Coker, Mrs. W.D. Montgomery, Emma Ivie, Iona Pittillo, and Bettie Davis; (third row) Lela Mae Settle, Sadie (Bud) Hutchins, Stella Stamford, Stella Hays, Jennie Pound, and Peachie Speed; (fourth row) Mrs. Blanton, Mildred Gaston, Annie Lou Hunter, Nellie Gray (Dr. J.S.H.) Allen, Lillie Whittle, and Mrs. Exa Alexander Morgan; (fifth row) Clara Windom, Tonie Garrett, Mrs. Ollie Abercrombie, Ida Braziel, and Mrs. Powell. All pictured are 70 years old.

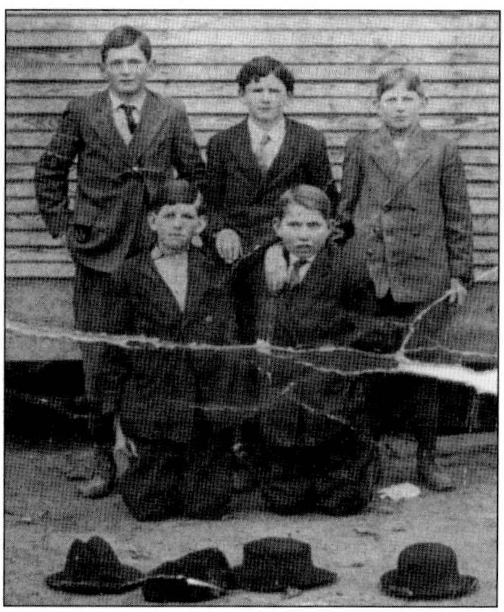

Bonanza School District No. 14 was established in 1890 and was located in northeastern Rains County just a short distance from the Hopkins County line. These students of the school, pictured about 1915, from left to right, are (first row) Jess Loftin and Austin Mitchell; (second row) Houston Asbill, Homer Asbill, and Van Loftin. (Courtesy of Mary Asbill Bishop.)

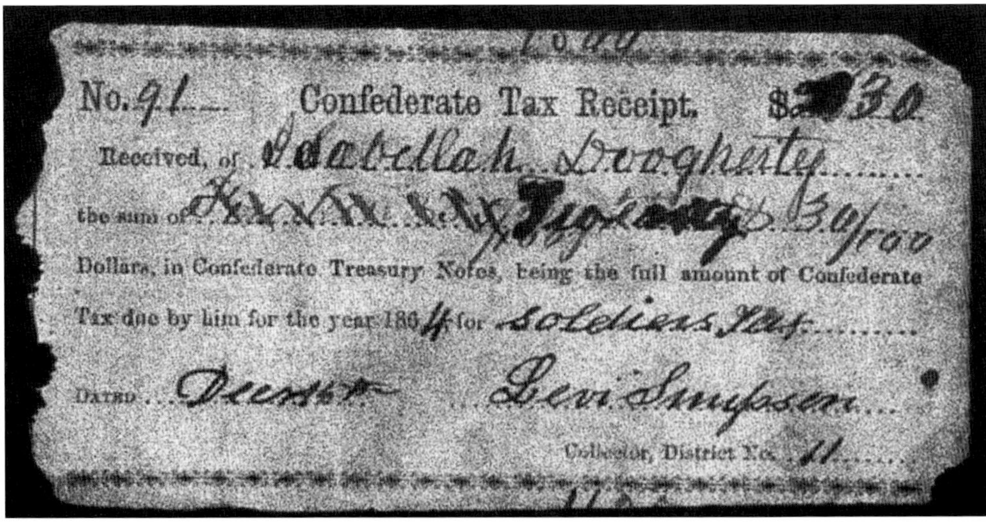

No. 91 Confederate Tax Receipt. $ 30

Received, of Isabellah Dougherty

the sum of 30/100

Dollars, in Confederate Treasury Notes, being the full amount of Confederate

Tax due by him for the year 1864 for soldiers tax

DATED Decr Levi Simpson

Collector, District No. 11

A 1864 Civil War soldier's tax receipt from James N. Dougherty's tanning business, located just east of his home place and on the nearby creek, hangs in the historical Dougherty home. The tannery made shoes and boots for the Confederate soldiers. (Courtesy of Maxanne Orsborn Potts.)

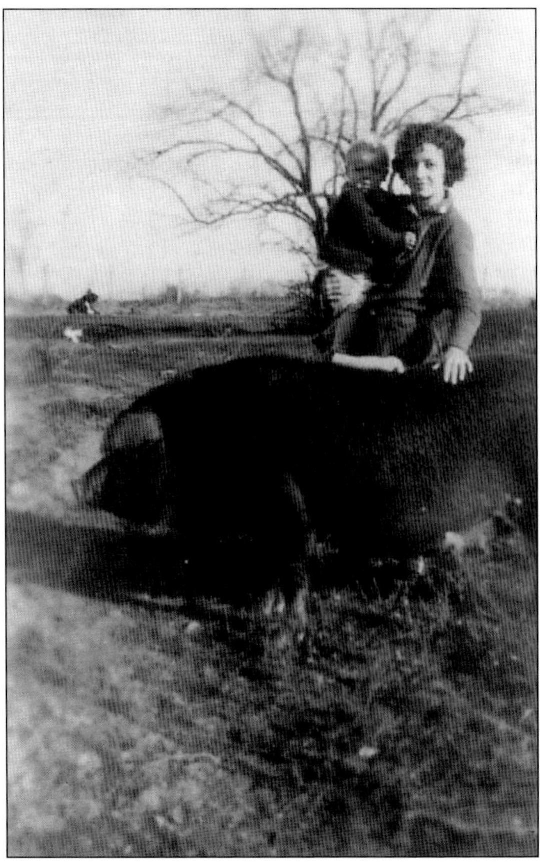

Ada Kerr Cain and son Jimmy posed with a pig. Family members raised pigs off of this root hog for their own use. (Courtesy of Ernest Cain.)

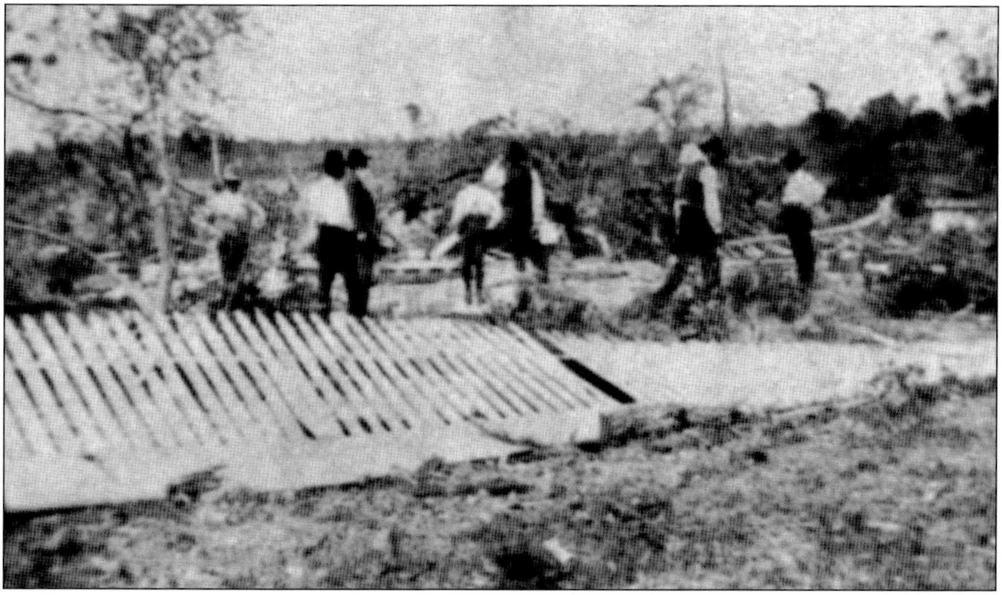

In March 1894, the first destructive tornado hit Rains County about 7:00 p.m. on a Saturday evening. The threatening tail of the cyclone dipped down with maddening fury. In its path, it left four dead, 30 injured, damage to every business, and complete destruction of the Baptist church and Masonic hall.

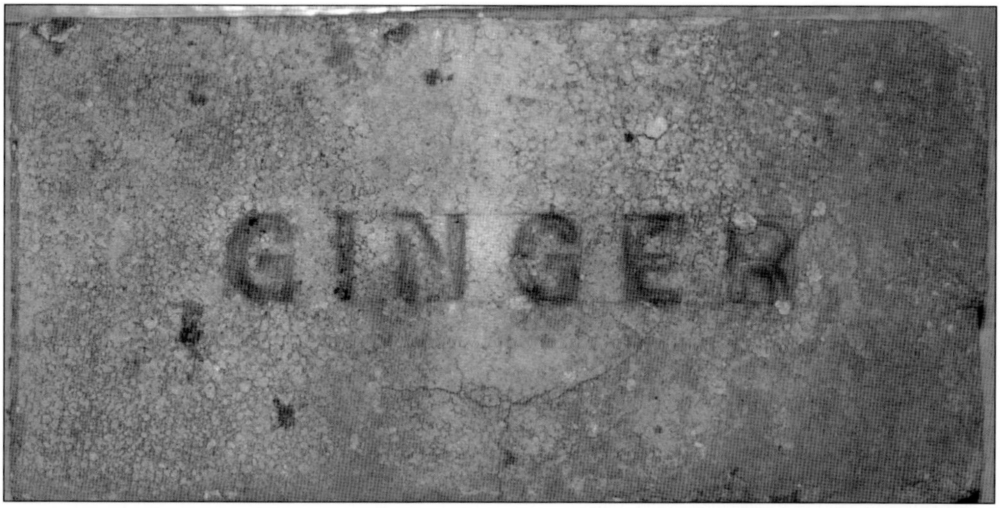


The Fraser Brick Company existed in Ginger, Rains County, Texas from 1905 to 1960. In 1961, the business was bought by Acme Brick Company. Walter B. Fraser was one of the first industrialists in Texas and in 1905 established the Fraser-Johnson Brick Company (later named Fraser Brick Company) in the area of what is today the Ginger community. An admixture of powdered or granulated manganese was added to the medium heat fire clay deposits found in Rains County. The result was a sticking face brick; Ginger brick became a much-desired product throughout the Southwest. The Ginger face brick was used to construct the Rice Hotel in Houston in 1912 as well as the Oklahoma City Post Office in 1909. The average number of employees was about 40. A Texas Historical Marker in honor of Walter B. Fraser was erected in 1969 near the site of the original Fraser Brick Company. These "Ginger" bricks are now collectables, especially for residents of Rains County. (Courtesy of Jeri McAree Humphrey.)

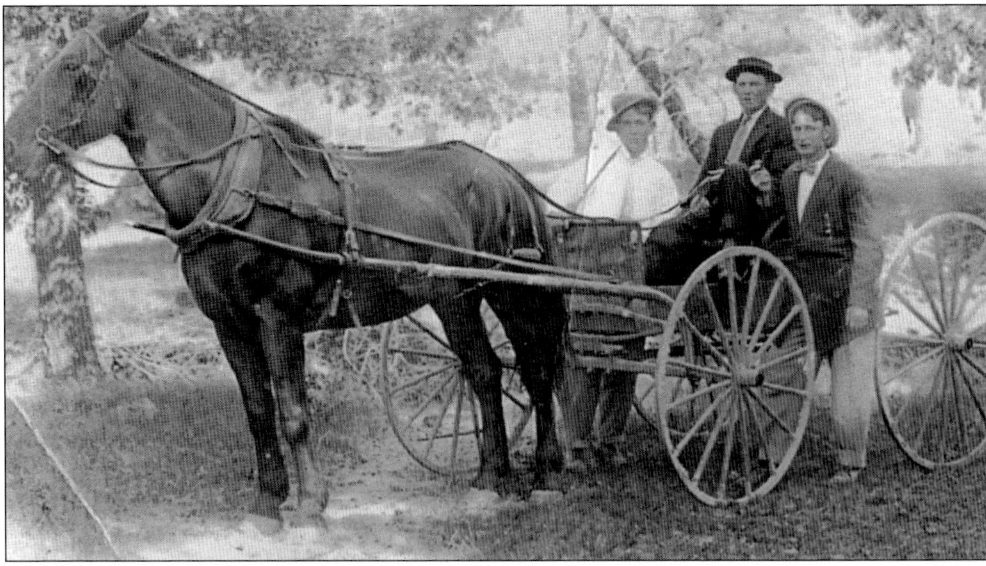

The Stuart brothers are all decked out to pick up their dates for a Saturday night party, singing, or card games. From left to right are Stephen Leon "Lon" Stuart (1887–1955), Grover Cleveland Stuart (1892–1973), and Guy Mortimer Stuart. All were sons of Stephen James and Janie Forbis Stuart. (Courtesy of Jo Ann Stuart Turman.)

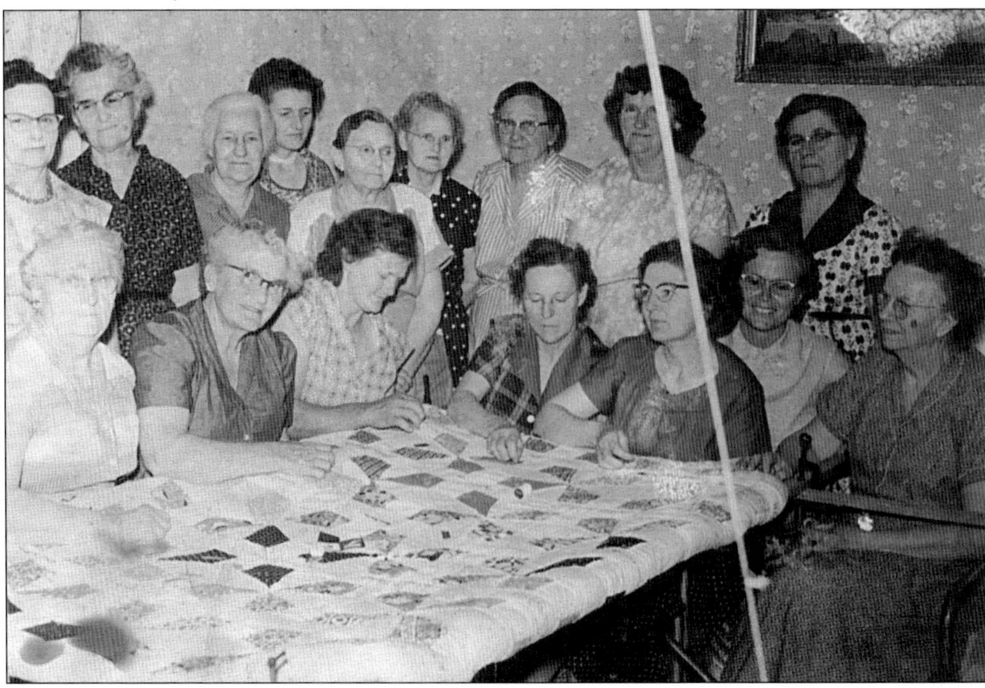

Quilting clubs were social events for many women in the 1940s and 1950s as well as a way to make the tedious job of the quilting process faster. Members of the Dougherty Quilting Club are, from left to right, (first row) Ms. McClain, Exa Adams, Mrs. Rastus Blanton, unidentified, Verna Barnett, Marie Garmon, and Flora Garrett; (second row, left to right) Alice Scott, Beadie Garrett, Grace Scott, unidentified, Luna Kerens, Cora Spradling, Della Blanton, Balmy Holman, and Mrs. Buck Watts. (Courtesy of Mary A. Cain White.)

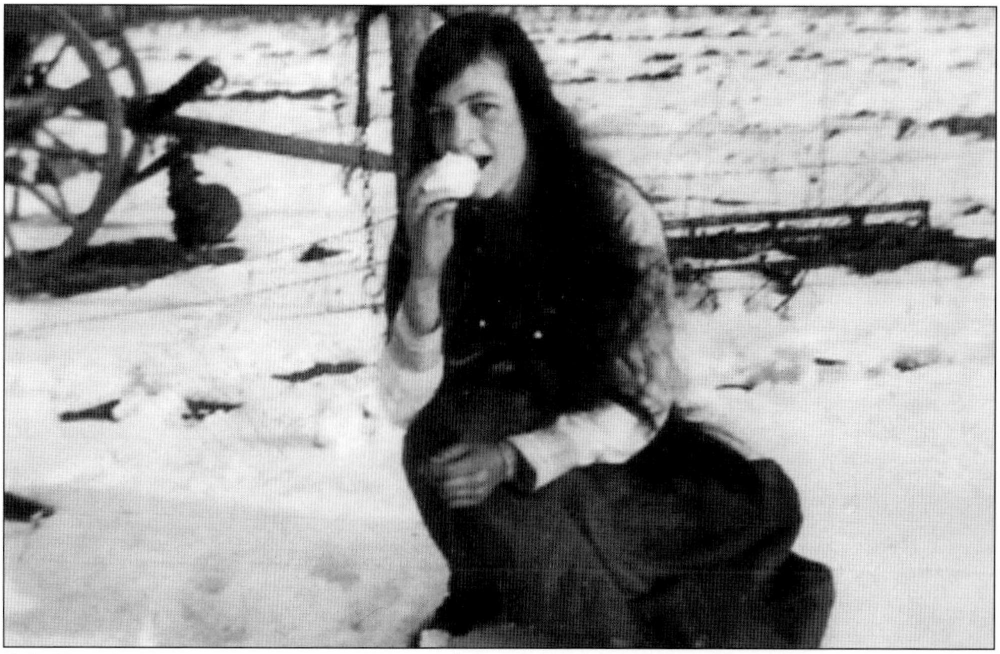

Ada Kerr Cain, age 14, is enjoying some infrequent snowy weather. Rains County had its share of rains and droughts, but the wind, dust, and mud were nothing compared to the extremely cold winters of 1887–1888 and 1898–1899. The story recounted is that during the winter of 1898–1899, pickles froze in the general store barrels and the combs froze clean off the chickens. In February 1889, milk froze solid in cans, vinegar in bottles, and bedroom water pitchers froze and burst. During these times, livestock literally froze to death where standing. An old-timer related that the wind was so strong, "you had to run backwards to spit." (Courtesy of Mary A. Cain White.)

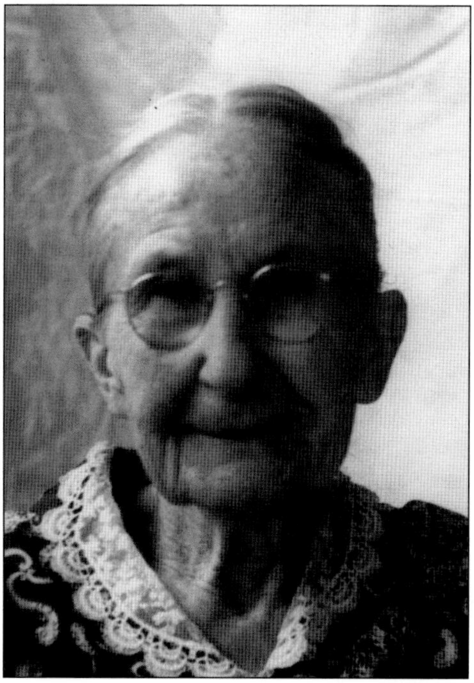

Ada Frances Cain, daughter of Thomas Mabry Cain and Elizabeth B. Hooker, was born August 11, 1867 in the Hooker Ridge community. Her childhood friends and playmates were Sicily Elizabeth Wafer, Laura Sullivan, Janie Forbis, and Emma Geary. Cain married Dr. William A. Duffey on May 21, 1884 in Rains County. From this union, seven children were born, six of whom grew to adulthood—Mary Tommie, Ruby Ellen, Nancy "Hankie," Willie Ada, Aldie, Samuel Cecil, and Bessie Lela. Ada was a very strong-willed and feisty woman for her petite, five-foot-two frame; being a wife and mother did not stop her from working outside the home. She became postmistress of Emory in July 1913, replacing Luther Cline; her deputy was E.V. Cooke. (Courtesy of Jo Ann Stuart Thurman.)

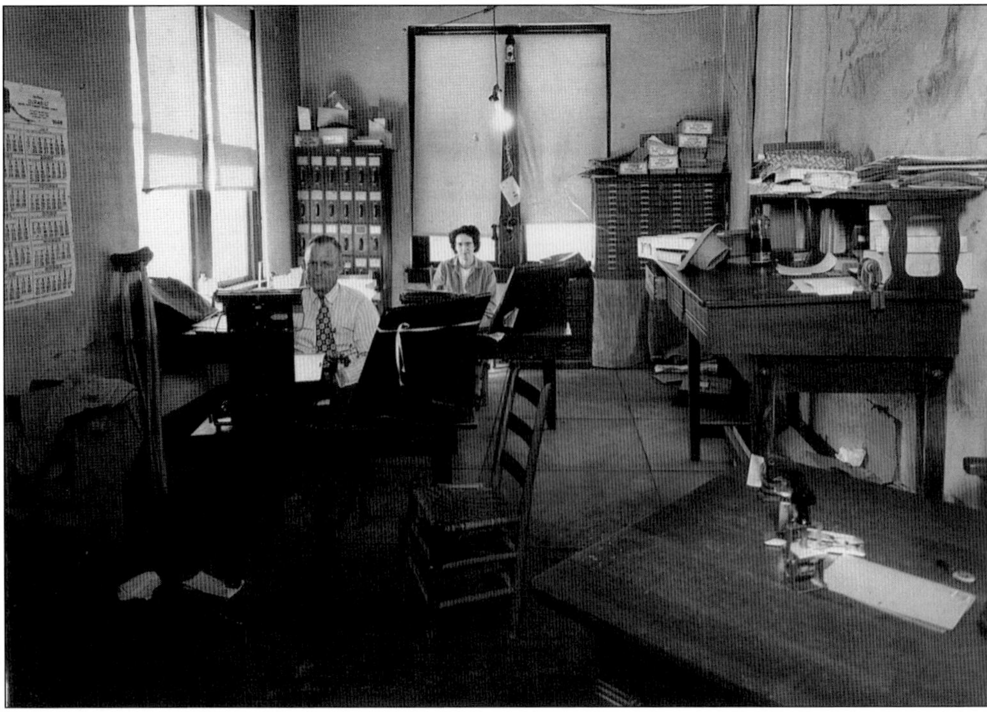

Olen and Grace Gilley are working in the Rains County clerk's office, located in the county courthouse around 1949. (Courtesy of Maxanne Orsborn Potts.)

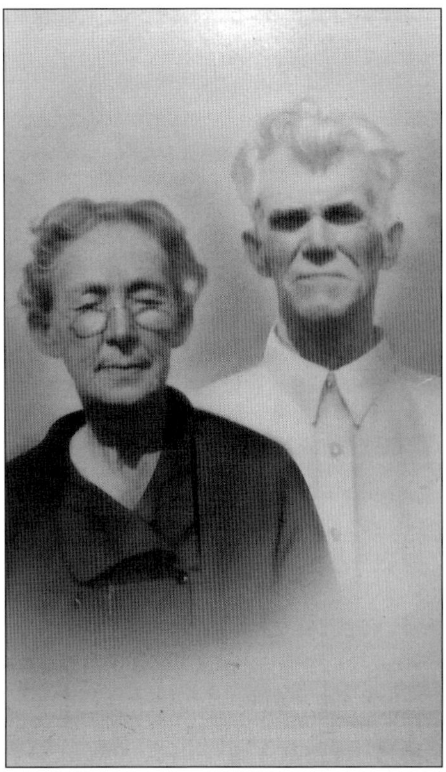

Richard L. Clewis Jr. (1866–1933) and Florentine Fryer Clewis (1867–1942) were early Rains County residents who settled near the Sabine River in the Willow Springs area. Fannie Hair Clewis (1851–1932) deeded two acres for the Clewis family cemetery. It is surrounded by private property, but the cemetery itself is dedicated to cemetery use on the Greene Ranch. According to Barbara King, "When Grandma sold the property, she reserved the right to bury in the cemetery, but gives 'title, full control and management' to the cemetery property to Mr. Green." Richard and Florentine are the grandparents of Maxanne Orsborn Potts, Jo Orsborn Williams, and Peggy Arnold Culpepper. (Courtesy of Maxanne Orsborn Potts.)

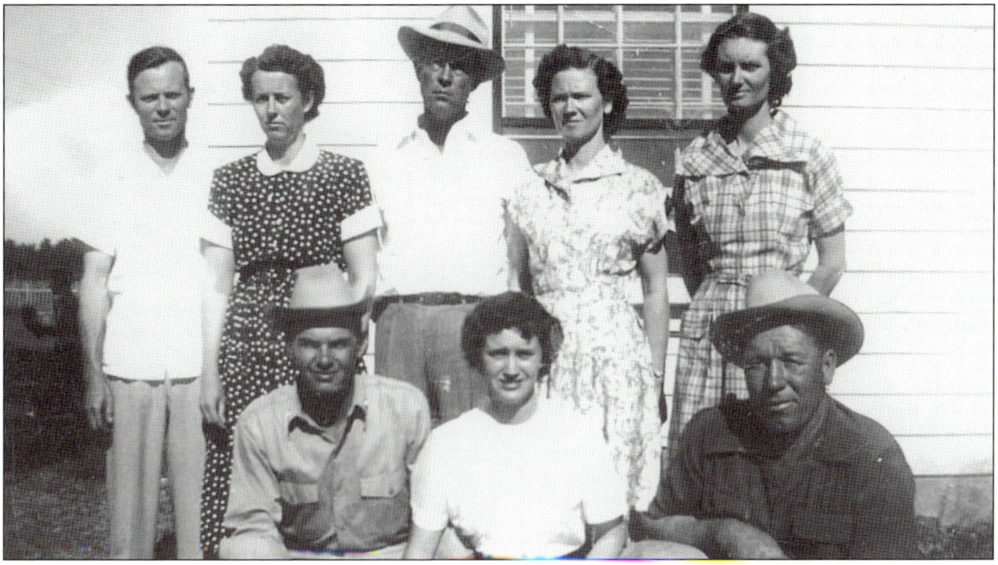

John Henry Jones and Susie Rebecca McKay were married in 1886 and moved to the Hogansville community. They had 10 children, five of whom died in 1937. The surviving children were Arthur, Alvis, Neely, and Mattie. Arthur Jones was elected Rains County tax assessor in 1928 and Rains County judge in 1949. The following descendants of John Henry and Susie Jones are pictured in a family group photograph at Joe and Velma Fletcher's home in the Prospect community. From left to right are (first row) Brevard Cheek, Bobbye Nell Jones (Cheek) Elkins, and Joe Fletcher; (second row) O.F. "Red" Jones, Mary Ellen Jones, Walter Coker, Johnnie Jones Coker, and Velma Jones Fletcher.

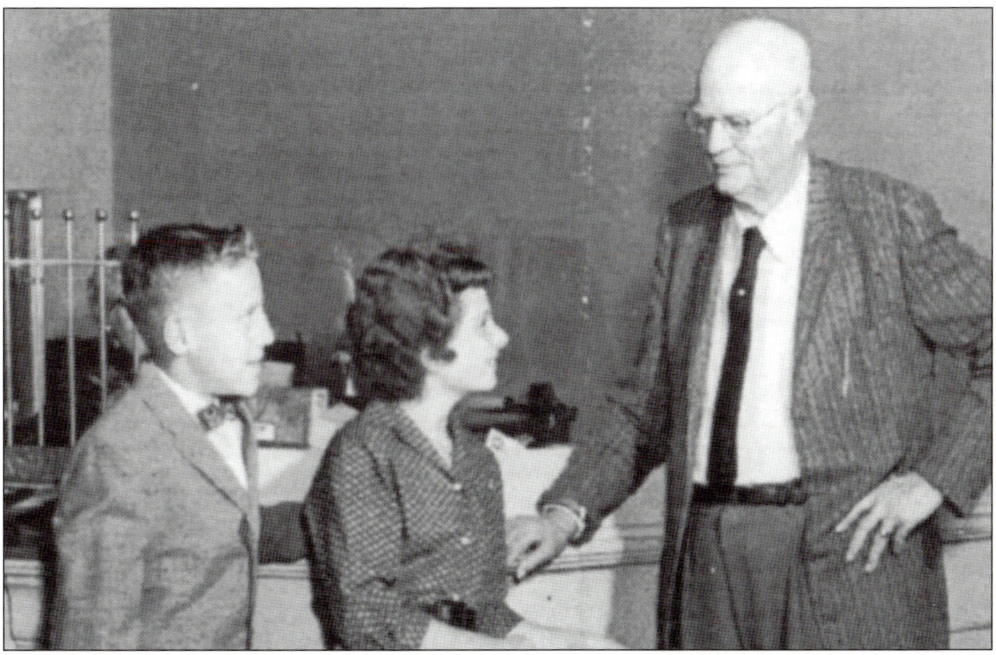

Caywood Montgomery, president of the Point Bank, posed with Emory Junior High class favorites Gayle Adcock and Pat Peeples, both of whom were in the seventh grade. (Courtesy of Cay Frances B. House.)

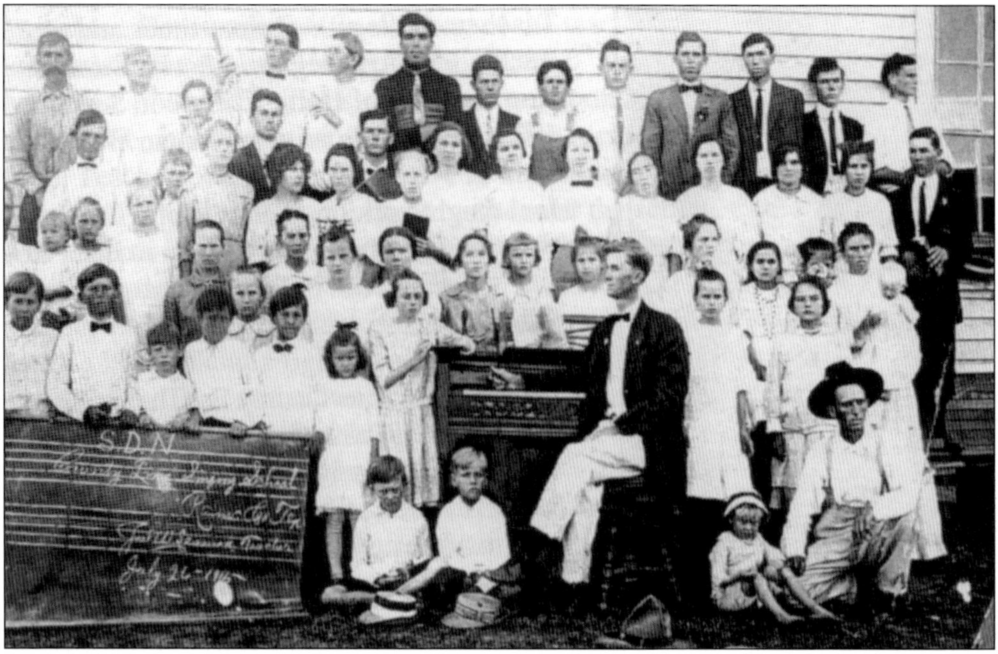


Joel Weaver Lennon (1893–1973) was known for his musical abilities. His first music class was at the Rocky Mountain community in 1914. Lennon held singing schools in different churches and schoolhouses during the summer months. These lasted all day for five days with a program as the finale. Constance Fenter Griffin made the statement, "He sort of leaned back and rocked back and forth on his toes as he sang." Lennon was drafted during World War I. At the end of his tour in France, the chaplain presented him with the violin that he had played all during his service.

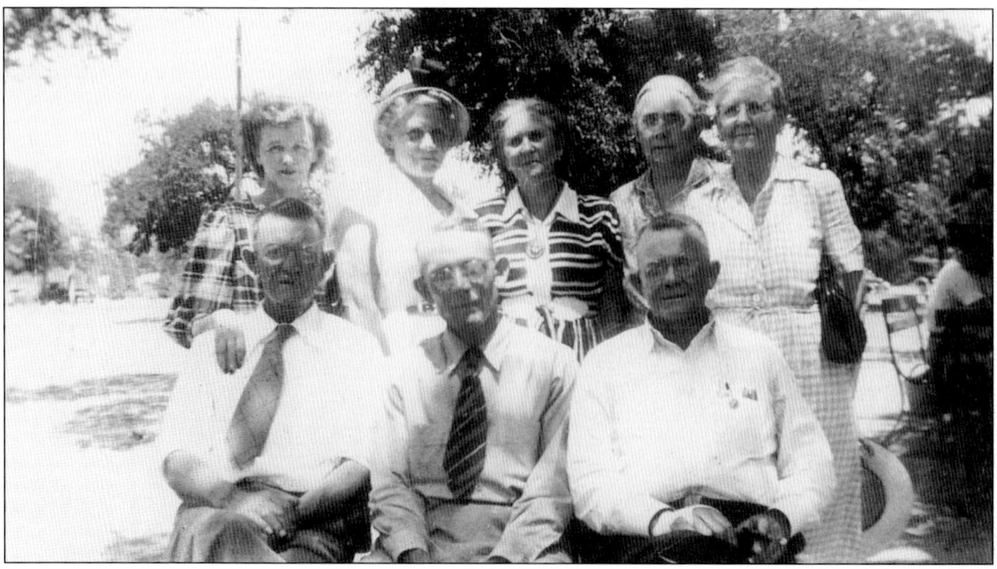

The children of S.J. Stuart and Janie Forbis gathered in 1947 for a Stuart family reunion. From left to right are (first row) Grover Cleveland Stuart, Guy Mortimer Stuart, and Stephen Leon "Lon" Stuart; (second row) Nell Stuart Arnsdale McKinney, Beulah Lee Stuart Herring, Mary Lou "Mitt" Stuart Barker, Minnie May Stuart Rodes, and Maude Stuart Hill. (Courtesy of Jo Ann Stuart Turman.)

A photographer came by the James Edward "Little Jim" Kennemer house in the Smyrna community around 1920. Bettie Kennemer had the dresser brought out on the front porch so that this unusual and memorable picture could be made of her daughter Esta Mae's hair. (Courtesy of Pat Peeples Adcock.)

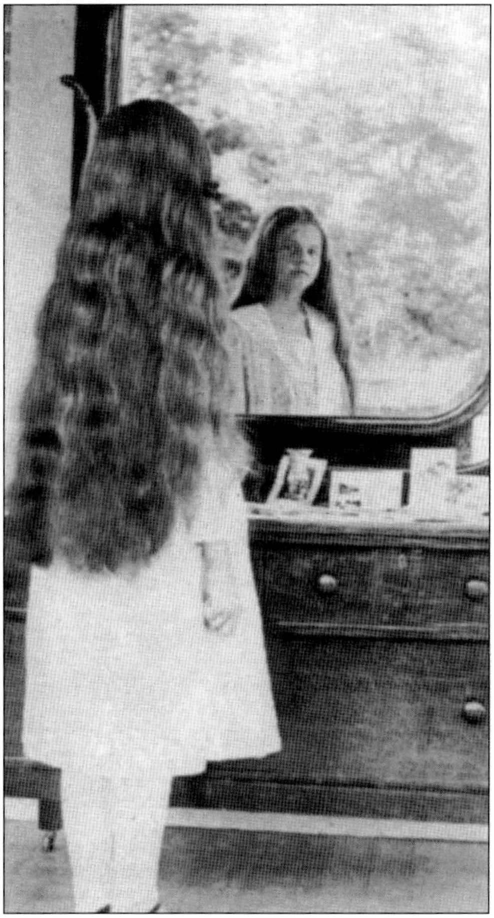

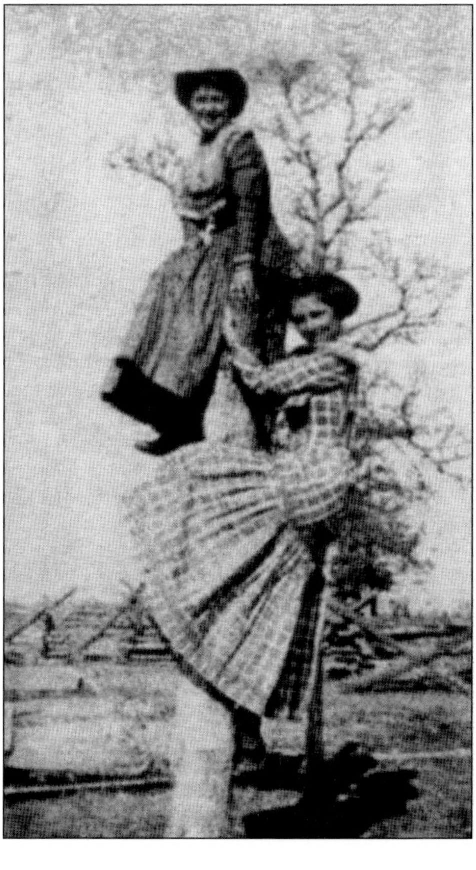

Mattie Lenora Glass (1891–1918) was the daughter of William James Foster and Mary Eugenia Rebecca Sheppard Glass. She attended the Emory Public School, and after attending the State Normal in Denton, began her teaching career at Center Point School for the 1909–1910 school year. In the photograph, Mattie is on the bottom limb of the tree, and her friend Mary Henry is at the top. Mattie died in the 1918 influenza epidemic. (Courtesy of Carolyn Glass Warren.)

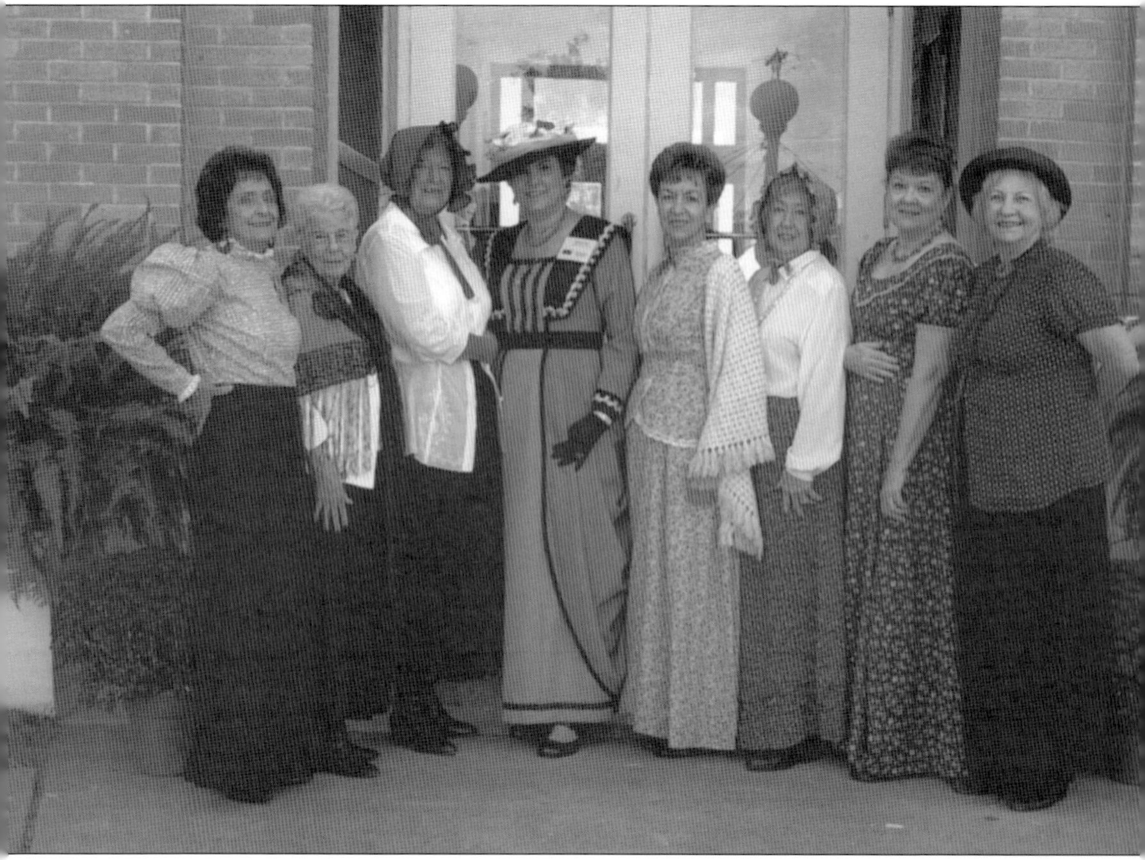

Members of the Rains County Historical Commission gathered at the 2009 dedication of the courthouse as it was restored to its 1908 construction. From left to right are Barbara Clifton, Juandell Weddle, Betty Lyles, Maxanne Orsborn Potts, Audnet Cody Largent, Loretta Potts Christian, Cay Frances B. House, and Mary A. Cain White. (Courtesy of Mary A. Cain White.)

# About the Organization

The Rains County Historical Commission was first appointed in the early 1960s. The purpose of the commission is historic preservation for current and future generations. Our vision is to get the community involved in preserving our past and being aware of the rich heritage that surrounds this county. Commission members serve as volunteers, and meetings are held quarterly, These meetings are open to the public. The commission has been active in preserving buildings, placing markers, compiling a book on the history of Rains County in 1980, and working diligently for grants to restore our grand old 1908 courthouse. Plans were made for its dedication October 17, 2009, and we conducted tours, dressed in period clothing from that era. Officials from the state government and the Texas Historical Commission attended. Many activities included a quilter quilting, a mill grinding cornmeal, and a grand parade with lots of ladies decked out in 1900s dresses, hats, and bonnets. It was a wonderful day.

Members of the Rains County Historical Commission are Mary A. Cain White (chairman), Juandell Weddle (vice-chairman), Loretta Potts Christian (secretary), Maxanne Orsborn Potts (treasurer), Cay Frances B. House (parliamentarian), Margaret Cain, Ernest Cain, Wayne Leshe, Betty Lyles, Glenda Harder, Georgia Potts Vititow, Tamara McLaughlin, Audie Cody Largent, Johnnie Laprade, Elaine Jenkins, Florene McMillan, Marvin Northcutt, Addine Thomas, Barbara Clifton, Ruby Jo Wade, and Pete Suits.